Gardening Under Glass

Gardening Under Glass

Alan Toogood

Weidenfeld and Nicolson

London

Typeset at Selwood Systems, Midsomer Norton

Made and printed in Great Britain by Butler & Tanner Ltd,
Frome and London

Weidenfeld & Nicolson
The Orion Publishing Group
Orion House
5 Upper St Martin's Lane
London WC2H 9EA

A catalogue record for this book is available from the British Library.

ISBN 0 297 83310 3

Contents

List of figures

Introduction

Greenhouse gardening is a very popular hobby today. Just take a train journey in the suburbs of any large town or city and you will see that many back gardens have a greenhouse, or maybe a conservatory. But why is greenhouse gardening so popular? I feel that there are several reasons. A greenhouse or conservatory allows one to become independent of the climate, so a very much wider range of plants can be grown, the range depending on the amount of heat that can be provided, A glass structure allows one to carry on gardening all the year round, and irrespective of what the weather is doing.

A greenhouse allows gardeners to raise all kinds of plants, such as summer bedding and many vegetables for the garden, and flowering pot plants for the house, instead of buying them from a garden centre or nursery, which can be expensive.

Most importantly, though, many gardeners find that they simply obtain a great deal of pleasure and satisfaction from growing plants under glass. And this is a good enough reason for me. Cultivation under glass calls for greater skills and care than in the garden and for most people, therefore, it represents a challenge. However, sound guidance is needed for successful results and that is the purpose of my book. But what does my book have to offer the amateur greenhouse gardener?

Being a plantsman I have placed great emphasis on plants and their cultivation because I feel that amateur gardeners should be aware of the vast range of plants available for growing under glass. The keen greenhouse gardener will soon become tired of growing all the usual plants like tomatoes, cucumbers, pelargoniums and fuchsias and will wish to try something different. I am not dismissing these popular plants by any means, and have indeed covered them thoroughly in this book, but I have included a great many more plants besides these – far more than are to be found in the average greenhouse book. In the appropriate chapters you will find plants that can be grown not only in heated greenhouses but also in cold or unheated structures. The last mentioned should interest many people for, due to the high cost of heating today, many gardeners are finding it impossible to heat their greenhouses during the winter and therefore close them down from mid-autumn to early spring. But there is no need for this: an unheated greenhouse can be (and should be) full of plants throughout the winter. However, those gardeners who can afford to heat their greenhouses will find a wide range of plants suited to different temperature levels.

I have included all the popular plants that are either raised or grown throughout their lives in a greenhouse, such as summer bedding plants, bulbs, flowering pot plants, foliage plants, fuchsias and flowering shrubs and climbers. Plants for the specialist are also covered: alpines, bromeliads, cacti and succulents, carnations, carnivorous plants, chrysanthemums, ferns, orchids and even water plants for a greenhouse pool.

A very wide range of fruits and vegetables can be grown in a greenhouse (very often in an unheated structure), as will be found in the section on utility crops. Many gardeners, I find, grow only tomatoes, and perhaps a grape vine, possibly because they are not aware of the wealth of vegetables and fruits that are suitable for protected cultivation. So I hope that the fruit and vegetable part of my book will encourage gardeners to be more adventurous in their choice of utility crops.

Garden frames and cloches offer another form of protected cultivation and again a very wide range of plants (utility and ornamental) can be grown under them, as will be seen in the appropriate chapters. Again many gardeners do not make maximum use of these valuable structures.

My book, however, is not only concerned with plants and their cultivation. Many readers will want sound guidance on choosing and equipping a greenhouse and therefore I have covered these aspects in detail. I have taken a look at all the types of greenhouse available, including lean-to types and conservatories. I have also included siting a greenhouse, putting it up and laying it out internally. All the equipment you are likely to need is discussed.

I have devoted a section of my book to plant raising and general care of greenhouse plants, not forgetting important pests and diseases and their control.

I hope that my book gives you plenty of new ideas and helps to make your greenhouse, frame and cloche gardening more enjoyable and productive.

Alan Toogood, Liss, Hampshire, 1994

Making the most of a covered area

As I indicated in my introduction, a greenhouse, conservatory, frames or cloches can give the gardener a great deal of pleasure and satisfaction. Many gardeners, however, show the greatest enthusiasm in the spring and summer, when their greenhouses, frames and so on are packed to capacity with plants. But when autumn arrives, and the summer flowers and crops are depleted and consequently relegated to the compost heap, the greenhouse and other structures invariably become devoid of plant life.

This is sad, for it means that the gardener is missing out on a great deal of pleasure: pleasure from ornamental plants as well as utility crops. Is it that enthusiasm wanes with the onset of colder weather and shorter days? Or is it that many gardeners think it possible to grow plants under cover in winter only if expensive artificial heat is provided? I do not really know the answer (indeed there may be several different reasons or a combination of reasons), but all I can say is, that to make the most of a covered area one should grow plants in it all the year round; irrespective of whether or not you can heat it.

Perhaps gardeners need plenty of encouragement to grow plants all the year round, or maybe they need suggestions and ideas. Let me, therefore, give you some idea of what can be grown in a greenhouse throughout the year.

Winter and spring There is certainly no lack of plants to give colour and interest during these seasons. Hardy bulbs like daffodils, tulips, hyacinths and crocuses will flower in the winter and spring and can be grown in a cold greenhouse, when they will flower later, or in a slightly heated greenhouse to encourage earlier flowering. Many people do not realise that several of the hardy annual flowers make excellent pot plants for the slightly heated or cold greenhouse, and they make a welcome show of colour in the spring. There are many pot plants which can be grown with the absolute minimum of artificial heat: among the most popular and easily grown are the primulas like *P. obconica* and *P. malacoides*.

Camellias are eminently suited to pot or tub culture and they can be flowered either in a cold greenhouse or in one which is kept just frost free. The greenhouse will protect the blooms from the weather and you will have a superb show of colour.

Many hardy shrubs and perennials can be forced into early bloom in a slightly heated greenhouse if they are potted in the autumn – and what a welcome splash of colour they make in the spring. No cold greenhouse should be without a selection of flowering alpines and dwarf bulbs; flowering starts in the winter and goes right on into the spring if you have a reasonable selection of plants. One should not forget vegetables for the winter and spring. In a cold greenhouse one can have lettuces and a selection of fresh herbs, for example.

Summer This is the time when most greenhouses are full of plants: pelargoniums, fuchsias, calceolarias, tomatoes, melons, cucumbers among others. Such pot plants and crops can be raised with minimum heat, and of course artificial heat is not necessary from late spring onwards. One can also have grapes and peaches fruiting in the summer, and with these it is not essential to provide artificial heat at any time of the year.

Autumn Following the summer plants should be a good range of autumn crops and flowers. Everyone should grow at least a few late-flowering chrysanthemums, either for greenhouse display or for cutting. Depending on cultivars grown, they will flower through to the end of the year. You will need to provide just sufficient artificial heat to keep the greenhouse atmosphere dry and so ensure perfect blooms. Also try the autumn-flowering bulbs, nerines, which are almost hardy and therefore require only slight heat. If you can provide a little heat for chrysanthemums you will find that perpetual-flowering carnations will also continue flowering in the autumn – these are well worth growing because they provide excellent cut flowers.

You will require no artificial heat at all for certain vegetables such as celery, sugar loaf chicory, Chinese cabbage and endive. Such crops fill a gap at the end of the summer season.

These are just a few of the many ideas you will find throughout my book. I hope they encourage you to become an all-the-year round gardener under cover.

PART ONE

The Greenhouse and its Equipment

1   Choosing a greenhouse

For most people a greenhouse is a fairly big item of expenditure and therefore needs to be chosen with great care. There are several points to consider as outlined in this chapter.

You should ask yourself the question: what is it to be used for? For instance, if you intend growing many plants at ground level, say in a soil bed or in growing-bags, then a glass-to-ground house would be ideal. This would ensure maximum light at ground level.

If a greenhouse is to be used mainly for pot plants grown on staging then solid sides and ends to bench height, such as timber cladding or a brick wall, would be a better choice as such a house retains heat better than a glass-to-ground model. Solid sides to bench height would also be a wise choice for an alpine house, together with plenty of ventilators top and bottom.

Or you may wish to compromise and buy a house with glass-to-ground on one side and timber cladding on the other. You can then successfully grow plants in the border on the glass-to-ground side and pot plants on the other.

You should also consider the appearance of greenhouses before making a final choice. If it is to be sited in the ornamental part of the garden you will need a good-looking house, but if it is to be in the vegetable garden then appearance is perhaps not so important. I consider that a house for the ornamental garden needs to blend with the surroundings and my choice would be a house with a framework of western red cedar, or aluminium with an anodized bronze finish. Plain aluminium, or a softwood greenhouse painted white, does not blend so well, with the exception of lean-to houses and conservatories against the house walls. However, all of this is a matter of personal choice.

If you are going for a lean-to greenhouse try to choose one with a framework and style that 'goes with the house'. For instance, aluminium looks well against a modern house, and perhaps cedar for a dwelling house in traditional style. If your choice is a conservatory, then again choose a style that is in keeping with the period of your house – for instance, if you have a Victorian house then choose a Victorian-style conservatory.

Coming now to size, always buy the biggest you can afford provided it does not dominate the garden. Even if it is too large at first you will soon fill it – that I can guarantee. Many people go in for a 1.8 by 2.4 m (6 by 8 ft) house but soon find that it is not big enough. If, however, you do not wish to be too ambitious to start with, then do at least choose a house that can at a later date be extended – many greenhouse manufacturers can supply extensions for their models.

Perhaps you are having difficulty in deciding whether to buy a free-standing greenhouse or a lean-to (or conservatory). This is a matter of personal choice but a structure against the house wall does offer several advantages over a free-standing house. It loses heat less quickly (so saving on fuel bills) and it can be easier to heat – for instance, it may be possible to run the domestic heating system into it. With access from the dwelling house a lean-to or conservatory can be used as an additional room and one does not have to walk down the garden in inclement weather to tend and enjoy the plants. A lean-to or conservatory blends better with the surroundings as it appears to be part of the house – that is, if it is chosen with care.

Where to buy is the next consideration. Greenhouses and conservatories can be bought from mail-order suppliers but first you would need to send for catalogues and price lists. Many garden centres have greenhouse show sites displaying a range of popular makes. I would strongly advise you to visit a show site so that you can compare makes. There are also special greenhouse centres, often offering substantial discounts, and with a wide range of makes to choose from.

Some chain stores offer greenhouses – again at very favourable prices.

Perhaps you want a greenhouse or conservatory built to your own specifications and requirements, or style (for instance, maybe you want a proper alpine house, or a Victorian-style conservatory), and this is where custom built structures come in. There are several companies in the UK who will design and build a greenhouse or conservatory for you.

How about cost and value for money? Buying a greenhouse or conservatory is like buying anything else – generally speaking, the more you pay the better the quality. Often it is like buying a car – the more you pay the more you get for your money in the way of extras. Try to buy a house that includes as much as possible in the price: like a prefabricated base, plenty of ventilators, guttering and downpipes and automatic ventilation.

Most manufacturers offer a range of optional extras like staging, blinds, extra ventilators, louvre ventilators, watering systems and the like. Some can supply extensions and internal partitioning. Sometimes prefabricated bases, guttering and downpipes and automatic ventilation are optional extras.

2   Materials used in construction

The framework

Timber This is the traditional material for construction of the greenhouse framework. It blends well with the surroundings, especially western red cedar, and is slightly warmer than aluminium alloy (heat is transmitted more quickly through metal). Condensation is consequently less of a problem in a timber-framed house.

It is easier to install equipment and insulation materials in a timber-framed house because there is no need for special fixings as with a metal-framed house. Glazing is usually very good – traditional putty and glazing sprigs (headless nails), giving a draught and leak-free structure.

Timber, of course, needs regular preservation treatment, which should be borne in mind when choosing a greenhouse. Softwoods, such as pine and spruce, need to be treated with a horticultural wood preservative annually, or painted white. Western red cedar is often used for the framework and has more resistance to decay than softwoods, but still needs treating regularly, for example with a special oil.

Timber is not as strong as metal and therefore the framework, including the glazing bars, is thicker than that of an aluminium house: this cuts down on the amount of light entering the house.

Aluminium alloy This is a popular material for the framework and has many advantages over timber: it does not split or rot, needs no preservative treatment, and is easily washed and cleaned. Some houses can be obtained with an acrylic or anodised finish. Framework members are thinner than those of timber houses and therefore light penetration is better. Erection is slower and more tedious than with a timber house as there are more parts to fit together.

Glass is bedded on to rubber or neoprene glazing strips and held in place with spring glazing clips. It is not so easy to install equipment in an aluminium house but there are special fixings available.

Steel This is not much used in greenhouse construction, except for polythene tunnel houses. These have galvanised tubular-steel hoops forming the framework and they are very strong.

Fittings All fittings like locks, catches, nails and screws should be made of copper, brass or galvanised/anodised steel. Untreated steel fittings quickly rust and will stain timber.

Cladding materials

Glass This is the traditional cladding material for greenhouses and there is still nothing to beat it. It is easy to clean, ensures excellent light penetration (up to 90%), has an indefinite life and retains heat reasonably well (certainly better than plastics). Of course, it is easily broken, is expensive and needs a really strong framework to support it. Manufacturers generally use 680 g (24 oz) horticultural glass (weighs 680 g per 09.3 sq deci (24 oz per sq ft)). Panes of glass are often 60 by 60 cm (2 by 2 ft) in amateur houses, or 50 by 45 cm (20 by 18 in). The larger the panes the better the light transmission.

Flexible plastic films These are cheaper than glass, do not break, are usually easy to patch if torn and are easy to replace. However, they discolour after a few years, become brittle, are more difficult to clean than glass, have poor heat retention and result in a bigger build-up of condensation. Plastic films have a short life – two to three years. Those with ultra-violet inhibitors are recommended as they do not deteriorate so quickly as untreated types. Films can, of course, be split and torn in very exposed or windy sites and to prevent damage must be stretched very tightly over the framework.

Rigid plastics These are quite popular, although they have many of the faults of flexible plastics, including discoloration. They are far more expensive than flexible plastics. They may be corrugated or smooth like glass.

3   Types available

Free-standing greenhouses

Traditional span roof This has a pitched roof (each side being of equal size and shape) sloping down to the eaves. The typical greenhouse shape, in fact. The house has straight sides, although sloping-sided models are now available which allow better light penetration.

One has a choice of solid sides to bench height or glass-to-ground.

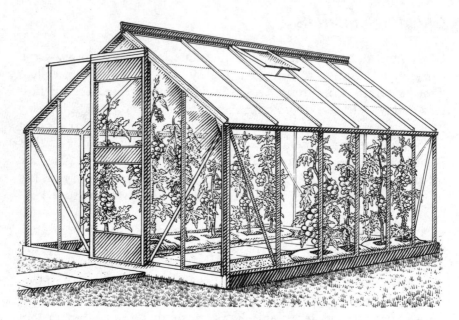

1 *Traditional span-roof greenhouse, glass-to-ground*

Solid sides are generally 60 to 91 cm (2 to 3 ft) high and are made of brick or timber (occasionally other materials are used). A house with solid sides to bench height is ideal for pot plants and alpines and it retains heat better than an all-glass house.

A glass-to-ground house is ideal for growing plants at ground level: for example, in soil beds or growing-bags. There are houses available with glass-to-ground on one side and solid material to bench height

2 *Traditional span-roof greenhouse, half-boarded*

on the other. Curved eaves represent a departure from the traditional span roof shape and create a very pleasing appearance. Traditional span-roof houses are made with either timber or aluminium framework.

Mansard Also known as a curvilinear greenhouse. As shown in the accompanying drawing, the roof panels are set at various angles which ensures very good light intensity within the house. Available glass-to-ground or with solid walls to bench height. Framework available only in aluminium. The mansard makes a very good display house for ornamental plants and there is plenty of width.

Dutch light house This is constructed of Dutch lights (see Chapter 30). The large panes of glass let in plenty of light, and light intensity is further increased by the sloping sides and glass right down to the ground. This is a useful general-purpose house but there is not much headroom for tall crops like tomatoes near the sides of the house. One can buy aluminium-framed houses of the same design.

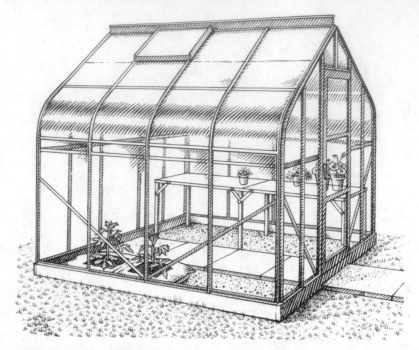

3 Greenhouse with curved eaves

Round houses Six, nine or twelve-sided houses are available and they are not so much round as lantern shaped. Although on the small side, they hold a surprisingly large number of plants and look very attractive in an ornamental setting or on a patio. Available with timber or aluminium framework, and glass-to-ground or half-timber sides.

Geodesic This is a dome-shaped greenhouse, with excellent light transmission and plenty of space. The panes of glass are triangular and generally there are solid panels at the base of the house. Available only with an aluminium framework. Looks superb in a very modern setting and excellent for ornamental plant displays.

Uneven span As shown in the accompanying drawing, this type of house has a high wall (which should face south) for maximum light penetration. The roof slopes back from the top of this. The framework may be timber or aluminium and may be clad with clear corrugated plastic. A conservation or energy-saving greenhouse also has uneven roof panels, angled to allow maximum light to enter. Mirrored

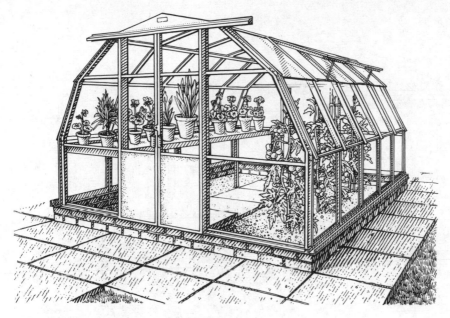

4 *Mansard* or *curvilinear greenhouse*

surfaces inside reflect light. Plastic double glazing and insulation are standard fittings.

Mini houses There are various makes of mini greenhouse. One cannot get inside them but they will hold a growing-bag for tomatoes, etc., and are also useful for plant raising. They generally have an aluminium framework and are glazed to ground level. An advantage is that they are easily moved but they can heat up quickly and excessively in warm weather unless careful attention is paid to ventilation.

Polythene tunnels The framework consists of galvanised tubular-steel hoops inserted in the ground, and these are covered with a flexible polythene 'skin'. Polythene tunnels are far cheaper than other types of greenhouse. They are excellent for growing vegetables and usually are not heated as they quickly lose heat. Generally there is a door at each end for ventilation although special 'tunnel ventilators' are available which are fixed to the plastic cladding. These help to solve the problem of excessive condensation.

5 *Round greenhouse*

Types requiring a back wall

We now come to structures which are erected against a wall – e.g. a wall of the dwelling house or a garden wall. These retain heat much better than free-standing houses and can be made accessible directly from the dwelling house. Also, a domestic heating system can be run into such a structure to provide the heat. Ideally they should be erected on a south- or west-facing wall so that they receive plenty of sun.

Lean-to Lean-to versions of the traditional span-roof greenhouse are available, together with the mansard. Available glazed to the ground or with solid sides to bench height. Mini lean-to houses are also available – ideal for a patio or balcony. One cannot get inside these but they have sliding doors for access. If you are not careful with ventilation they can quickly heat up to excessive levels.

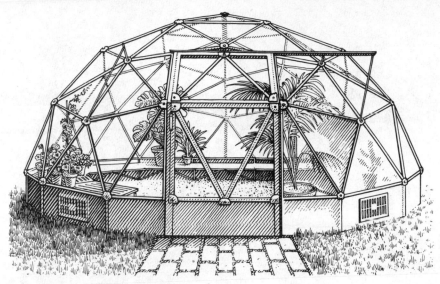

6 *Geodesic or dome-shaped greenhouse*

7 *Uneven-span greenhouse*

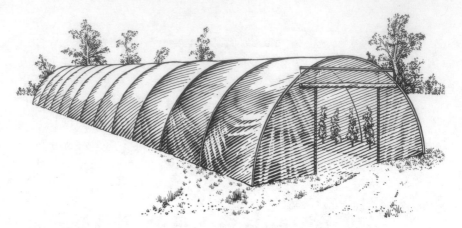

8 Polythene tunnel

9 Lean-to greenhouse

Conservatories I find it difficult to differentiate between a lean-to and a conservatory and in fact there is a certain amount of overlap. The true conservatory should appear as an integral part of the house and not look as though it has been added as an afterthought. Conservatories are available as modular systems or they can be custom built. Virtually any shape or size is available. A conservatory generally has brick sides up to 91 cm (3 ft) in height, or it may have timber sides to the same height. It is best to buy one, or to have one designed and built, to suit the style or period of your house; for example, a Victorian style for a Victorian house.

10 A conservatory in traditional style

Sun rooms Really these are prefabricated home extensions to provide an extra room. However, many of them include a large area of glass, and the roof (generally flat) is made of clear corrugated plastic, so letting in plenty of light, certainly enough to allow you to grow a good range of house plants.

4 Siting

Planning permission Before putting up any building it is always advisable to check with the planning department of your local council to find out whether or not planning permission is required. Although not generally required for a free-standing greenhouse it often is for a lean-to or conservatory against the house. Planning permission is definitely required if there is to be access from the dwelling house to the lean-to, conservatory or sun-room.

Orientation Wherever possible site a free-standing greenhouse so that its ridge runs from east to west. But if this is not possible do not worry too much because provided the house is situated in a spot which receives plenty of sunshine you will be able to grow plants well. A lean-to, conservatory or sun-room is ideally sited on a south- or west-facing wall where it will receive plenty of sun. However, if you have to site it on a north- or east-facing wall you will still be able to grow plants provided you choose those kinds which thrive in shade.

Considering light and shade Never erect a greenhouse where it will be overshadowed by trees or large buildings which cast a great amount of shade. Instead opt for an open situation which receives plenty of sunshine. Try to find a site which receives sunshine for as much of the day as possible.

Wind protection The greenhouse must be sheltered from winds, because high winds will considerably lower the temperature within the house resulting in very high fuel bills as the heater will keep running to maintain the desired temperature. Therefore avoid a very exposed situation and at all costs do not site the greenhouse where it will be subjected to wind funnelling – such as between two houses. If necessary, I would advise the use of a windbreak of some kind on the windward side of the house, but some distance from it. For example, a temporary windbreak could be constructed from windbreak netting supported on a wooden framework at least 1.8 m (6 ft) high. A permanent windbreak could be in the form of a hedge or screen of conifers. Suitable conifers include the Leyland cypress, × *Cupressocyparis leylandii*, strong-growing cultivars of the Lawson cypress, *Chamaecyparis lawsoniana*, and *Thuja plicata*. These are quick growing and will form a good hedge or screen within a few years.

Frost pockets These are low-lying areas, dips and hollows and the foot of a slope, and they should be avoided for cold air drains down into them. This will mean higher fuel bills and a slower start for plants in the spring. If you have to erect your house on sloping ground it is best to site it half way up the slope. Ideally choose a perfectly level piece of ground for the greenhouse.

Soils and drainage If you intend growing plants in soil beds and borders in the greenhouse you should try to choose a site which has good fertile soil. The drainage should be good so that you are able to cultivate the soil at any time of the year. Also, a well-drained soil will warm up more quickly in the spring. It is time-consuming, and can also be expensive, if you have to install an artificial drainage system.

Services The services that you may need to run to a greenhouse are electricity, mains gas and water. If you are considering any of these it is very sensible to site the greenhouse as close as possible to the dwelling house. Laying on these services is expensive and will be increasingly costly the further away from the dwelling house the greenhouse is sited. Also it will no doubt be more convenient for you if the greenhouse is close to the dwelling house – it means that you will not have to traipse down the garden in cold or wet weather to tend to your plants.

5   Construction and erection

Preparing the site The site should be prepared well in advance of delivery of the greenhouse for it may entail more work than you envisage – but on the other hand you may have very little in the way of preparation.

First of all the site should be made completely level. This can be done with the aid of wooden pegs, a straight-edge board and a spirit level. A peg is banged into the ground until the top is at the required level. Then, working from this peg with your board and spirit level, insert pegs all over the site, a convenient distance apart being about 1.8 m (6 ft). If you use the spirit level accurately, the tops of all the pegs should be at the same level. Then it is a case of adding or taking away soil until the soil level over the entire site is level with the tops of the pegs.

If drainage is required it is best to lay a system of tile drains to take excess water into a soakaway, as shown on the next page.

Base and foundations I strongly recommend buying a ready-made base for the greenhouse – most manufacturers supply them for their houses. There are various kinds: pre-cast concrete, steel and even strong plastic. Generally the corners are anchored in concrete – follow the maker's instructions. You must ensure that the corners of the base are at right angles otherwise the house will not fit properly. Use a large set square for this. The base must be laid on a perfectly level site and the soil should be well rammed to ensure it is really firm. The greenhouse is generally bolted on to the base – but again the instructions will be provided.

You may, however, prefer to make your own base but this entails much more work. Again the site should first be made level. Then accurately mark out the area of the greenhouse, using four wooden stakes (one for each corner) and strong twine, ensuring the corners are at right angles. Take out a trench all round, the depth and width of a garden spade, half fill it with brick rubble and ram it really well. Then place bricks at each corner (one on each side) and, using a straight-edge board and spirit level, adjust them until they are perfectly level. These eight bricks will indicate the final level of the concrete which is used to form the foundation.

Then mix some concrete – one part cement to five parts ballast. Fill the trench with it and tamp it down, making sure the final level corresponds with the level of the eight bricks. When it has set, lay a single row of bricks on this foundation on which to stand the house. Use mortar – one part cement to four parts builders' sand. Use a spirit level to ensure they are laid perfectly level and again make sure the corners are at right angles. You can make sure they are laid in a straight line by stretching a length of string down each side of the foundation. When laying the bricks, insert metal coach bolts into

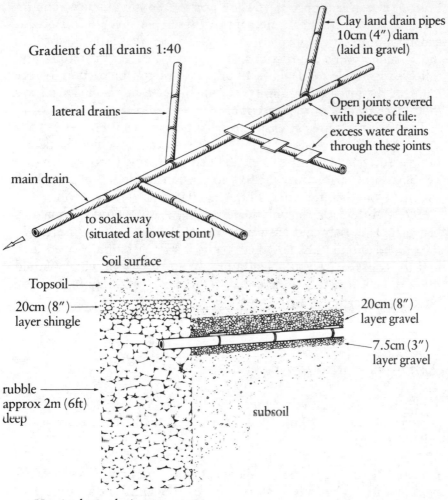

Gradient of all drains 1:40

← Clay land drain pipes
10cm (4″) diam
(laid in gravel)

lateral drains ————→

Open joints covered
with piece of tile:
excess water drains
through these joints

main drain

to soakaway
(situated at lowest point)

Soil surface

Topsoil ————→

20cm (8″)
layer shingle

20cm (8″)
layer gravel

7.5cm (3″)
layer gravel

rubble
approx 2m (6ft)
deep

subsoil

11 Herringbone drainage system

the mortar between the bricks, about every 91 cm (3 ft), so that the greenhouse can be bolted down to this base. Before erecting the greenhouse cover the bricks with strips of bituminised roofing felt to act as a damp-proof course, preventing rising damp.

If you require brick walls to bench height, prepare the foundation in the way described above but continue building with bricks until the desired height has been reached. If you are not too skilled at brick laying you may wish to employ the services of a local builder who will soon put it up for you.

Erecting the greenhouse If you are not too happy about erecting a greenhouse yourself, ask the supplier about an erection service. It usually requires two people to put up a greenhouse and first of all the manufacturer's instructions must be studied very carefully and followed to the letter. It pays, I find, to sit down the evening before and read the instructions until you fully understand them. Then have them close by you during erection.

Timber houses are far easier to put up than metal houses as they are supplied in sections which are simply bolted together. Some are pre-glazed. Metal houses are supplied in many parts which are bundled into various packages – for instance, all the glazing bars should be bundled together, all the ventilator parts, and so on.

If you are erecting a polythene tunnel again follow the maker's instructions closely and ensure the metal hoops are well inserted in the ground and that the polythene 'skin' is stretched tightly over them and the edges buried sufficiently deeply into the soil, which should then be well firmed. It is essential to choose a calm day for putting on the polythene 'skin' – it will be virtually impossible in windy conditions because it will keep 'ballooning'.

The greenhouse floor

When the greenhouse or conservatory has been erected you can consider the type of floor you require. Let us look at the various possibilities.

Concrete If you wish to grow plants only in containers like growing-bags and pots you may wish to concrete the entire floor area. This makes for a very hygienic greenhouse as the floor is easily washed. The concrete should be laid on well-rammed rubble as described under Bases and Foundations. In fact, you may find it more convenient to lay a concrete floor before the house is erected.

Paving slabs Instead of using concrete you could pave the entire floor area, using pre-cast concrete paving slabs. Lay them on at least 15 cm (6 in) of well-rammed rubble, topped with builders' sand to create a smooth level 'bed'. Lay the slabs on dollops of mortar – one dollop for each corner. Lightly tap down and ensure each is perfectly level by using a spirit level. Slabs can be obtained in various shapes and sizes and in a range of colours. There should be a slight gap between each, which is filled with mortar when the bedding mortar has hardened.

Quarry tiles For a conservatory or lean-to greenhouse you may wish to indulge in the luxury of quarry floor tiles. They are very expensive but create a superb appearance. This is the traditional type of floor for a conservatory. Again they must be laid on a solid level foundation. Many designs and colours are available.

Paths You may simply wish to have a central path in your greenhouse, maybe with soil borders or staging on each side. The path should be at least 30 cm (12 in) wide and can be made from concrete, laid as described under Concrete above. Or you could use 30 cm (12 in) square paving slabs, laid as described under Paving Slabs above. Or they could be laid loosely on a bed of sand over rammed soil. Duckboards, made of slatted timber, make useful temporary paths and are especially useful in a polythene tunnel house where vegetables are being grown direct in the soil. You can make them easily at home, using 2.5 by 7.5 cm (1 by 3 in) timber. Treat with a horticultural wood preservative before use.

Shingle or gravel areas Shingle or gravel is useful for areas which are not to be cropped, such as under the staging, or either side of the path to make a good base for standing growing-bags and pots. I generally use pea shingle which is readily available from builders' merchants. Do not lay shingle or gravel direct on the soil but first put down a sheet of thick polythene and then place on this a 5–7.5 cm (2–3 in) layer. Do not allow the edges of the polythene to turn up because excess water will not be able to drain away. Alternatively, you could use one of the horticultural aggregates for the same purpose.

Soil borders and beds

Soil borders and beds are often used for growing utility crops like tomatoes, but they are equally to be recommended for growing ornamental plants like shrubs and perennials. Plants grow far better in good soil beds or borders than in containers and the ornamentals look far more natural. In my opinion a more pleasing appearance is created in a conservatory if the shrubs and other plants are grown in beds rather than in pots or tubs. A disadvantage of growing ornamentals in a soil bed is that due to unrestricted root growth they can quickly become too large and outgrow their allotted space. However, even this problem can be overcome if plants of suitable size for the structure are chosen.

Preparation Firstly the land on which the greenhouse or conservatory is to be built should be well drained and the soil in good heart. (I have commented on this in Chapters 4 and 5.) Initially the bed or border should be dug deeply, ideally by double digging (to two depths of the spade, breaking up the subsoil with a fork). Into each trench add a generous quantity of well-rotted farmyard manure, garden compost, composted bark or spent hops. If you are growing utility crops like tomatoes, the border should be dug once a year in autumn after the crops have been cleared. However, there is no need to carry out double digging every year – after the initial preparation single digging (to the depth of the spade) will be sufficient. But it is still a good idea to add organic matter to each trench.

Decorative beds To give you ideas on creating beds for ornamental plants in a conservatory (or indeed in a free-standing greenhouse) visit the greenhouses of famous gardens. Beds can be formal (square or rectangular) or informal (of irregular shape). They can be constructed around the edges of the conservatory or greenhouse and even in the centre if the structure is large enough.

Beds do not have to be completely flat – indeed a more pleasing effect is created if they are built up or contoured. For instance you can create a terraced bed (several different levels, like steps) using logs or rocks to retain the terraces. Or you could, more simply, have a gently undulating bed. You will probably need more soil to achieve these effects; if you do not have any spare garden soil buy in some really good-quality topsoil – a lightish to medium loam. If you create an undulating bed, consider placing a few well-shaped pieces of rock in it over which some of the low-growing plants can scramble. The rocks should be partially sunk in the soil.

Of course, if you are an alpine enthusiast you may even like the idea of building a small rock garden in the greenhouse.

Generally, as the bed is higher than the floor of the conservatory or greenhouse, the edges will need to be retained. For this purpose you can again use logs or rocks.

If you are fortunate enough to have a large conservatory and consequently a large bed or beds, you could consider running paths through them so that you can easily get to the plants to admire and care for them. Such paths should not be straight but meander and wind through the bed. I like to use sections of tree trunk for creating paths – circular pieces about 7.5 cm (3 in) thick. These can be laid like stepping stones and should be sunk into the soil so that their surfaces are level with the soil surface. Or you could make a path from pea shingle, horticultural aggregate or a very coarse grade of pulverised pine bark.

After planting, the surface of the bed can be covered with a suitable material to give a pleasing effect. If you are growing shrubs, perennials, bulbs and so on you could mulch the surface with pulverised pine bark 5–7.5 cm (2–3 in) deep. This will not only prevent the soil from drying out rapidly in warm weather but will help to suppress weeds. For cacti you could cover the soil with a layer of coarse sand, gravel or shingle. Shingle is also recommended for alpines, or even stone chippings. Plants like bromeliads and orchids could have a mulch of pulverised bark.

6 Heating equipment

As well as gaining a great deal of pleasure from a heated greenhouse one can also expect good returns from it in the form of early or out-of-season fruits and vegetables, pot plants and cut flowers, together with summer bedding plants for the garden. Heating, indeed, greatly increases the range of plants that can be grown. I am not saying that an unheated greenhouse should not be considered if you really cannot afford to run a heater – I have an unheated greenhouse which is kept full of plants throughout the year – but I can say that your pleasure will be greatly increased if you provide heat.

Most gardeners these days provide heat from early autumn through to late spring and from then until early autumn rely on natural warmth.

Exactly what you can grow in a greenhouse depends on the minimum winter temperature you are able to provide. There are three recommended temperature ranges, these being minimum night temperatures in winter.

The cool greenhouse This has a minimum temperature of 4.5°C (40°F) or 7°C (45°F). A wide range of plants can be grown in this house and this is probably the most popular temperature to maintain. This is considered a general-purpose house with flowering pot plants throughout the year together with utility crops all year.

The intermediate house This has a minimum temperature of 10°C (50°F) and allows an even wider range of plants to be grown.

The warm greenhouse This has a minimum temperature of 15.5°C (60°F) and will ensure that many of the available tropical plants will flourish. It is interesting to note, however, that many tropical plants will 'tick over' in a minimum of 10°C, although they will certainly not 'do much' in the winter.

Stove house Years ago gardeners grew tropical plants in what was termed a stove house, with temperatures of 21°C (70°F) and above, but it has been found (mostly through necessity) that many will survive in lower temperatures. However there are still some tropical plants that need stove conditions and a few examples will be found in the plant chapters – although not many, I hasten to add.

   It should be borne in mind that it costs twice as much to maintain 10°C as 4.5°C and three times as much to maintain 15.5°C.

Dividing a house If you have a reasonably large greenhouse, say 3 to 3.6 m (10 to 12 ft) in length, you could consider dividing it into two sections by means of a permanent glass partition with an access door. This would allow you to have two temperature ranges. Some greenhouse manufacturers supply partitions for their houses.

Types of heaters

There is a choice of paraffin, gas and electric heaters, as well as boiler and hot-water-pipe systems. In the near future solar heating may be widely used. Greenhouse heaters are summarised in the accompanying chart.

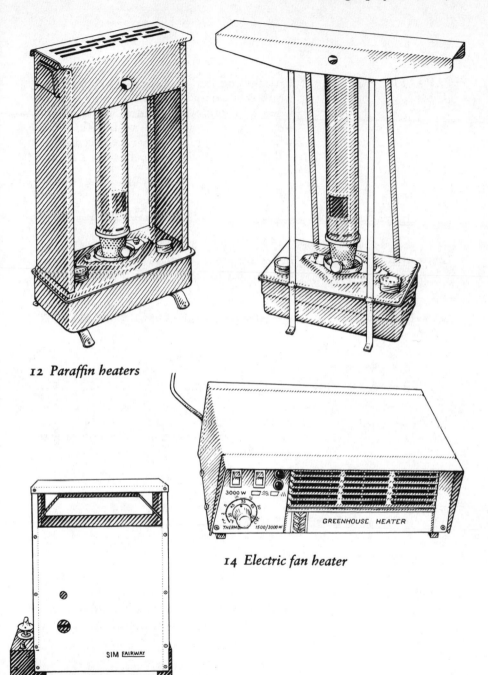

12 *Paraffin heaters*

14 *Electric fan heater*

13 *Portable gas heater*

Type	Description
PARAFFIN (Fig. 12)	Basically consists of a reservoir of paraffin which is taken up by a wick, giving off heat when lit. Thermostatic control available on some models. Two types available – blue flame, with less risk of fumes being produced, and yellow flame which is almost as good as blue-flame types
Convection type	In the form of a cabinet. Draws in cold air at bottom and gives off warm air at top
GAS HEATERS Natural-gas types	Basically a warm-air cabinet. Thermostatically controlled
Bottled-gas types (Fig. 13)	Basically a warm-air cabinet. Portable. Thermostatically controlled. Runs off propane or butane
ELECTRICITY	—
Fan Heaters (Fig. 14)	Small portable cabinet with fan and heating element inside. Blows out warm air
Tubular heaters (Fig. 15)	Hollow tubes with heating elements within. Generally installed in 'banks', the number of tubes depending on heat output required

Advantages	Disadvantages	Comments
Provides carbon dioxide. Portable. Not too expensive to buy	Frequent attention needed. Produces water vapour (results in condensation). Some ventilation must be provided at all times. Can produce harmful fumes if not cleaned regularly. Fuel expensive	Very popular. Use pipes or ducts if available to distribute heat more efficiently. Use high-grade paraffin. Avoid placing in draughts. Clean regularly
Keeps air circulating in greenhouse	Can produce fumes if not kept clean	
Cheaper to run than bottled gas. Gives off carbon dioxide. Minimum attention and maintenance	Needs a gas supply to greenhouse (can be expensive). Gives off water vapour	Becoming more popular. Employ a professional to install gas supply and to connect up heater
Portable. Gives off carbon dioxide. Minimum attention and maintenance	Gives off water vapour. More expensive to run than natural gas	Almost as popular as paraffin heaters. Buy large gas cylinders – more economical
Most efficient fuel – none wasted. Reliable. Automatic. Convenient. Gives off dry heat. Clean	A very expensive fuel. Needs mains supply (can be expensive to install). Problems during power cuts	All heaters must have thermostatic control for economic running. Employ a professional electrician to install power supply, and control panel etc. inside the greenhouse
Neat and compact	None, apart from being expensive to run	Can mount along sides of greenhouse or under staging
Circulates the air. Small, portable	None, except expensive to run	Stand on path in greenhouse – do not allow to blow directly at plants

Type	Description
Convection heaters	Basically cabinets with heating elements within to warm the air. Warm air rises and comes out at the top, drawing in cool air from the bottom
Soil-warming cables (Fig. 16)	Electric warming cables which are laid out and buried in soil bed, or in sand on greenhouse staging. Provide desirable bottom heat for plants, cuttings and for seed raising
Air-warming cables	Cables which are fitted to walls of small greenhouses – e.g. mini houses and mini lean-to types
BOILER SYSTEMS WITH HOT- WATER PIPES (Fig. 17)	Boiler, fired by solid fuel, oil or mains gas. Pipes mounted around walls of greenhouse. Boiler outside but under cover
SOLAR HEATING	A system which stores natural heat, to be given off at night when most needed

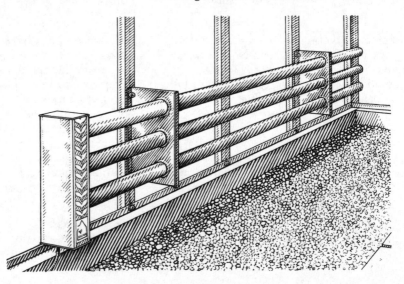

Advantages	Disadvantages	Comments
Keeps air moving	None, apart from running costs	Useful for the larger greenhouse
Cheaper to run than fan, tubular or convection heaters	Provide only localised heat. You will need another heater to warm the air	Ensure thermostatic control – some kits are not supplied with this
,, ,, ,,	Will only keep the structure frost free	,, ,, ,,
Solid fuel ideal if you want to maintain high temperatures with realistic running costs. Automation with oil or gas. Minimum attention needed even with solid fuel. Gives out dry heat. Modern systems easy to install	System does not respond quite so quickly to temperature changes as with electric or gas heaters. Rather bulky. Daily stoking and ash clearing with solid fuel	Ideal for large houses, but also suitable for smaller house. Manufacturers advise on size of boiler of your greenhouse, and necessary pipe length according to temperature you wish to maintain. They will also recommend suitable fuels.
Free heat	Lack of sun in some areas. A conventional heater would be required to ensure sufficient heat at certain times, especially in winter	Not widely used. Solar heating for greenhouses is still very much in the experimental stages

15 (opposite) *Electric tubular heater*

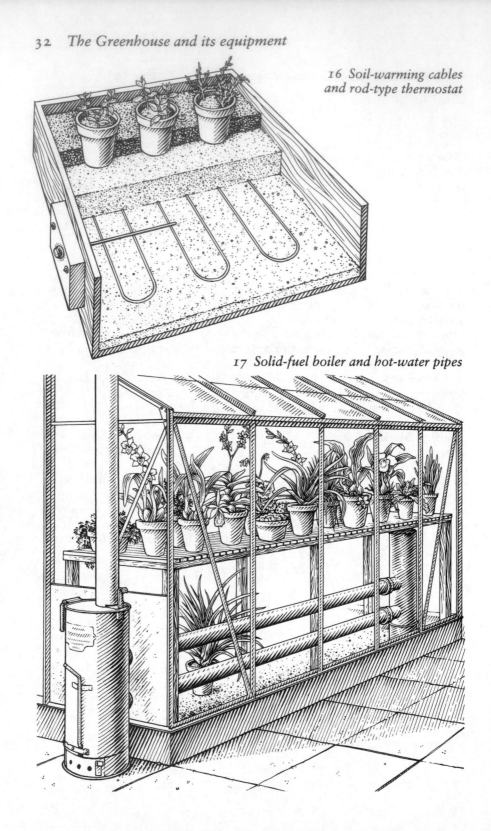

16 Soil-warming cables and rod-type thermostat

17 Solid-fuel boiler and hot-water pipes

Calculating size of heater

Calculating costs Before I go on to discuss how to calculate the size of heater for a greenhouse, let me first say something about calculating the cost of heating a greenhouse. It is possible to estimate the cost if you know the present unit price of the fuel in your area (the price per kg, litre, therm or kilowatt). You must also know both the heat output or yield of the chosen fuel – which is expressed in terms of British Thermal Units (BTU) – and the rating of your heater – the amount of heat needed per hour is again expressed in BTUs. Here, then, are the BTU heat yields of fuels:

Paraffin – 157,000 BTU per 4.5 litres (1 gallon)
Gas, natural – 100,000 BTU per therm
Gas, propane/butane – 21,500 BTU per 0.45 kilos (1 lb)
Electricity 3,412 BTU per unit (1 kilowatt)
Solid fuels – 12–14,000 BTU per 0.45 kilos (1 lb)
Oil – 165,000 BTU per 4.5 litres (1 gallon)

These figures are based on the efficient use of fuel and assume that equipment is in good working order, properly installed, thermostatically controlled and used correctly. The cheapest fuel is generally considered to be solid fuel, followed by natural gas, then paraffin, propane/butane gas, and finally electricity.

Calculating size of heater To determine this we must calculate the heat loss of the greenhouse. In the following calculations I have used only imperial measurements to simplify things. There are standard figures for the rate of heat loss (thermal conductivity) of materials. These are expressed in BTUs per hour per square foot for each degree Fahrenheit of temperature difference between inside and outside:

Glass (including the greenhouse framework, whether wood or aluminium) – 1.1 BTU per hour.
Brick wall ($4\frac{1}{2}$ in thick) – 0.5 BTU per hour.
Wood (1 in) thick – 0.5 BTU per hour.

First accurately measure the greenhouse to find out the total area of glass (and other materials if applicable) in square feet. For example, I will take a popular size and type of greenhouse: a glass-to-ground house, 6 by 8 ft, with 6 ft to the eaves and 8 ft to the ridge.
Each side (to the eaves) measures 8 by 6 ft, which equals 48 sq ft. As we have two sides, the total is 96 sq ft.

Each end (to the eaves) measures 6 by 6 ft, which equals 36 sq ft. As we have two ends, the total is 72 sq ft.

Each roof section measures 8 by $3\frac{1}{2}$ ft, which equals 28 sq ft. As we have two roof sections, the total is 56 sq ft.

Finally measure the gable ends – the triangular shapes. We can take each as being 3 by 2 ft which equals 6 sq ft. As we have two, the total is 12 sq ft.

Now add all of these figures together to arrive at the total glass area of 236 sq ft.

We already know that we have a heat loss of 1.1 BTU per square foot of glass area, so multiply 236 by 1.1. This equals 259 BTUs. This is the heat loss of the house, provided it is completely draught-free (no cracks, gaps, etc), well insulated and it is not in an exposed or windy situation where heat loss will be even more rapid. However, we do not often have such perfect conditions, so to compensate it is advisable to add one-third to our figure to allow for additional heat losses. Therefore, 259 BTUs becomes 343 BTUs.

However, if you are certain that your house is completely draught free, very well insulated, and in a very sheltered, warm aspect, you may neglect to add a third to the figure.

Now we have to decide on the minimum temperature required in the greenhouse. We shall assume that the outside temperature could fall as low as minus 7° C (20° F). A greenhouse maintained at 10° C (50° F) minimum would therefore need a temperature 'lift' of 17° C (30° F).

So, to calculate the heat input needed, multiply 343 by 30 (30° F). The answer is 10,290. This is the heat requirement in BTUs. The heat output of heaters is generally expressed in BTUs, so in this example we would need a heater with an output of 10,290 BTUs.

However, you may wish to use an electric heater. The heat output in this case is expressed in kilowatts, so we must convert our 10,290 BTUs to kilowatts. 1 kw of electricity is 3,412 BTUs, so therefore we would need a 3 kw electric heater (divide 10,290 by 3,412).

This may seem a high-output heater, but remember that it would not be running all the time (it will be thermostatically controlled), so do not be alarmed by the capacity of the heater required for the desired temperature lift. Remember that for most of the time in winter the minimum outside temperature will be much higher than the minus 7° C (20° F) quoted. However, should it fall to this at times, the heater will be able to cope.

If you do not wish to dabble in these calculations and are seeking an easier way of determining the right size of heater, you should refer to the accompanying table. But for a fully accurate figure it will be necessary to do your own calculations.

Choose your heater the easy way

Greenhouse size		Minimum temperature required					
		WARM 15.5°C (60°F) Temp lift 22°C (40°F) Heat/energy needed		INTERMEDIATE 10°C (50°F) Temp lift 17°C (30°F) Heat/energy needed		COOL 4.5°C (40°F) Temp lift 11°C (20°F) Heat/energy needed	
(metres)	(feet)	Kw	BTUs	Kw	BTUs	Kw	BTUs
1.8 by 1.5	6 by 5	2.4	7,800	1.8	5,600	1.3	4,200
1.8 by 1.8	6 by 6	3.1	9,500	2.2	7,000	1.6	4,800
2.4 by 1.8	8 by 6	3.7	11,400	3.0	9,000	2.0	6,000
3.0 by 1.8	10 by 6	4.3	13,600	3.3	10,100	2.3	7,500
2.4 by 2.4	8 by 8	4.7	14,400	3.5	10,400	2.4	7,800
3.0 by 2.4	10 by 8	4.8	15,000	3.8	11,500	2.8	8,400
3.6 by 2.4	12 by 8	5.3	16,500	4.2	13,200	3.3	10,000
3.0 by 3.0	10 by 10	6.0	18,500	4.6	14,000	3.6	11,200

(Assuming minimum outdoor temperature of $-7°C$ (20°F)). Figures approximate only.

NOTES: Temp lift – difference between indoor and outdoor temperatures Figures approximate only as greenhouse height/shape affect surface area, speed of wind/draughts and type of cladding, all influence energy requirements.

(Reproduced by courtesy of David Carr)

---

7 Controlling the environment

Ventilators

It is essential for a greenhouse or conservatory to have adequate ventilators. Most greenhouses are fitted with roof and side ventilators, and perhaps louvres. It is also possible to have automatic ventilation which can be left to its own devices. The following table summarises what is available for greenhouse ventilation.

Ventilators

Type	Position	Comments
Ridge (Fig. 18)	Roof – hinged at the ridge on both sides of house	Minimum number is one every 2 m (6 ft) length of house. Area of ridge vents should be equal to at least one-sixth of floor area. On long houses continuous vents are recommended, running the entire length of the house. Side vents are also needed in all houses – see below.
Side (Fig. 19)	Positioned on side walls, usually hinged, generally near ground level	Minimum number is one every 2 m length of house. Or continuous vents for long houses
Louvre vents (Fig. 20)	Positioned on side walls, near ground level. An alternative to normal hinged side vents	Less draught-proof than traditional vents. They generally replace panes of glass so you can have as many as you like

Automatic ventilation

Type	Position	Comments
Automatic ventilator arms (Fig. 21)	Fixed to hinged vents and greenhouse framework. Versions for louvre vents available	Automatically open and close the vents according to temperature. Reasonably priced. No power source needed – powered by natural heat. Can be pre-set to open at required temperature
Electric circulating fans	Mounted in roof, at one end of greenhouse, usually opposite end to door	Need supply of electricity. Useful for keeping air moving. Additional to side and ridge vents

Type	Position	Comments
Electric extractor fans	End of greenhouse – opposite end to door. Useful in plastic tunnel houses	Create through-flow of cool air, by pushing the warm air out of the house. Need supply of electricity. Additional to side and ridge vents

18 Ridge ventilators

Thermometers

Type	Function	Comments
Ordinary	Simply indicate present temperature in greenhouse	Place where direct sunlight does not fall on it (this would give a false reading). Ensure good air circulation around it
Maximum/ minimum	Consists of two columns of mercury with a metal needle in each. These are moved by the mercury and stay in place when the mercury falls, thus indicating highest and lowest temperature in a 24 hour period	Reset needles each morning. Place where direct sunlight does not fall on it. Ensure good air circulation around it. Far more useful than ordinary thermometer

19 *Side ventilator*

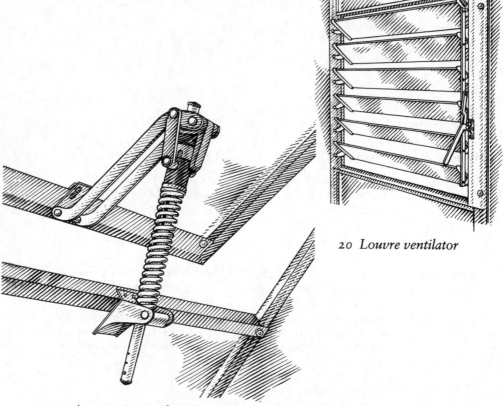

20 *Louvre ventilator*

21 *Automatic ventilator opener*

Insulation

To reduce heat loss and therefore save on fuel bills it is essential to insulate a greenhouse. This involves lining it inside with some suitable material, as indicated in the table below. It slightly reduces light – the percentage loss depending on the type of material. The reduction in heat loss also depends on the type of material used.

Leave a 12–25 mm ($\frac{1}{2}$–1 in) gap between the insulation material and the glass to create a cushioning layer of air. Most manufacturers of greenhouse insulation materials supply special fittings to hold the material in place, both in aluminium and timber houses. Do not seal vents, but insulate them separately so that they can be opened.

Insulation materials

Type	Specifications	Comments
Glass	Clear horticultural glass. The most effective insulation material	Permanent double glazing. There are greenhouses specially designed to be double glazed – it is an optional extra
Clear single plastic sheeting	Usually 150 gauge. Not so effective in reducing heat loss as, for example, bubble plastic. Can save up to 40% of heating costs	Plastic linings collect condensation which further reduces light intensity. Can be taken down for the summer
Bubble plastic	Two sheets of clear polythene sheeting with air bubbles between. Considerably reduces heat loss. Can reduce heating costs by up to 60%	Very popular. Can be taken down for the summer
Rigid clear plastics and other materials	Sheets of rigid clear plastic for horticultural use. Considerably reduces heat loss: up to 60%. There is also a polyester resin-based sheet material reinforced with glass fibres: can reduce heat loss by up to 60%, with 93% light transmission	For permanent 'double glazing'

Type	Specifications	Comments
Thermal screens	Sheets of transparent plastic or translucent fabric forming an internal horizontal screen between eaves which reduces amount of heat rising into roof area	Screen is drawn in the evening and pulled back in the morning
Insulating panels	Timber or polystyrene panels to provide half-cladding in winter for glass-to-ground houses	Take down in spring before you plant summer crops

Shading

There are various ways of providing shade from the sun, as outlined in the table below.

Shading materials

Type	Specifications	Comments
Liquid (proprietary products)	Paste: mixed with water and 'painted' on to outside of glass. Available green or white – the latter is recommended	Put on in spring, remove early autumn
External blinds (Fig. 22)	Fixed to ridge of greenhouse. Available in various materials: wooden lath blinds, plastic reeds, shading netting and woven polyethylene	Can be pulled up and down as required
Internal blinds	Generally made from green or white polythene film (white recommended), polypropylene netting, polyester material (also provides insulation in winter), or fibreglass	Not so convenient as external blinds, since plants can get in the way of operation

22 *Lath-type roller blinds*

8 Other accessories

Staging and shelving

Staging provides a convenient way of growing potted plants. It allows a maximum use of space, especially if tiered staging (two or more levels) is used. The main level should be at waist height, and recommended maximum width is 91 cm (3 ft). Leave a gap between staging and greenhouse walls to allow good air circulation and heat to rise. Staging can run down one or both sides of greenhouse, depending on the amount required.

In a wide greenhouse, say 3.6 m (12 ft), central as well as side staging could be used: all should be about 76 cm ($2\frac{1}{2}$ ft) wide. Side staging must not be wider than door opening.

Staging does not have to be a permanent fixture – most kinds are

23 *Aluminium staging – two-tier*

easily dismantled and moved out to make room for tall summer crops like tomatoes. Most greenhouse manufacturers supply staging for their models.

Shelving This allows you to make maximum use of space, particularly in the roof area. It can be positioned below the eaves and/or down the centre of the house in the roof area. Shelves can also be mounted on the back wall of a greenhouse, one above the other. Several greenhouse manufacturers offer shelving.

Other accessories 43

24 *Aluminium staging – single tier*

Types of staging

Type	Specifications	Comments
Aluminium alloy (Fig. 23) (Fig. 24)	Framework is often of tubular aluminium. Many systems available. Can have single tier or several tiers, the latter ideal for pot-plant displays. Can have aluminium or plastic tops	Ideal for aluminium houses
Timber (Fig. 25)	Deal or cedarwood. Single level or tiered. Often with slatted timber top	Looks best in timber houses

25 *Timber staging with slatted surface*

Staging surfaces or tops

Type	Specifications	Comments
Slatted or open-work top	May be timber slats or strong plastic open-work top	Allows surplus water to drain quickly. Ensures good air circulation between plants. Allows heat to rise. Often recommended for cool and intermediate orchids, and many other pot plants (e.g. pelargoniums)
Gravel trays	Staging can often be supplied with gravel trays to hold gravel, shingle or horticultural aggregate	Either stand pots on these material or plunge them. Framework must be strong
Capillary staging	Needs a solid top, ideally with raised edges, for capillary watering. Can use sand (bench must be strong) or capillary matting. Gravel trays can be used for capillary watering	For further details of capillary watering see Watering Equipment further on in this chapter

Watering and spraying equipment

Greenhouse water supply Ideally mains water should be run to the greenhouse. Nowadays this is a simple matter as an alkathene supply pipe can be used. It should be laid underground not less than 60 cm (2 ft) deep. I recommend employing the services of a plumber for this job. A screw-thread tap can be fitted inside the greenhouse to take a hosepipe if necessary.

Collecting rainwater A greenhouse should have guttering and down-pipes. It is a good idea to collect rainwater from these in a water-butt as it is ideal for watering plants. Rainwater can either be used for hand watering or used in a header-tank or other container in a semi-automatic watering system (one that does not run off mains water). A water-butt should have a lid to prevent debris from falling into the water and contaminating it.

Hosepipes A hosepipe offers a convenient means of hand watering. Connect it to the greenhouse tap. You could fit a fine sprinkler head on the end of the hose for watering soil beds, or even pots and seed trays. But do not turn the tap on too far or the water could disturb the compost. Also available are watering lances for hosepipes complete with an on/off trigger. These are ideal for the controlled watering of pot plants. A seep hose, which has a fine spray, could be attached to a hosepipe and laid on the surface of the greenhouse soil border to gently water the soil.

Watering cans These represent the traditional way of watering greenhouse plants and are available in metal or plastic. A convenient size is a 4.5 litre (1 gal) can. Choose a can with a long spout so that it is easy to water plants at the back of the staging. Have a selection of roses to fit on the spout – fine, medium and coarse. Use the fine one for watering seed trays and seedlings.

Automatic and semi-automatic watering systems A fully automatic watering system runs from the mains water supply, via a header-tank fitted with a ballcock valve. A semi-automatic system is fed from a header-tank or some other container which has to be manually filled. However, such a system can generally be left for a few days without any attention. Some semi-automatic systems are connected to a tap by means of a hosepipe and the water is turned on by hand when required. None of these systems is selective – all plants get watered whether they need it or not.

Let us look at the main greenhouse watering systems in a little more detail.

Capillary watering – pots are placed on a water-retentive medium and take up moisture as required. Grow plants in plastic pots when using this system. The medium can be sand, kept moist via a pipe from a header-tank or other container, or via a tank with a ballcock valve connected to the mains water supply. Sand is heavy and bulky and needs strong staging with raised edges and lined with polythene sheeting.

More popular is capillary matting (a fibre matting) which is light in weight. It can be laid in shallow plastic trays. Water can be supplied to the matting as for the sand system. Complete capillary watering systems are available and are easy to install.

Trickle irrigation – this can be semi-automatic or fully automatic as outlined above. It consists of a main plastic supply pipe from which 'sprout' small-bore tubes (consequently known as the 'spaghetti system'). Each tube is positioned over a pot or other container, and therefore each one is watered when the supply is turned on.

Overhead sprinklers and misting equipment – several systems are available, and are mainly used for damping down a greenhouse. Useful when plenty of humidity is required, such as in a tropical house. Overhead watering systems are either connected directly to a tap so that you can turn on the water when it is needed, or are fully automatic.

Propagation equipment

To enable you to raise plants from seeds and cuttings you will need some form of propagation equipment. Most amateurs go for a heated propagating case, while the more ambitious gardeners may well opt for a sophisticated mist-propagation unit.

Propagating cases and mist-propagation units are generally placed or installed on the greenhouse staging; indeed, it is best to reserve a section of the staging specially for propagation and for growing on young plants. Even if you have a conservatory in which you grow only decorative plants, it is sensible to devote an area or an odd corner to propagation. It is certainly not necessary for the amateur

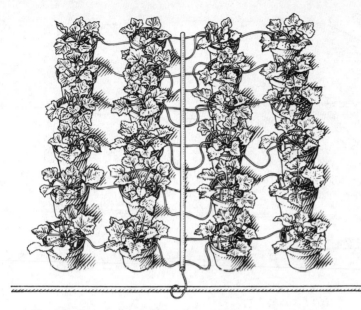

26 Trickle or spaghetti irrigation system

gardener to have a separate greenhouse for propagation, because the volume of plants raised from seeds or cuttings is not likely to warrant such an expense.

Propagating cases – unheated These simply consist of a box with a clear plastic or glass top. Useful for summer propagation, relying on natural warmth; for example, seed sowing and rooting of semi-ripe cuttings. The desirable humid atmosphere builds up within the case. There are many proprietary models available.

Propagating cases – heated There is a wide range of electrically heated propagating cases. They have electric heating cables in the base controlled by a thermostat. To retain heat and ensure the desirable high humidity, propagating cases are fitted with a glass or clear plastic top or lid. Such propagating cases are cheap to run, and are essential for keen gardeners who want to raise plants from seeds and cuttings in the spring – or indeed all the year round. There are also very simple versions available, consisting of a heated base on which stand one or two seed trays.

Soil-warming cables (See also table in Chapter 6.) Electric soil-

27 *Electrically heated propagating case*

warming cables can be laid in sand or shingle on the greenhouse staging to provide bottom heat for seed raising and rooting cuttings. To ensure high humidity, propagation can be carried out under a 'tent' of clear polythene sheeting supported on a light wooden or heavy galvanised-wire framework. This is a useful system, especially if you want a large heated propagation area that is economical to run.

Mist-propagation unit A familiar sight on commercial nurseries, but small versions are available for amateur gardeners. Installed on the greenhouse staging, a mist-propagation unit consists of a number of spray heads which periodically spray cuttings with a fine mist-like spray of water to prevent them from wilting. The spray heads run off the main water supply and are generally controlled automatically: as soon as the leaves of the cuttings start to dry off they are sprayed with water.

The water supply is generally operated by a moisture-sensitive device which is placed among the cuttings and which dries out at the same rate as the leaves of the cuttings. In such a unit bottom heat is provided by soil-warming cables laid in sand or shingle on the staging and controlled by a thermostat.

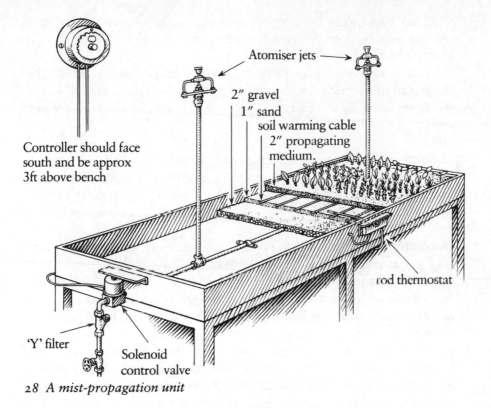

Atomiser jets →

2" gravel
1" sand
soil warming cable
2" propagating
medium.

Controller should face
south and be approx
3ft above bench

rod thermostat

'Y' filter

Solenoid
control valve

28 *A mist-propagation unit*

Lighting

Supplementary lighting Poor natural light in winter and early spring
means that plant growth is slow and coupled with high temperatures
results in weak and etiolated ('drawn') plants. Artificial light (by the
use of electric lamps) can be used in a heated greenhouse to accelerate
plant growth. Mercury vapour lamps can be used. Or, more popularly,
banks of fluorescent tubes mounted about 60 cm (2 ft) above the
staging. Such lighting is ideally used for raising plants, so therefore
each lamp is able to illuminate many small plants. Supplementary
lighting is frequently used in raising lettuces, tomatoes and cucumbers
among others.

Carnations can be given supplementary lighting to ensure flowering
all the year round. In this instance tungsten (incandescent) bulbs are
used, particularly in the winter to extend daylength. Commercially
such bulbs are also used in all-the-year-round chrysanthemum production to speed growth and to ensure flowering at required times.

As supplementary lighting is a complex subject (plants have very specific requirements) it will be necessary for readers to refer to a specialised book on the subject.

Some greenhouse gardeners install fluorescent tubes under the staging to allow plants to be grown in this often dark area. Always use tubes specially designed for horticultural use, or the warm-white ones.

Lighting for working If lighting is required simply for working at night, use a fluorescent tube fitted in the roof of the greenhouse, ideally over the staging or other working areas to prevent shadows while you are working.

Decorative lighting You may wish to illuminate ornamental plant displays at night simply for decorative effect, particularly in a conservatory or sun-room. Spot lights could perhaps be used, especially for plants that are in full flower or those with attractive foliage. There are various ornamental lighting systems available for greenhouse and conservatory use. Do make sure that lighting (as well as all other electrical equipment) is designed specifically for greenhouse use. Ideally all electrical apparatus should be installed by a qualified electrician. Fittings and wiring must be suitable for the moist conditions found in greenhouses and conservatories.

Plant Raising and General Care

9 Containers and composts

Having purchased a greenhouse or conservatory and fitted it out according to requirements you are no doubt eager to start raising and growing plants. In Part Two I shall consider how to raise plants and how to care for them properly. But first you will need to buy some suitable containers for both propagation and growing on plants, together with composts, and you will find there is a wide range of both on the market, as I have indicated in this chapter.

Containers

A selection of pots These days there is a wide range of plant pots available to the amateur gardener, many of which were first used by commercial growers. It is good to see that many products, so successfully used by professionals, are coming on to the amateur market.

Plastic – I think it safe to say that the majority of pots used today are plastic, either traditional terracotta colour (which I much prefer) or black and various other colours. I go for terracotta colour or black because they do not detract from the natural beauty of the plants. To my mind there is nothing more vulgar than to put a plant into a bright red or yellow pot.

Plastic pots come in all sizes, from small 'thumb' pots to 30 cm (12 in) in diameter and over. Unlike clay pots they will not break if dropped and in fact will give many years' service. After some years, however, they do tend to become brittle. Plastic pots are not porous like clays and therefore they do not dry out so quickly, a point that must be borne in mind when watering. If you saturate the compost in a plastic pot you will find that it remains wet for quite a long time, which can result in root rot. Plastic pots generally have plenty of drainage holes in the base and the trend is not to use drainage material in them like crocks (broken clay flower pots) or shingle.

Clay – terracotta clay flower pots are the traditional plant containers but unfortunately have been largely superseded by plastic pots. However, many gardeners still prefer to use clays and I am glad to say there are still some manufacturers of them. A wide range of sizes is available. So what are their advantages? Firstly they are porous so if you are heavy handed with the watering you can be sure that the compost will quickly lose surplus moisture. However, do bear in mind that the compost in clay pots can dry out quickly, especially in warm weather, so you will need to keep a more regular eye on water requirements. Clays are heavier than plastics and so there is less chance of plants toppling over. Clay pots are able to 'breathe' so the plants' roots are well supplied with air. The main disadvantage with clay pots is that they are easily broken. And they are more difficult to clean than plastics – it is not too easy to remove the green algae that build up on them. It is usual to provide drainage material in the base, such as crocks.

Pans and half pots – pans are shallow containers, generally only about one-third the height of pots. They can be obtained in plastic or clay and are particularly suitable for low-growing plants like alpines and dwarf bulbs. They are also very useful for seed sowing, when a great depth of compost is not required. Half pots are, as the name implies, about half the depth of ordinary flower pots. Clay and plastic versions are available in a good range of sizes. Half pots are especially useful for fairly low-growing plants, such as dwarf pot chrysanthemums, as they are in proportion to the plants. It looks slightly ridiculous to put a low-growing plant in a tall pot. Half pots are also recommended for shallow-rooting plants, such as some of the orchids, peperomias and others.

Compressed peat – these are especially useful for plant raising because plants receive no root disturbance when they are planted out, or potted on, because the pot is also planted. It rots away in the soil. I would suggest you use compressed-peat pots for potting seedlings or plants which are later to be planted out – such as tomatoes, capsicums, aubergines, melons, cucumbers, summer-bedding plants, and vegetables generally. In any event peat pots are intended only for short-term use and therefore only small ones are manufactured, such as 7.5 and 9 cm (3 and $3\frac{1}{2}$ in) diameter. The roots of the plants grow into the pot walls, so do not attempt to remove pots.

Bituminised paper – these have the same uses as peat pots – that is, they are ideal for raising young plants which are to be planted out, as the pot is planted with the plant, so eliminating root disturbance. Again they are intended only for short-term use.

Polythene bags – these are pots which are made of flexible polythene and they are widely used in the nursery industry for growing on young plants for sale. In recent years they have become available to amateur gardeners. They are supplied folded flat, but of course open out when filled with compost. They have drainage holes in the bottom as with normal pots.

Bags are comparatively cheap to buy and their main use is for growing on young plants prior to planting out. For instance, they could be used for seedling vegetables such as cabbages and tomatoes, and for summer bedding plants which benefit from pots rather than seed trays. It is essential to remove them before planting and this is done by slitting them down one side and underneath and peeling them away from the soil ball. You may find potting is more difficult than with rigid pots, until you become used to bags.

Peat pellets These are supplied as flat compressed peat discs and before use they have to be soaked in water so that they swell up. Each 'unit' is approximately 4 cm ($1\frac{1}{2}$ in) in diameter and depth. They are used for propagation, and you will find that each one has a hole in the centre. Seeds can be sown in them, one per unit, or cuttings rooted in them, again one per pellet. The young plants receive no root disturbance when they are potted or planted out because the pellet is planted with the plant. Make sure you keep them moist because once they dry out they are difficult to moisten again. They are useful for raising all kinds of plants, including vegetables and summer bedding, as well as pot plants.

Unexpanded   1 minute   2 minutes   3 minutes

29 Peat pellets

Soil blocks These have the same uses as peat pellets and in fact are just another version of it. Whereas peat pellets are bought, soil blocks are made at home. You will need to purchase a small soil-blocking tool. Basically what they do is to press out compost in small blocks, generally with a hole in the centre. Some blocking tools press out only one block at a time, while others press out four or five at one 'pass'. Various composts can be 'blocked', but most people prefer to use a soilless potting compost, or even a special blocking compost if available, which must be thoroughly wetted before use. Soil blocks are not as popular as they once were with amateurs – they have been superseded by modular systems.

Seed trays Seed trays are used not only for sowing seeds but also for pricking out or transplanting seedlings to give them more room to grow. For instance, many summer bedding plants, pot plants and seedling vegetables can be pricked out into trays, from which they are either planted out or potted.

Wood – wooden seed trays are almost a thing of the past, their place having been taken by moulded-plastic versions. Wooden trays are more difficult to clean than plastic ones and they have a shorter life, unless you treat them with a horticultural wood preservative. However, they give good results and as with clay pots the compost dries out more quickly than with plastic trays. Generally you have to cover the gaps in the bottom with crocks to prevent compost falling through. The standard size is 38 by 23 cm (15 by 9 in). Depth may be 2.5 to 7.5 cm (1 to 3 in). Use the shallowest for seed sowing, the deepest for pricking out.

Plastic – most gardeners these days use plastic trays which really have the same characteristics as plastic pots (see above). The standard size is as quoted above, but one can also purchase half trays (half the length of standard ones) for small quantities of seeds or seedlings. Unlike wooden trays, the plastic versions can be stacked one inside the other. Some of the cheaper plastic trays are very flimsy (or should I say flexible) and are best not moved around too much when full of compost. More expensive ones are very rigid.

Modular systems These are plastic trays, rather like seed trays, except that they are divided into a number of compartments, the number depending on the particular model. They are used for growing young plants – seedlings are pricked out into them, one seedling per compartment. Modules are especially useful for growing on vegetables and summer bedding plants which are later to be planted out. They prevent the roots of plants from becoming entangled and therefore minimise root disturbance when planting out. The plants are removed by pushing each one up from the bottom. Unit containers are often made from fairly flexible plastic and generally need to be placed in a rigid seed tray for support.

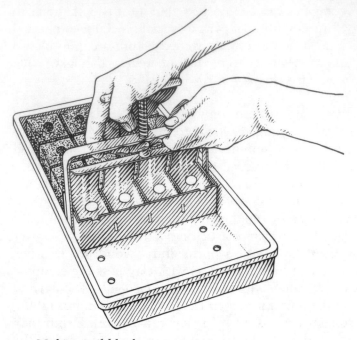

30 *Making soil blocks*

Ring-culture containers With ring culture, plants are grown in bot-tomless pots or 'rings'. These have a diameter of about 23 cm (9 in) and are available from garden centres, generally in whalehide or some kind of fibre. One can easily make plastic rings by cutting out the bottoms of plastic pots with a hacksaw. Plastic rings are serviceable for many years, while whalehide varieties last only for one growing season. The most popular crop for ring culture is the tomato, although others also can be grown by this method, such as capsicums and aubergines.

Ring culture has several benefits. For example, it ensures even uptake of water (one of the greatest problems with tomato growing is erratic watering) and isolates plants from soil-borne pests and diseases. Ring culture is carried out on the floor of the greenhouse such as over a soil border. In this instance, first cover the soil with a sheet of polythene. You will need to lay down a 15 cm (6 in) deep layer of aggregate which can be retained with timber planks. The aggregate can be used for several years in succession if it is flooded and sterilised after the crop has been cleared in the autumn. Several

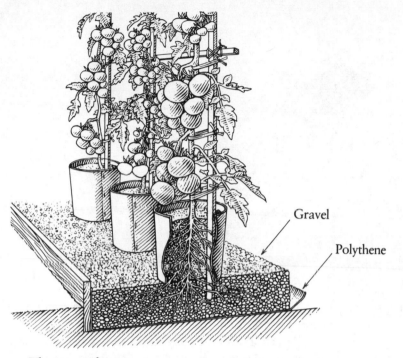

31 *The ring-culture system*

kinds of material can be used such as washed pea shingle or proprietary lightweight horticultural aggregates.

Place the rings firmly on the aggregate, spacing them about 45 cm (18 in) apart each way, and fill to within 5 cm (2 in) of the top with John Innes potting compost No. 2 or 3 or a similar soil-based type. Plant the tomatoes or other plants and water well. Thereafter water only the aggregate to encourage the plants to root into it. You will need to check daily for water requirements as the aggregate should be kept steadily moist. Feeding of the plants is via the compost in the rings –generally a liquid fertiliser is used.

Growing-bags These are specially made long narrow polythene bags filled with compost, generally a soilless type, in which to grow plants. There are several proprietary growing bags on the market and they are readily available from garden centres. They are placed on a firm level surface and a hole for each plant is made in the top. Plant in the normal way. The average-size growing bag is 1.2 m (4 ft) long and will hold four tomato, capsicum or aubergine plants, or two melons

32 *A growing-bag*

or cucumbers. Any short term greenhouse plant can be grown in them, but most gardeners use them for greenhouse vegetables.

The makers generally recommend that you do not make drainage holes in the bottom, so you have to be careful with watering or you will end up with saturated compost. Bamboo canes cannot, therefore, be used to support plants, but there are available special growing-bag crop supports, generally made of strong plastic-coated wire.

So what are the advantages of growing-bags? They are ideal if your greenhouse border soil is not of very good quality, or is infested with pests and diseases. Many gardeners do not wish to have a soil border, for its maintenance can be time-consuming, and therefore bags are probably the next best thing. They produce very good plant growth, provided you feed plants regularly when established. I find that bags do not dry out as quickly as pots. They should be used only for one season, after which the compost can be spread on the garden. However, I must admit that after a crop of tomatoes I plant them with winter lettuce, which always seem to grow satisfactorily.

Special display materials So far I have been discussing utility containers, although plastic and clay pots are widely used for growing decorative or display plants. However, let us now have a look at various containers and materials that are used for displaying ornamental plants.

Hanging baskets – these are used mainly for plants with a pendulous or trailing habit of growth, some popular examples of which are pendulous fuchsias and begonias, ivy-leaf pelargoniums, ivies and chlorophytums. There are many less well-known plants that are suited to basket culture, such as columneas. Remember that many epiphytic plants can be grown in baskets, such as the forest cacti, including the Christmas and Easter cacti.

Basically there are two types of hanging basket: the traditional wire basket (galvanised, or plastic-coated in the modern versions) and the moulded-plastic types, sometimes with a dish for catching drips. The wire baskets have to be lined before adding compost and traditionally this is done with sphagnum moss. Alternatively you could line the basket with a sheet of black polythene, with some holes punched in it to ensure drainage of surplus water, or with a proprietary foam-plastic liner. With a moulded-plastic basket simply fill with compost.

Plants are generally set around the edge of the basket as well as in the centre. With a wire basket you can also plant some through the wire to make more of a show. The way to do this is as follows: partially fill the basket with compost and firm it, then carefully push the roots of the plants through the wire and spread them out on the compost surface. Then fill up with compost and plant the rest of the plants in the top. Always leave room for watering when preparing a basket – a space of at least 2.5 cm (1 in) between the compost surface and the rim of the basket. Compost can dry out very rapidly in warm weather, so check daily for water requirements.

Hanging pots – one sometimes sees these offered for sale and they have the same uses as baskets. I am a great advocate of hanging containers in the greenhouse for they utilise space that would otherwise be wasted – the roof area. And the provide the most satisfactory method of displaying pendulous and hanging plants.

Plant-trees – an excellent way of displaying epiphytic plants (those which grow naturally on trees) is to grow them on a plant-tree. Many of the bromeliads can be displayed in this way, together with many orchids and the forest cacti like *Rhipsalis*. The tree should be dead and well branched and is best firmly secured in the greenhouse border. Insert it fairly deeply in the soil and ram well all round. I am saying use a 'tree', but rather a stout branch is what is generally used. Some of the botanic gardens use artificial trees made of cork bark and polyurethane foam filler, but these are expensive to make and do not look as pleasing as a real tree or branch.

Small-growing plants can be secured to a separate piece of bark before being fixed to the tree, thereby allowing you to move them around. Larger plants, such as some of the heavy bromeliads, need to be more securely fixed and a small planting pocket (using, for instance, pieces of bark or cork bark nailed to the tree) should be made and filled with suitable compost. Plants can be secured to pieces of bark or direct to the tree with thin nylon string, after the roots have been covered with some live sphagnum moss. The best way to water plants growing on a tree is to spray or syringe the whole thing with water. Ideas on how to display plants in this way can be gained by a visit to the greenhouses of botanic and other gardens.

Moss poles and columns – although not containers as such, moss poles provide an attractive means of supporting climbing plants which produce aerial roots, like *Monstera* and *Philodendron* species. The roots will eventually penetrate the moss. The easiest way to make a moss pole or column is to insert a broom handle of suitable length into the soil (or pot) and to slip over this a small-mesh wire netting cylinder. Ideally this should extend below the soil surface. The cylinder is then packed with live sphagnum moss. This moss should be kept moist at all times by spraying or syringing it with tepid water. Although I have not tried it myself, I have seen very thick moss columns, presumably with compost inside, with anthuriums planted in them. I see no reason why various epiphytic plants, like the forest cacti, should not grow directly in a thick moss column. It would be worth trying.

Plant labels It is convenient here to mention labels, for ideally all plants should be adequately labelled with their full botanical name. Most gardeners use white plastic or thin metal labels, and either a pencil or a waterproof pen. I find that those written with a pencil remain legible for longer than those marked with a waterproof pen. For permanent labelling you may find someone who can supply engraved plastic labels (white lettering and black background) but these are very expensive.

Composts

One can either buy ready-made proprietary potting and seed composts or purchase the ingredients and mix them at home. The latter, of course, works out cheaper – or at least you get more compost for your money. Here I shall consider both types: first, the ingredients used in home-made composts.

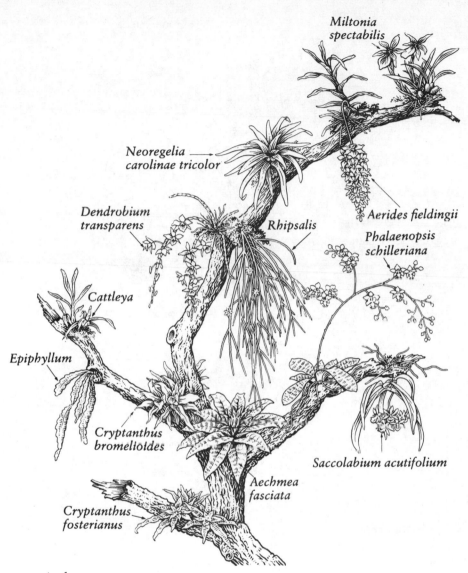

Miltonia spectabilis

Neoregelia carolinae tricolor

Dendrobium transparens

Rhipsalis

Aerides fieldingii

Phalaenopsis schilleriana

Cattleya

Epiphyllum

Cryptanthus bromelioides

Saccolabium acutifolium

Aechmea fasciata

Cryptanthus fosterianus

33 *A plant-tree*

Major compost ingredients All of the following are easily obtained from garden centres.

Loam – this is simply a term for soil which is used in loam-based composts, such as the John Innes types. Good quality loam can be bought from garden centres in plastic bags but it can also be made at home. Loam is produced by rotting down turves, which are lifted

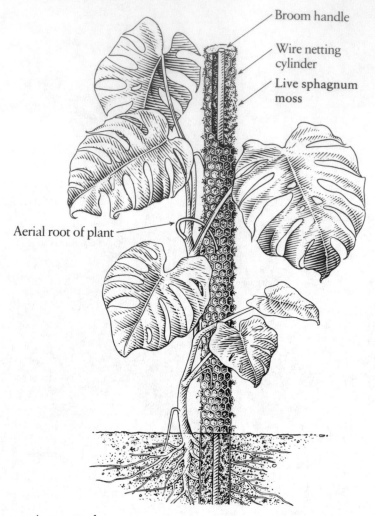

Broom handle

Wire netting
cylinder

Live sphagnum
moss

Aerial root of plant

34 A moss pole

from land which is of a good medium loam. They are stacked for up
to 12 months, grass side down, by which time they should be well
rotted. You will then have a fibrous loam for your composts – the
fibres are the partially decomposed roots of the turves.

Loam must be partially sterilised before use to kill weed seeds and
soil-borne pests and diseases. This is easily accomplished with a small
electric soil steriliser. The soil should be heated to a temperature of
82°C (180°F) – it should not go above this, or beneficial organisms

will be killed. If this temperature is not reached weed seeds and harmful organisms may survive.

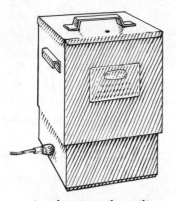

35 An electric soil steriliser

Before using loam pass it through a 9 mm ($\frac{3}{8}$ in) sieve. Loam for composts should be slightly acid, with a pH of 6 to 6.5.

Peat – use granulated moss peat for all composts. It should be quite acid, with a pH of 4 to 4.5. Pass it through a 9 mm sieve before use and make sure it is thoroughly moist.

Bark – pulverised or shredded bark is a comparatively new ingredient of composts. I like it because it gives an open, well-aerated and drained compost. Many growers at the moment are replacing up to 50% of the peat with bark.

Coconut fibre – this is a major ingredient of some proprietary soilless composts and is an alternative to peat.

Sand – use only horticultural sand in composts, not builders' sand. It should be washed (done by the suppliers) so that it is free from silt, lime or chalk. Generally a sharp of coarse sand is used – 60–70% of the particles should be between 1.5 and 3 mm ($\frac{1}{16}$ and $\frac{1}{8}$ in) in diameter. Horticultural grits are also used in composts. Buy whatever is available locally.

Perlite – this consists of inert granules of volcanic origin and is a very popular ingredient of composts, replacing the sand content. It is very light in weight and results in a well-aerated and drained compost.

Vermiculite – this is of mineral origin and has similar properties to Perlite. Again it is used instead of sand.

Fertilisers – of course, when making composts you must add fertilisers to supply the necessary plant foods. The main ones used are as follows: sulphate of ammonia and ammonium nitrate which supply nitrogen, a major nutrient; superphosphate of lime which provides phosphorus, another major plant food; sulphate of potash and nitrate of potash which supply the third major nutrient, potassium; chalk, ground limestone and magnesium limestone which supply calcium (the latter also magnesium); and fritted trace elements which supply a wide range of minor though important nutrients.

John Innes base fertiliser is the one used in the John Innes potting composts and it can either be bought ready for use or mixed at home. It consists of 2 parts hoof and horn, 2 parts superphosphate of lime and 1 part sulphate of potash (parts by weight). Hoof and horn supply the nitrogen.

John Innes seed compost:
This can either be bought ready for use or mixed at home. It is used mainly for seed sowing. The formula is as follows:

2 parts loam
1 part peat
1 part sand
Parts by volume, thoroughly mixed

To each bushel (see 'bushel' p. 66) of this mixture add the following fertilisers:

42 g ($1\frac{1}{2}$ oz) superphosphate of lime
21 g ($\frac{3}{4}$ oz) chalk or ground limestone

John Innes potting composts:
John Innes potting compost No. 1 is used for initial potting of young plants, for pricking out seedlings and for potting plants which do not need much fertiliser. Again it can be bought or mixed at home. The formula is as follows:

7 parts loam
3 parts peat
2 parts sand
Parts by volume, thoroughly mixed

To each bushel of this mixture add the following fertilisers:

113 g (4 oz) John Innes base
21 g ($\frac{3}{4}$ oz) chalk or ground limestone

John Innes potting compost No. 2 is used for potting plants into larger pots and is ideal for those which like a richer compost. Formula as above but add double the amount of JI base and chalk or ground limestone per bushel – 226 g (8 oz) and 42 g (1½ oz) respectively.

John Innes potting compost No. 3 is a very rich compost and is used only for comparatively few plants, such as chrysanthemums, during their final potting into large pots. Formula as for No. 1 but add treble the amount of JI base and chalk or ground limestone per bushel – 340 g (12 oz) and 63 g (2¼ oz) respectively.

John Innes lime-free compost. For acid-loving plants use a chalk- or lime-free compost. The JI seed compost may be used, but omit the chalk or limestone and use instead flowers of sulphur at 21 g (¾ oz) per bushel. The loam should be acid or lime free.

Soilless composts These can be made from peat with fertilisers added, peat and sand with fertilisers, peat and Perlite with fertilisers, or peat and Vermiculite with fertilisers. One can also replace 50% of the peat with pulverised bark if desired, or replace it completely with coconut fibre. A few home-made mixtures are given below, but remember that one can also buy proprietary soilless composts from garden centres.

A soilless seed compost:

Equal parts by volume of peat and sand (or peat and Perlite, or peat and Vermiculite), thoroughly mixed

To each bushel of this mix add the following fertilisers:

14 g (½ oz) sulphate of ammonia
28 g (1 oz) superphosphate of lime
14 g (½ oz) sulphate of potash
113 g (4 oz) ground chalk or limestone

A soilless potting or pricking-out compost:

3 parts peat
1 part sand
Or replace sand with either Perlite or Vermiculite
Parts by volume, thoroughly mixed

To each bushel of this mix add the following fertilisers:

14 g (½ oz) ammonium nitrate
28 g (1 oz) nitrate of potash
56 g (2 oz) superphosphate of lime
85 g (3 oz) chalk or ground limestone
85 g (3 oz) magnesium limestone
14 g (½ oz) fritted trace elements

With these soilless composts it is necessary to start liquid feeding as soon as the plants are well established because the foods do not last as long as with JI composts.

Cutting composts For the rooting of cuttings use one of the following, which are easily mixed at home:

Equal parts by volume peat and sand
Equal parts by volume peat and Perlite
Equal parts by volume peat and Vermiculite
Perlite or Vermiculite can also be used alone

Do not add fertilisers, but pot the cuttings as soon as rooted, for there are no nutrients in these composts. In each case, the peat can be replaced with coconut fibre.

Mixing composts In the above formulae I have used the bushel as a measure, as it is a convenient quantity for the amateur gardener to mix. It is 1.28 cu ft or 2,200 cu in. I make no apologies for reverting to imperial measurements here for the bushel is such a well-known unit. One can make a wooden bushel box for measuring composts: the size is 22 in by 10 in by 10 in. A bushel also equals 8 gal; therefore, one can, for instance, use a 2 gal bucket for measuring even smaller quantities – this would give you $\frac{1}{4}$ bushel

Now a few hints on mixing your own composts. I prefer to mix first the major ingredients – e.g. the loam, peat and sand. These can be measured by the shovelful, bucketful, etc., as they must be measured out in volume. Thoroughly mix them on a clean surface such as dry concrete. It is best to place the different ingredients in layers to form a cone-shaped heap: for instance, a layer of loam, topped with a layer of sand, topped with a layer of peat. The way to mix is to turn the heap with a shovel, at least three times – rather like mixing concrete. If you mix more than you need at the time, remember that a compost mix can be stored until required (but do not add the fertilisers until required for use). Ideally store in a clean plastic sack or dustbin as you must prevent it from becoming wet.

When the major ingredients are well mixed measure out in bushel units (using your box) and add the appropriate amounts of fertiliser. Again mix thoroughly by turning the heap several times. Use the compost as soon as possible after adding the fertilisers.

10 Propagation

Raising plants from seeds and by vegetative means, such as cuttings and division, is a major aspect of greenhouse cultivation. However, I am covering only the basic techniques here, for plant raising is discussed in detail in my book *Plant Propagation Made Easy* (J. M. Dent, 1993).

Raising plants from seeds

Sowing and germination For guidance on suitable containers and composts, see Chapter 9. Moderately firm the compost in the containers by pressing all over with the fingers, paying particular attention to the corners and sides of the trays or pans. The surface should be made perfectly smooth and level by pressing it with a flat piece of wood, ideally the size of the container. If you are sowing fine dust-like seeds, use a small-mesh sieve to sift a layer of fine compost over the surface before finally firming it. The final level of the compost should be 6–12 mm ($\frac{1}{4}$–$\frac{1}{2}$ in) below the top of the container.

Sow seeds thinly and evenly. The best way to ensure even sowing of very fine dust-like seeds is to mix them with a quantity of dry, very fine silver sand to make handling easier.

I can recommend the following procedure for thin even sowing. In the palm of one hand hold enough seeds for the container. Raise this hand 10–15 cm (4–6 in) above the surface of the compost. Now move your hand to and fro across the surface of the compost, at the same time gently tapping it with your other hand to release the seeds slowly. I must emphasize the *slow* release of the seeds to avoid thick patches. You should find that the seeds scatter evenly over the surface of the compost. Sow half the quantity of seeds in one direction, from one end of the seed tray to the other, and then sow the remaining half in the other direction, from one side of the tray to the other. If very small seeds stick to the palm of your hand you could place them on a sheet of paper and again sow as above.

Most seeds need to be covered with a layer of compost, but very fine dust-like seeds should not be covered because this would prevent germination. Seeds which need it should be covered with a layer of

36 *Sowing seeds*

compost equal to twice the diameter of the seeds. Sift a layer of
compost over them, using a fine or medium sieve, making sure the
compost is of a uniform depth all over the seeds otherwise germination
will be uneven.

Very large seeds and pelleted seeds can be hand-spaced evenly on
the surface of the compost. If you are sowing in soil blocks or peat
pellets, or in modules, insert one seed per unit and cover with a little
sand or fine compost.

After sowing, stand seed trays and pans in shallow trays of water
and leave them until the surface of the compost becomes moist – then
remove and allow to drain before transferring them to germination
conditions.

Seeds are best germinated in an electrically heated propagating case
in the greenhouse, maintaining a temperature of 18–21° C (65–70° F).
Cover the containers with sheets of newspaper, brown paper or black
polythene to prevent the compost drying before germination occurs
and to keep an even temperature over the surface of the compost. As
soon as seeds germinate transfer them to a part of the greenhouse
where they will receive maximum light, but shade them from strong
sunshine.

Pricking out seedlings When the seedlings are large enough to handle
easily they should be pricked out or transplanted into other containers
to give them room to develop. One can use standard seed trays for
pricking out, inserting 40 to 54 seedlings per tray. Or you could prick

out into soil blocks, peat pellets or modules, or even small pots. Use 5 cm (2 in) deep seed trays as a reasonable depth of soil is required.

Use John Innes potting compost No. 1 for pricking out or an equivalent loamless type. Seedlings should always be handled by the seed leaves or cotyledons (the first leaves produced) and must be carefully lifted out of the seed trays with a dibber or pencil. Insert it under the roots and lift out a few at a time.

37 *Pricking out seedlings*

Trays or pots should be filled with compost and then a hole for each seedling made with the dibber or pencil. Make sure the hole is deep enough to allow the roots of the seedlings to dangle straight down. Each seedling should be inserted almost up to its cotyledons and then very gently firmed in with the dibber. After pricking out thoroughly water the seedlings with a fine-rosed watering can. The seedlings are now grown, in the greenhouse, in conditions suited to the particular plants, shading them from strong sunshine to prevent leaf scorch.

Stem cuttings

A great many greenhouse plants can be raised from stem cuttings, both softwood and semi-ripe cuttings, and this is one of the most popular methods of producing new plants.

Softwood cuttings These are prepared from the current year's shoots before they become fully ripened, or hard and woody: the cuttings are soft or unripened. They are rooted mainly in the early part of the year – from mid-winter to early summer.

Collection and preparation Choose soft new side shoots for cuttings, removing complete shoots with a sharp knife. Prepare and insert immediately to prevent wilting. Use a sharp knife or razor blade for final preparation, which consists of cutting the shoots immediately below a node or leaf joint at the base. Leave the tips of the shoots intact. Cuttings should be approximately 7.5 cm (3 in) in length. The lower third or even half of the cuttings should be cleanly stripped of leaves.

The lower 6 mm ($\frac{1}{4}$ in) of each cutting should be dipped in a hormone rooting power (one formulated for softwood cuttings) to encourage quicker rooting.

38 Preparing a softwood cutting

Insertion and rooting conditions Insert either in a cutting compost in seed trays, modules, or pots or pans; or in soil blocks or peat pellets (see Chapter 9).

Insert cuttings in holes made with a wooden dibber or pencil and ensure that the base of each touches the bottom of the hole and that the lower leaves are just above compost level. Firm lightly and then water with a rosed can.

Softwood cuttings need heat and high humidity to root well. It is best, if possible, to provide heat at the base of cuttings, where a temperature of 18° C (65° F) is suitable for most. There is no doubt that an electrically heated propagating case provides the ideal conditions. The mist-propagation unit is a more sophisticated piece of equipment which gives ideal conditions for cuttings. Bottom heat is provided by means of soil-warming cables. Another system is to install soil-warming cables on the greenhouse bench and to root the cuttings on this, covering them with a clear-polythene 'tent' to ensure humid conditions.

As soon as cuttings have rooted, remove them from the rooting medium and pot in small pots of John Innes potting compost No. 1, or a soilless equivalent.

Semi-ripe cuttings These are usually rooted in the summer and early autumn and are prepared from the current year's shoots which are becoming ripe and firm (or woody) at the base, while the tops are still soft or unripened. Semi-ripe cuttings are generally easier to root than softwoods.

Collection and preparation Semi-ripe cuttings are collected and prepared in the same way as softwoods (see above) and benefit from being dipped in a hormone rooting powder formulated for this type of plant material.

Insertion and rooting conditions Again refer to softwood cuttings as the same comments apply. Remember to pot as soon as rooted because there are no nutrients in the rooting medium.

Leaf cuttings

Certain plants can be propagated from leaves used as cuttings. When inserted, the leaves form roots and eventually young plants. Leaf cuttings are generally taken in the spring and summer and they need heat to root, so use a propagating case, a mist-propagating unit or a bench warmed with soil-warming cables. Leaf cuttings can be prepared in various ways according to the plant.

Preparation and insertion Sometimes whole leaves are used complete with leaf stalk: for example, *Peperomia* and *Saintpaulia*. Cleanly remove some healthy leaves and dip the ends of the stalks in a hormone rooting powder formulated for softwood cuttings. Insert in cutting compost, the entire stalk being below the surface.

Some begonias can be propagated from leaves, like *B. masoniana*, *B. rex* and similar species. Take an entire leaf and remove the stalk. Turn the leaf upside down and with a sharp knife slice right through

39 *Leaf cuttings of* Peperomia

the veins. Lay the leaf on the surface of cutting compost in a seed tray, top side facing upwards. It is important to ensure the cut veins are in close contact with the compost: this can be achieved by weighting the leaf with small stones, or some small wire pegs could be pushed through the leaf to hold it down. Roots will be produced where the veins have been cut and new plants will develop on the upper side of the leaf.

With plants like *Sinningia* (gloxinia) and *Streptocarpus* entire leaves are used but, because of their length, they are best cut in half, the lower half being used as a cutting. Treat with hormone rooting powder and insert upright, in pots or seed trays.

The leaves of *Sansevieria* are cut into 5 cm (2 in) long sections. Remove an entire leaf and cut it into a number of sections. This method is used for *S. trifasciata* and other species, but do not propagate the yellow-edged *S. trifasciata* 'Laurentii' by this method because the result will be all-green plants – the yellow edge will disappear. Use division instead as a method of increase. Dip the bases of cuttings

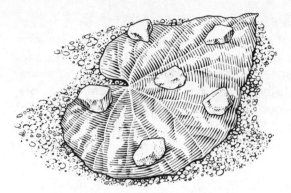

40 *Leaf cutting of* Begonia rex

in a hormone rooting powder and insert them vertically (making sure they are the right way up) to half their length in pots or trays of cutting compost.

There are a number of succulent plants than can be increased from leaves and these include *Aloe, Crassula, Echeveria* and *Sedum*. Use whole leaves as cuttings and insert them in an upright position, shallowly, in pots or trays of cutting compost.

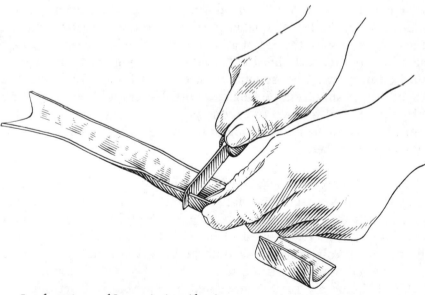

41 *Leaf cuttings of* Sansevieria trifasciata

Rooting conditions Provide a temperature of 18–21° C (65–70° F) to ensure that leaf cuttings of all types root successfully. High humidity is also desirable. Use one of the items of equipment described under softwood cuttings. When leaf cuttings have rooted and the young plants have formed, carefully lift and pot them in 7.5 cm (3 in) pots, using either John Innes potting compost No. 1 or an equivalent loamless type.

Division of plants

Division, or splitting plants into a number of smaller portions, is an easy method of increase for many greenhouse plants. Plants which form clumps, and mats or carpets of growth, can often be divided. Spring is the best time, especially during potting on or re-potting. Many clump-forming greenhouse plants become very large after a number of years and they need to be reduced in size so that they fit into reasonable-sized pots. Among the clump formers are *Aspidistra*, bromeliads, some of the cacti, *Chlorophytum*, many ferns, a wide range of orchids, *Sansevieria* and *Saintpaulia*.

The method Plants should be removed from their pots and as much soil as possible teased away from the roots to make division easy and to avoid too much root damage during the operation. Then split the plants into a number of smaller portions, either by carefully pulling them apart or with the use of a knife if the crowns are on the tough side. Ensure that each division has adequate top growth plus a good portion of roots. Choose suitable-sized pots for the divisions and repot them, using fresh potting compost. Water and keep in a warm place for a week or two to encourage them to put forth new roots quickly. Shading from the strongest sun will also help them to become quickly established.

Dividing orchids Divide plants when they have two or more new growths, but do make sure that sufficient pseudobulbs remain after division. Pseudobulbs are the large green bulb-like growths. Some orchids can be increased by detaching offshoots which are produced by the parent plants. These should be potted in small pots. *Vanda* species often produce offshoots.

Cymbidiums are often propagated by backbulbs. These are the older, leafless pseudobulbs behind the leading pseudobulbs. They should be carefully removed (generally they have no roots) and potted individually into suitable-sized pots.

11   Plant care

Having raised plants for your greenhouse you must ensure they are cared for properly. In this chapter, therefore, I shall deal with basic but very important aspects of plant care, such as potting and planting, watering and damping down, ventilating and shading, feeding plants and supporting them, stopping and hardening, and maintaining hygienic conditions in the greenhouse.

Potting

This is the correct term used for the initial potting of things like rooted cuttings and seedlings. Many people refer to this stage of potting as 'potting up', and it is also referred to as potting off.

Always use small pots when potting, just large enough to take the root system without cramping it. Over-large pots should not be used, because plants do not like a large volume of compost around their roots – it will hold more water than the plants need and it is liable to remain too wet. This could inhibit rooting and may even result in rotting of the roots. So for the majority of small plants pots in the region of 7.5–9 cm (3–3½ in) in diameter are suitable for the initial potting. Do not use too rich a compost for initial potting – John Innes potting compost No. 1 is suitable, or a soilless equivalent.

It is generally considered unnecessary to place a layer of drainage material in the bottom of plastic pots which have adequate drainage holes in the base and therefore ensure excellent drainage. Clay pots usually have crocks (broken clay pots) placed in the bottom to ensure good drainage.

The young plants, like rooted cuttings and seedlings, should be carefully lifted from their trays, or other containers, because the new roots may be brittle. Many people use an old table fork to lift young plants. If roots are exceptionally long they may be cut back by one-third to half their length to make potting easier – this also stimulates a good fibrous root system.

To pot a young plant, first put a layer of compost in the bottom of the pot and firm it moderately with your fingers. Place the plant so that it is central in the pot and the roots are dangling downwards and are not cramped, then fill up to the top with more compost. Tap the pot on the bench to get the compost well down, and finish by firming it all round with your fingers. You may need to add a little more compost, but make sure that you leave space at the top of the pot for watering. Having mentioned moderate firming with the fingers, I should say that some of the soilless composts do not need any firming, so be sure to refer to the manufacturer's instructions on the bag. However, the traditional loam-based types, like John Innes, do need moderate firming. Finally water newly potted plants to settle the compost around them, particularly if using soilless composts.

Potting on Potting on involves moving a plant from a smaller to a larger pot, generally to the next size, say from a 7.5 cm (3 in) to a 10 cm (4 in) pot; or from a 12.5 cm (5 in) to a 15 cm (6 in) pot. The aim is to avoid a very large volume of compost around the roots. The time to pot on is when the present pot is full of roots – but before the plant becomes pot-bound (when the pot is crammed full of roots), because plants in this condition do not make good growth. There are a few exceptions, since some plants like to be rather pot-bound and this is indicated in the plant chapters. To find out whether or not a plant needs potting on, invert the pot, tap the rim on a bench to loosen the soil ball and slide the pot off so that root development can be seen clearly.

When potting on a stronger compost is generally used, such as John Innes potting compost No. 2 or an equivalent soilless type. If you find that the roots are very tightly packed when you remove the plants from their existing pots, gently tease them out, avoiding damage as much as possible, to ensure that they quickly root in the new compost. The technique of potting on is the same as described above, except that the plant will have a ball of soil around its roots. Simply trickle compost between the soil ball and the pot wall, tap the pot on the bench to get the compost well down, and firm with the fingers (unless you are using one of the soilless composts which does not need firming).

The term re-potting simply means removing a plant from its pot, teasing away some of the old compost and putting it back into the

42 *Potting on a young plant*

same size of pot, using fresh compost. This is necessary for plants which have not made much growth and therefore do not need a larger pot, but which need a supply of fresh compost because they have been in their existing pots for several years. Examples are well-established greenhouse shrubs, perennials and some of the bulbous plants, particularly if they are in large final pots.

Planting

Planting pot-grown plants in a soil bed or border, in growing-bags or even in ring-culture containers is really straightforward, but I can offer a few helpful hints to gain complete success. First, thoroughly water the plants in their pots several hours before planting out. If plants are planted out with a dry soil ball it is often impossible to moisten it again, no matter how much water you apply subsequently, and the plants therefore may fail to become established and grow well; they could even die.

See that the soil is moderately moist before planting but certainly not wet and sticky. Greenhouse plants should always be planted in soil that has had a chance to warm up – cold soil will inhibit establishment. The hole for each plant should be made wide and deep enough to take the soil ball. Remember that plants should be planted to the same depth that they were in their pots – or very slightly deeper so that the top of the rootball is just covered with soil. Return the soil into the space between the soil ball and the sides of the hole and firm well with your fingers, hands or heels, depending on the size of the plant and the situation. After planting, lightly prick over the soil surface to relieve any compaction.

Watering

Even if you have an automatic watering system it is still advisable to know how and when to water plants by hand. For instance you might not be using the system in the autumn and winter, or it might not be working properly, so that you would have to resort to hand watering. There are in any case many gardeners who do not like automatic watering systems, preferring to water plants according to their own judgment.

Hand watering, however, is a highly skilled task which can be learned only through experience. Understandably, many beginners simply do not know when plants need water and how much is needed. Unfortunately it is all too easy to allow plants to suffer or die from too much water or too little.

When to water Water requirements are given where applicable in the plant chapters and you will see that plants differ widely in their requirements. Some like the soil to be steadily on the moist side and others may like rather dry conditions. However, the bulk of greenhouse plants prefer it somewhere between the two extremes. As a general rule for watering (one can only give general guidelines in a subject such as this), and particularly to help beginners, apply water when the surface (say the top 6 mm or $\frac{1}{4}$ in) of the compost or soil starts to become dry. It is a case of feeling the surface with your fingers – if it feels dry then apply water. If moist, leave well alone. Also, most composts turn a lighter colour when dry, so if the surface becomes lighter then it is an indication that water is needed.

In warm weather soils and composts will dry out more rapidly than in cool or cold conditions. Plants well rooted in their pots will also dry out more quickly than those whose roots have not fully ramified the compost. Soilless composts often dry out more quickly than soil-based kinds, and compost in clay pots will lose its moisture more quickly than in plastic pots.

How to water plants When watering potted plants, completely fill the space between the compost surface and the rim of the pot with water to ensure the compost becomes moistened right the way through. If compost has become bone dry in a pot, it is best to stand the pot up to its rim in water until the compost is thoroughly moist again – until air bubbles cease to rise through the water.

When watering soil beds and borders use a gently running hosepipe fitted with a rose or sprinkler attachment to prevent panning of the soil surface and mud splashes on plants. Water soil beds when they feel dry on the surface – again use your fingers. You must add enough water for it to penetrate at least 15 cm (6 in) deep. This means applying the equivalent of 2.5 cm (1 in) of rain. This is about 27 litres of water per m² (4¾ gallons per square yard). About half an hour after watering it is a good idea to check that the water has penetrated sufficiently deeply. Simply dig a small hole with a trowel about 15 cm deep – if the soil is still dry at the bottom, apply more water.

There are quite a few proprietary soil-moisture indicators available, the more expensive ones being fairly accurate. They are generally battery-operated and contain a probe which is pushed into the soil. This activates a needle in front of a calibrated dial and you simply read off the state of the soil – dry, moist or wet. Reliable soil-moisture meters are especially useful to beginners and they can be used in pots or soil beds.

43 *A soil-moisture indicator*

Water quality Many gardeners use rainwater for watering greenhouse plants; this is excellent provided it is not contaminated by a dirty water butt, storage tank, gutters and greenhouse glass. Ideally, water should be at greenhouse temperature for watering plants and this can be achieved by having a water-storage tank inside the house, which can be used to catch rainwater from the greenhouse roof, via gutter and downpipe.

Other gardeners, however, use tap water for watering their plants and this is extremely variable in quality. In some areas it is 'soft' or on the acid side (highly desirable), while in other areas it is 'hard' or alkaline, containing calcium or chalk. This is not so good for some plants. If you grow lime-hating plants it is best not to water them with hard water for it can result in a build-up of calcium in the compost (which should be acid or lime-free). The calcium will render iron unavailable to plants and they will consequently suffer from lime-induced chlorosis – the leaves will turn yellow and growth may be stunted.

If you have no choice but to water lime-hating plants with hard tap water, then periodically apply a solution of sequestered iron to the compost to prevent the plants becoming chlorotic. Apply according to the manufacturer's instructions on the packet.

I do not recommend spraying the leaves of plants with hard or alkaline water because it deposits calcium on them which is unsightly and will inhibit growth; use rainwater instead.

If you have a mist propagation unit you may find that the mist heads become coated with lime scale after some time if you are in a hard-water area, and the nozzles may become blocked. Metal mist heads can be soaked in concentrated hydrochloric acid until all the calcium scale has been removed. The heads should then be washed thoroughly in plain water. The alternative is to rub the heads with fine emery paper to remove the scale and to unblock the nozzles with a pin. In a hard-water area, cuttings in a mist-propagation unit may be subjected to a deposit of calcium. In this instance sponge off the leaves with soft water.

Damping down

The purpose of damping down a greenhouse is simply to create a moist or humid atmosphere. You will see in the plant chapters that I have indicated whether or not plants like these conditions. Many of the tropical plants, for instance, especially those from rain forests, like high humidity, while plants from deserts and semi-deserts need a dry atmosphere.

Generally speaking one should create humid conditions only when temperatures are fairly high, say 15.5° C (60° F) and above. I would not damp down in temperatures below 15.5° C – it is then a case of keeping the atmosphere as dry as possible. If you are running a tropical greenhouse then obviously you can with advantage carry out damping down all the year round, but otherwise the spring and summer are the main periods for creating a humid atmosphere, provided temperatures are high enough.

Damping down can also be used to lower temperatures. For instance, if you are finding it difficult to keep the temperature down in your greenhouse during very hot weather despite the fact the door and ventilators are fully open, it is best to damp down several times throughout the day. The evaporating moisture has a cooling effect.

Damping down simply consists of wetting the floor of the greenhouse and the staging, either with a rosed watering-can or with a hosepipe. In very warm conditions plants also can have their leaves sprayed with water. Damping down is generally carried out first thing in the morning, and in the late afternoon, to allow plants to dry off before nightfall and ensuing lower temperatures.

Ventilating

There are several very good reasons for opening the greenhouse ventilators to provide ventilation. First, it is a means of reducing the temperature; for example, when the sun is shining and the temperature in the greenhouse is soaring to an excessively high level. Opening the vents also ensures that the air in the house is kept fresh, thereby preventing a stale, stagnant atmosphere. Ventilating also helps to reduce humidity, which is particularly important in the winter when the temperatures are low. If excess condensation forms on the glass then this is an indication of insufficient ventilation.

The usual way in which a greenhouse is ventilated is to open the ridge vents to allow the rising warm air to escape, thereby sucking in cool air from the side vents and/or louvres. Fans can also be used for ventilation. (For details of these and other types of ventilators see Chapter 7.)

Ventilation is needed all the year round and must be geared to

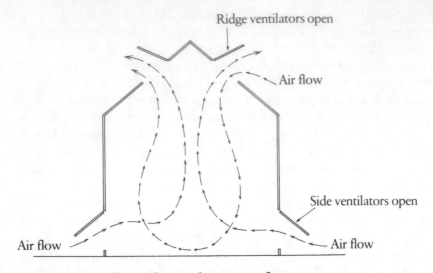

44　*Ventilation of greenhouse, showing air flow*

maintaining the minimum temperatures. Even in winter a little ventilation whenever the weather is fine helps to keep the air dry. If you are using a paraffin heater a little ventilation should be kept on at all times to allow any harmful fumes to escape and to ensure efficient combustion of the fuel. On windy days open only those vents on the lee side of the greenhouse.

Shading

Shading is necessary in spring and summer to prevent excessive temperatures – it goes hand in hand with ventilation in controlling the greenhouse atmosphere. It is also used to prevent scorching of the plants, for strong sun shining through the glass can severely scorch many plants and quickly kill seedlings, especially if there are droplets of water on the leaves. Shading is not required in the autumn and winter and during these seasons one must make sure that the plants receive maximum light.

Plants vary in the amount of shade needed – for example, cacti and many other succulents like plenty of sun, whereas ferns and many tropical plants need to be shaded well from strong sunshine. It is best to try to group plants in the greenhouse according to their requirements: those which need shade can all be placed together in one part, and those which need plenty of light grouped in another part. Then you can conveniently provide shade only for those plants which need it. In the plant chapters I have shown the needs of plants in respect of light and shade.

The ideal system is to provide shade only when it is needed and to remove it in dull conditions so that plants receive maximum light, and this means the use of roller blinds. But, of course, these are not practical propositions if you are out all day; the alternative is to apply a liquid shading material to the glass, which remains in place all spring and summer. (See Chapter 7 for shading materials.)

Feeding plants

Potted and border plants Feed plants only when they are actively growing, which for most is in the spring and summer. Ideally carry out a regular feeding programme during the growing season – most plants benefit from feeding every seven to fourteen days. Use the same type of fertiliser throughout the season.

Start a feeding programme only when plants are well established: in other words, when the roots of potted plants have ramified the volume of compost – it is a mistake to feed newly potted plants, for the new compost will provide sufficient plant foods for many weeks. With border plants, start to feed in the summer after autumn/winter/early spring planting, by which time they should be established and putting forth new roots. As a general rule apply fertilisers only to moist soil or compost and never when dry, or when the plants are suffering from lack of moisture.

Types of fertilisers and application There are several types or groups of fertilisers which can be used under glass and these are described below.

Liquids – most gardeners these days prefer to use proprietary liquid fertilisers for their spring and summer feeding programme. Use a general-purpose fertiliser for most plants and a specific one for certain others – for instance, there are special tomato, chrysanthemum and carnation fertilisers available, as well as other 'specifics'. Liquid fertilisers should be dissolved/diluted and used according to the maker's instructions and applied to moist soil or compost where they are quickly absorbed by the plants.

Foliar – foliar fertilisers are again liquid but are applied to the leaves to give a boost to growth. They are particularly useful if plants are making slow or poor growth. They are absorbed even more quickly than liquid fertilisers applied to the soil or compost.

Dry fertilisers – proprietary dry fertilisers, both general-purpose and specific, are sprinkled around plants as a top dressing and pricked into the surface. Use according to instructions on the packet. They can be used in a spring and summer feeding programme instead of liquid fertilisers.

Fertiliser pellets and spikes – these are inserted in the soil or compost where they release plant foods over a long period – mostly for the entire growing season – so reducing time spent on feeding plants. Use them as an alternative to applying liquid or dry fertilisers in the spring and summer.

Base dressing – this is an application of dry fertiliser to a soil bed or border before sowing or planting to ensure there are sufficient plant foods in the soil. The fertiliser is sprinkled on the surface of the dug soil and pricked into the top few centimetres. One can either use a compound fertiliser (supplying all the major plant foods like nitrogen, phosphorus and potash) or 'straight' fertilisers which supply only one type of plant food.

Ideally a base dressing should be applied according to the results of a soil test – use one of the proprietary soil-testing kits which come complete with instructions. You can then rectify nutrient deficiencies by applying the correct amount of the right type of fertiliser. For instance, you may find you need to add more nitrogen than, say, potash. Never apply a base dressing haphazardly without making a soil test, for you will not know which nutrients are deficient or how much fertiliser to apply to make up these deficiencies.

Also test the soil for lime content (the pH) and apply lime if this proves necessary (but not if you are growing lime-hating plants). The best time to apply lime is in the winter after the soil border has been dug. The ideal pH for most plants is 6.5.

Supporting plants

Many greenhouse plants need some kind of support, not only to keep them neat and tidy and to prevent them toppling over, but also to ensure optimum growth. In the plant chapters I have recommended supports wherever applicable. The most widely used plant supports are listed below.

Canes – bamboo canes are suitable for supporting many crops like tomatoes, chrysanthemums and carnations. Generally only one cane is needed per plant. For these kinds of plants use stout canes about 1.8 m (6 ft) in length. Always push canes well down into the soil. Thin or split canes, 30–45 cm (12–18 in) long, are useful for supporting smaller plants in pots. Tie plants to canes with raffia or soft string. Plastic canes are also now available.

Horizontal wires – these provide a good means of supporting many climbing plants, both ornamentals and crops like melons and cucumbers. They are fixed to a greenhouse wall or the back wall of a lean-to or conservatory, generally spaced 30 cm (12 in) apart. Use galvanised or plastic-coated wire. But how do you fix wires to the glazing bars in metal houses? Fortunately there are special plugs or fixings available. Use wall nails or eyes for fixing them to a brick wall, while for a wooden-frame greenhouse there are metal eye hooks which are screwed into the woodwork. Tie in plants with raffia or soft string.

Tying materials – raffia is the traditional tying material and is highly recommended because it does not damage even the softest stems. These days plastic 'raffia' is also available. Soft garden twine is widely used for tying in plants, as is plastic 'string'. Never tie in growths tightly – leave space for stems to thicken.

Growing-bag crop supports – these are proprietary metal supports which can be placed alongside growing-bags (with their 'feet' under the bag) to which plants can be tied.

Vertical strings – these are sometimes used for supporting tomatoes. Use lengths of strong garden twine, attaching one end to a horizontal wire in the roof and burying the other end under a plant when planting. The string is then twisted around the stem as it grows; therefore, it must not be too tight or too loose.

Miscellaneous – finally a few odds and ends you may find useful. Hazel sticks make good supports for things like freesias and dwarf French beans. Push the sticks into the compost between and around the plants, and let the plants grow up through them. Trellis is useful for climbing plants. Panels can be obtained in timber, plastic-coated wire and plastic, and are generally fixed to the back wall of a lean-to or conservatory. There are many shapes and sizes to choose from. There are also mini-trellises for pots. Split wire rings can be used to 'clip' plant stems to canes and other supports; it is far quicker to use these than, say, raffia or string, especially if you have a lot of tying in to do.

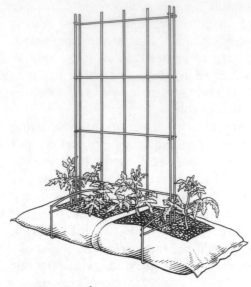

45 *Growing-bag crop supports*

Stopping or pinching

This involves pinching out the tip of a plant to encourage side or lateral shoots to form, so giving a bushier plant with more flowers than would occur if left to its own devices. Many plants make better specimens if they are stopped at an early stage in their life, like fuchsias, carnations, chrysanthemums and capsicums. In the plant chapters stopping is recommended wherever applicable.

Simply pinch out the top 12 mm ($\frac{1}{2}$ in) or so between finger and thumb, just above a node or leaf joint, or use a sharp knife. With some plants, like fuchsias, the resultant lateral shoots are also stopped to ensure really bunchy specimens with plenty of flowers.

Hardening plants

Plants which have been raised in heat and which are intended eventually to be planted out of doors must be gradually acclimatised to outdoor conditions. This process is known as hardening. The idea is to avoid giving plants a nasty shock which would happen if they were to be suddenly transferred from a high temperature to much cooler conditions.

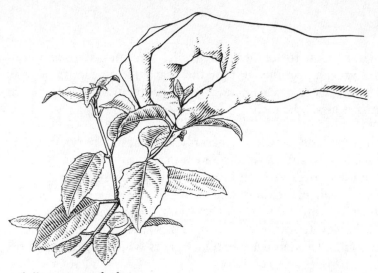

46 Stopping a fuchsia

If plants have been raised in a heated propagating case, on a heated bench under polythene, or in a mist unit, the first stage is to transfer them to the normal greenhouse atmosphere to allow them to become established after potting, or pricking out in the case of seedlings. When the plants are obviously growing well the next stage is to transfer them to a cold frame to complete the acclimatisation process. They should be moved to a frame three to four weeks before you wish to plant them out in the garden.

For the first few days the glass frame lights should be kept closed; then they can be opened very slightly during the day but closed again at night. Over a period of several weeks the lights can be gradually opened wider during the day until eventually they can be left off altogether, but they should still be closed at night. Several days before you wish to plant out, the lights can be left off at night too.

If the plants you are hardening are half-hardy annuals and perennials intended for outdoor summer bedding, or even tender vegetables, then remember that these should not be planted out until all danger of frost is over (late spring or early summer). If a frost is forecast when these subjects are hardening in cold frames, it is wise to cover the lights at night with matting or some similar material to ensure the plants are not frosted. Do not leave the lights open at night until you are sure that there is no longer danger of frost.

Hygiene

It is most important to maintain hygienic, scrupulously clean conditions in a greenhouse throughout the year to keep plants healthy and free from pests, diseases and other problems. All aspects of hygiene are discussed below.

Annual cleaning and repairs A greenhouse should be thoroughly cleaned once a year and most gardeners find autumn the ideal time, after the summer crops like tomatoes have been cleared out.

First, remove all plants and return them only when the house is completely free from the fumes of sterilant, wood preservative and the like. If, however, you have permanent plants in the greenhouse, planted in soil beds, then use cleaning agents which do not give off fumes, like soft soap.

All the old crops like tomatoes, cucumbers, etc., should first of all be cleared out and put on the compost heap, or burnt if pest- or disease-ridden.

Using a horticultural disinfectant and plenty of warm water, scrub the house thoroughly inside and out, paying attention to all parts, including staging, floor, etc. The glass should also be scrubbed. To remove the green slime and debris from between the glass overlaps, use a thin plastic plant label. After scrubbing, forcefully hose down the whole structure, including the glass overlaps.

If you have gravel on the staging this can be washed in a sieve of suitable mesh size – place a small amount at a time in the sieve and play the hosepipe over it. Do this outside. If you have sand on the bench this can be drenched with a horticultural soil sterilant as can shingle or gravel on the floor of the house. Capillary matting should also be drenched with disinfectant.

Take the opportunity, if necessary, to treat timber houses and staging with a horticultural wood preservative; for instance, there is a special cedarwood preservative for western red cedar greenhouses. If you have a softwood greenhouse then use good-quality white gloss paint, first priming any bare wood, followed by an undercoat. Always rub down existing paintwork with glass paper and remove any flaking paint first. Brick walls can be painted inside the house with white masonry paint to help reflect the light.

Replace broken or cracked panes of glass after cleaning the house to prevent draughts. Also have electrical systems and fittings checked every few years by a qualified electrician to ensure they are safe to use. Heaters of all kinds should be serviced and cleaned well before they are required for use. Dirty paraffin heaters, for example, can give off harmful fumes when in use.

General considerations Throughout the year pay attention to hygiene. Pick up regularly any plant debris – fallen leaves, flowers and the like. Pick off any dead or dying leaves and flowers and discard plants which appear sickly and beyond recovery. Sweep the floor regularly to keep it free from plant debris and spilled compost. Remove regularly any dead or dying cuttings from the propagating case. Do not store dirty pots or seed trays in the greenhouse. Keep pests and diseases under control (see Chapter 12).

Sterilising a soil border A soil border which is used for temporary utility crops like tomatoes, cucumbers, melons, capsicums and aubergines needs rather special treatment if it is to be kept free from soil-born pests and diseases. After removing these crops in the autumn, first dig the border (see Chapter 5). It should then be flooded with plain water to wash out any harmful salts (the residues of fertilisers) which are inclined to build up in the soil.

After allowing some time for the border to dry out a bit, but still in the autumn, it is advisable to sterilise the soil to kill pests and diseases. Chemical sterilisation is the most practical method for amateur gardeners, using a proprietary soil sterilant.

If you do not want to be bothered with annual soil sterilisation you could instead consider soil replacement every few years. Dig out the soil to a depth of 30 cm (12 in) and place on the garden. Fill the excavation with good-quality topsoil bought from a reliable local supplier. Fill up a few inches higher than the original level to allow for settlement.

Washing pots and trays Scrub thoroughly in plain water immediately after use and allow to dry. Store in a dry place. If you have to store them under the greenhouse staging, cover them with a sheet of polythene to keep them dry.

Weed control Weeds should be regularly removed because they can harbour pests and diseases which could then spread to your plants. Hoe or hand-weed borders. To prevent weed growth through gravel placed over soil, first lay a sheet of thick polythene on the soil.

Algae control Algae, or green slime, which forms on staging, pots,

trays, paths, walls, glass, etc., is unsightly and not very hygienic. To
remove it, scrub all hard surfaces with a stiff brush, using plenty of
warm water. Afterwards a horticultural algicide could be applied to
keep it under control. Pots, trays and other containers should also be
scrubbed well to remove algae and again treated with an algicide.
Capillary matting quickly becomes green with algae and this can be
soaked in an algicide solution.

Many gardeners are worried by growth of moss and/or liverwort on soil and compost surfaces. These do not harm plants (although they could smother tiny slow-growing seedlings). Simply
scrape off these growths and, if necessary, top up with fresh soil
or compost.

12   Pests and diseases

In a greenhouse, as in the garden, pests and diseases can become a
problem and in these protected, warmer conditions they can rapidly
spread. My policy is to try to prevent pests and diseases taking a
hold rather than to resort to the vast range of chemicals which
are now available to control them. I do not use pesticides unless all
else fails.

There are various ways of trying to prevent trouble. If plants are
grown really well, then they are less likely to succumb to diseases and
they are better able to stand up to attacks by pests. If you practise
greenhouse cultivation as I have recommended throughout this book
you should have comparatively few troubles.

If you maintain hygienic conditions under glass, pests and diseases
will be far less of a problem. Any sickly-looking plants should be
removed from the greenhouse and put on the bonfire and you should
act as soon as any pest or disease is seen to prevent it from spreading.
Do not propagate from plants infected with virus, disease or even
pests. Grow disease-resistant cultivars if available.

However, if pests and diseases do appear in the house, there are
various ways of eliminating them, as discussed below.

Ways of eliminating pests and diseases

Spraying Liquid pesticides are widely used under glass and they are best applied to plants with a sprayer fitted with a fine spray nozzle. Thoroughly wet the plants, particularly the shoot tips and the undersides of the leaves. Dilute and use these pesticides strictly according to the maker's instructions – this applies to all chemicals used for pest and disease control.

Dusting Some pesticides can be bought as dusts and these are generally applied from puffer packs. Dusts are especially useful for plants which do not like to have their foliage wetted, for flowers, and for stored plant material which needs to be kept dry. Dusts are useful for pest and disease control in the winter when one is aiming to keep leaves and the atmosphere as dry as possible.

Fumigation With this method pesticides are applied in smoke. One can buy smoke cones (rather like fireworks) which are ignited and which burn slowly, releasing a large amount of smoke. First close down all the vents and seal any cracks. Then light the cones and quickly leave the greenhouse – not forgetting to close the door. The smoke will penetrate every nook and cranny. It is better to fumigate in the evening and leave the house closed all night.

Electric fumigator This vaporises insecticides and fungicides. It is a permanent fixture in the house and dispenses fine particles of chemical throughout the greenhouse. A range of chemicals is supplied with it and replacements are available as required. Most pests and fungal diseases can be controlled by means of an electric fumigator.

Manual control I recommend this whenever possible rather than the use of chemicals. For instance, you can hand-pick caterpillars and you can squash between finger and thumb various plant bugs like aphids and mealy bugs. If some of the leaves on a plant are badly infested with a pest, I generally pick them off and burn them. If a plant is really badly diseased I tend to remove it from the house and burn it. Very often pests, like aphids, can simply be washed off plants with the use of tepid water and a sponge or soft paint brush.

Some serious pests and diseases of greenhouse plants

PESTS

Name	Description	Plants attacked
Aphids	Small green or black plant bugs	Very wide range
Caterpillars (including tortrix)	Butterfly or moth larvae or 'grubs', often greenish	Very wide range, e.g. carnations
Earwigs	Brown insects with rear 'pincers'	Chrysanthemums, carnations, etc.
Eelworms	Microscopic 'worms' living on or in the plants	Many, including tomatoes and chrysanthemums
Leaf miners	Small white grubs	Chrysanthemums and cinerarias
Mealy bug	Soft bugs covered in white 'meal'	Many, especially woody plants
Red spider mites	Reddish-brown, spider-like, barely visible with naked eye	Very wide range
Scale insects	Brown, scale-like	Many, especially woody kinds
Slugs and snails	Very well known, hardly needing to be described	Many, especially soft plants like lettuces
Symphilids	Tiny white insects in soil	Many plants attacked
Thrips	Tiny dark insects	Many plants attacked
Whitefly	Small white flies	Very wide range

Damage	Control
Suck sap and weaken plants; spread viruses	Rub off; spray with malathion or fumigate with permethrin. Biological
Eat leaves	Hand-pick; spray with derris, malathion or pirimiphos-methyl. Biological
Eat flower petals	Spray with pirimiphos-methyl
Sickly looking plants, weakened growth	Sterilise soil; burn affected plants; practise crop rotation
Tunnel in leaves, weakening the foliage	Pick off affected leaves; spray with malathion or pirimiphos-methyl
Suck sap and weaken plants	Hand-pick; biological control; spray with malathion
Suck sap, weaken plants, pale mottling on leaves	Biological. Maintain humid atmosphere if possible, which they dislike. Spray with pirimiphos-methyl
Suck sap, weaken plants	Biological, or spray with malathion or pirimiphos-methyl
Eat leaves and stems, also fruits	Place methiocarb slug pellets around plants
Weaken root system by feeding on fine roots	Incorporate gamma-HCH dust into the soil
Suck sap, resulting in speckled leaves and flowers	Spray with malathion. Biological
Suck sap and weaken plants	Biological control is the best method, or spray with pirimiphos-methyl

DISEASES

Name	Symptoms
Botrytis	Grey mould on stems, leaves, fruits and flowers, which quickly rot. Stems of some plants turn black and rot at ground level
Damping off	Seedlings collapse and die
Mildew	White powdery covering on foliage and shoot tips. Cripples foliage and growth
Peach leaf curl	Leaves curled and puckered, turn bright red
Potato blight	Dark brown patches on fruits, which then rot
Root rot	Plants wilt because roots rot
Rust	Brown-orange spots on leaves
Stem rot	Stems rot near ground level and plants collapse
Tomato leaf-mould	Brownish-yellow mould on leaves, cripples foliage and weakens plants
Wilt	Plants wilt and collapse
Viruses	Leaves mottled or streaked yellow, leaves and growth may be distorted and stunted, fruits may be deformed. Plants generally weakened

Plants attacked	Control
Very wide range indeed, including cuttings, seedlings, etc.	Maintain scrupulously clean and hygienic conditions and a healthy atmosphere. Avoid damp stale conditions. Remove all affected material. Spray plants with benomyl or carbendazim
Any seedlings	Use sterilised containers and compost. Water compost with a copper sulphate fungicide after sowing and pricking out
Grapes, cinerarias, lettuces and many others	Provide good ventilation, spray with benomyl or fumigate with tecnazene
Peaches and nectarines	Spray with copper sulphate in late winter
Tomatoes	Spray with mancozeb in early summer
Tomatoes	Avoid overwatering
Carnations, chrysanthemums, pelargoniums, etc.	Pick off badly affected leaves; spray with mancozeb
Cucumbers, melons and tomatoes	Water carefully and do not wet base of stems
Tomatoes	Spray with benomyl or mancozeb
Tomatoes	Maintain optimum growing conditions; burn affected plants; sterilise soil
Wide range, including cucumbers and tomatoes	Destroy affected plants; keep aphids under control (they spread viruses)

Biological control This is highly recommended wherever possible, particularly as some pests (especially whitefly and glasshouse red spider mite) become immune to pesticides and cannot be controlled by spraying or fumigating.

Biological control consists of introducing parasitic or predatory insects (or mites) into the greenhouse to destroy the pests.

If you have whitefly problems, introduce the whitefly parasite *Encarsia formosa* (a parasitic wasp) at the beginning of the growing season – early to mid-spring – and reintroduce throughout the season. The parasites are supplied on a leaf which is cut into strips and these are hung up in the greenhouse.

For red spider mite control, use the predatory mite *Phytoseiulus persimilis*, as described above, but place the pieces of leaf on the plants in this instance. For mealy bug an Australian ladybird predator is used – *Cryptolaemus montrouzieri* – supplied in a small test tube. Release the ladybirds into the greenhouse. It is now possible to deal with various other greenhouse pests by biological control, including soft scale, aphids, thrips, vine weevil and caterpillars.

Introduce parasites and predators only when pests are found on the plants otherwise they will have nothing to live on and will quickly die – they do not live on plant material. Do not use chemicals if you have introduced parasites or predators – you may wipe out these beneficial creatures.

PART THREE

Greenhouse Plants and their Cultivation

13 Summer bedding plants

Botanical Name	Common Name	Sowing Time	Germination Temperature °C (°F)
Acroclinium (syn *Helipterum*)	Everlasting flower	Early spring	15.5 (60)
Ageratum	Floss flower	Late winter/ early spring	18–21 (65–70)
Amaranthus (foliage types)	—	Late winter/early spring	18–21 (65–70)
Antirrhinum	Snapdragon	Mid/late winter	18–21 (65–70)
Arctotis	African daisy	Late winter/early spring	15.5 (60)
Begonia(fibrous and tuberous rooted)	—	Mid/late winter	18–21 (65–70)
Calceolaria (shrubby bedding type)	Slipper wort	Mid/late winter	18–21 (65–70)
Callistephus	China aster	Early spring	18–21 (65–70)
Centaurea cineraria ssp. *cineraria*	—	Late winter	21 (70)
Cleome	Spider flower	Late winter/early spring	21 (70)
Cosmea	Cosmos	Early spring	15.5–18 (60–65)
Dahlia (bedding types)	—	Late winter	18–21 (65–70)

Raising summer bedding plants from seeds

Growing Conditions	Comments
Heated greenhouse, then cold frame when young plants established	Grow 45 plants per standard seed tray
Warm conditions – 15.5°C (60°F)	Cover seeds very lightly with compost. Grow 45 plants per standard seed tray
Warm conditions – 15.5°C (60°F)	Cover seeds very lightly with compost. Grow in 9 cm ($3\frac{1}{2}$ in) pots
Heated greenhouse, then cold frame when young plants established	Cover seeds very lightly with compost. Grow 45 plants per standard seed tray
Greenhouse – about 10°C (50°F)	Grow 45 plants per standard seed tray
Warm greenhouse – 15.5°C (60°F)	Do not cover seeds with compost. Grow 45 plants per standard seed tray
Heated greenhouse – 10°C (50°F), or cold frame when established	Do not cover seeds with compost. Grow 45 plants per standard seed tray
Heated greenhouse – 10°C (50°F)	Grow 45 plants per standard seed tray
Heated greenhouse – 10°C (50°F), or cold frame when established	Grow 45 plants per standard seed tray, or individually in 9 cm ($3\frac{1}{2}$ in) pots
Heated greenhouse – 10°C (50°F)	Cover seeds very lightly with compost. Grow 45 plants per standard seed tray
Heated greenhouse – about 10°C (50°F), or cold frame when established	Grow 45 plants per standard seed tray
Warm greenhouse – about 15.5°C (60°F)	Grow in 7.5 or 9 cm (3 or $3\frac{1}{2}$ in) pots

Botanical Name	Common Name	Sowing Time	Germination Temperature °C (°F)
Dianthus	Pinks and Carnations (Chabaud type)	Mid-winter	18–21 (65–70)
Dorotheanthus bellidiformis	Livingstone daisy	Late winter/early spring	18–21 (65–70)
Felicia	Kingfisher daisy	Late winter to mid-spring	10–15.5 (50–60)
Gaillardia (annual types)	Blanket flower	Late winter/early spring	10–15.5 (50–60)
Gazania	—	Late winter/early spring	18–21 (65–70)
Gomphrena	Globe amaranth	Early/mid-spring	18–21 (65–70)
Heliotropium	Heliotrope	Late winter/early spring	18–21 (65–70)
Impatiens	Busy lizzie, balsam	Late winter/early spring	21 (70)
Limonium sinuatum	Sea lavender	Mid/late winter	18–21 (65–70)
Lobelia	—	Mid/late winter	18–21 (65–70)
Lobularia (syn *Alyssum*)	Madwort	Early spring	15.5–18 (60–65)
Matthiola	Stock	Late winter/early spring	18 (65)
Mimulus	Monkey flower	Late winter/early spring	18–21 (65–70)
Nemesia	—	Late winter/early spring	18–21 (65–70)
Nicotiana	Tobacco flower	Late winter/early spring	18–21 (65–70)

Growing Conditions	Comments
Heated greenhouse – about 10° C (50° F), then cold frame when established	Cover seeds very lightly with compost. Grow 45 plants per standard seed tray
Heated greenhouse – 10–15.5° C (50–60° F)	Cover seeds very lightly with compost. Grow 45 plants per standard seed tray
Cool greenhouse or cold frame	Cover seeds very lightly with compost. Grow 45 plants per standard seed tray
Cool greenhouse or cold frame	Grow 45 plants per standard seed tray
Heated greenhouse – about 10° C (50° F)	Grow 45 plants per standard seed tray
Warm greenhouse – 15.5° C (60° F)	Grow 45 plants per standard seed tray
Heated greenhouse – about 10° C (50° F)	Grow 45 plants per standard seed tray
Heated greenhouse – about 10° C (50° F)	Cover seeds very lightly with compost. Grow 45 plants per standard seed tray
Heated greenhouse 10–15.5° C (50–60° F)	Grow 45 plants per standard seed tray
Heated greenhouse, then cold frame when established	Do not cover seeds with compost. Grow 45 plants per standard seed tray. Prick out small clumps of seedlings
Heated greenhouse, then cold frame when young plants established	Grow 45 plants per standard seed tray. Relatively hardy
Heated greenhouse – 10° C (50° F), or cold frame when established	Grow 45 plants per standard seed tray
Heated greenhouse – 10° C (50° F), or cold frame when established	Do not cover seeds with compost. Grow 45 plants per standard seed tray. Keep compost steadily moist
Heated greenhouse – about 10° C (50° F)	Cover seeds very lightly with compost. Grow 45 plants per standard seed tray. Avoid checks to growth – results in premature flowering
Grow steadily at 10° C (50° F)	Cover seeds very lightly with compost. Grow 45 plants per standard seed tray

Botanical Name	Common Name	Sowing Time	Germination Temperature °C (°F)
Pelargonium (F1 hybrids)	Geranium	Early/mid winter	21–25 (70–77)
Petunia	—	Late winter/early spring	18–21 (65–70)
Phlox drummondii	Annual phlox	Late winter/early spring	15.5 (60)
Rudbeckia	Coneflower	Late winter/early spring	18–21 (65–70)
Salvia	Scarlet sage	Late winter/early spring	21–25 (70–77)
Tagetes	Marigolds – African, French and Afro-French	Early spring	18–21 (65–70)
Tagetes signata 'Pumila'	—	Early spring	18–21 (65–70)
Tanacetum	—	Mid/late winter	18–21 (65–70)
Verbena	Vervain	Late winter/early spring	18–21 (65–70)
Zinnia	—	Early/mid spring	18–21 (65–70)

One of the most popular uses of an amateur greenhouse is the raising of summer bedding plants from seeds in winter and spring. Summer bedding plants include many kinds of half-hardy annuals and perennials which are sown between mid-winter and mid-spring, depending on their rate of growth.

Sowing and pricking out The basic technique of sowing summer bedding plants need not be discussed here – see the advice given in Chapter 10 on propagation from seeds (see p. 67). Pricking out is also discussed in that chapter (see p. 68).

The table above gives specific details of raising a wide range of

Growing Conditions	Comments
Warm greenhouse – 15.5–18°C (60–65°F)	Essential to sow at these times to ensure flowering in same year. Grow in 9 cm (3½ in) pots
Heated greenhouse – 10°C (50°F), then cold frame when established	Do not cover seeds with compost. Grow 45 plants per standard seed tray
Heated greenhouse – 10°C (50°F), or cold frame when established	Grow 45 plants per standard seed tray
Heated greenhouse – 10°C (50°F)	Cover seeds very lightly with compost. Grow 45 plants per standard seed tray
Warm greenhouse – 15.5°C (60°F) for satisfactory growth	Growth poor in low temperature. Grow 45 plants per standard seed tray
Heated greenhouse – 10°C (50°F), then cold frame when established	Quick germination and growth. Grow 45 plants per standard seed tray
Heated greenhouse – 10°C (50°F), then cold frame when established	Quick germination and growth. Grow 45 plants per standard seed tray
Heated greenhouse – 10°C (50°F), or cold frame when established	Cover seeds very lightly with compost. Grow 45 plants per standard seed tray
Heated greenhouse – 10°C (50°F), then cold frame when established	Cover seeds very lightly with compost. Grow 45 plants per standard seed tray. Do not keep compost too wet
Heated greenhouse – 10°C (50°F), then cold frame when established	Grow 45 plants per standard seed tray

popular plants and gives the optimum sowing time for each. It is necessary to sow at the times recommended to ensure you have plants which are ready for planting out of doors in late spring or early summer. Many will be starting to come into flower.

By providing the newly sown seeds with the temperatures indicated in the table you will ensure good germination. For this an electric propagator is recommended. Newly germinated seedlings also need the temperatures recommended.

Growing conditions suitable growing conditions are included in the table. After the seedlings have been pricked out – generally 45 per standard seed tray, although some are grown in pots – they are generally grown in a heated greenhouse until two or three weeks before planting time, at which stage they need to be transferred to a cold frame to harden off thoroughly. It will be noted from the table, however, that tougher or hardier plants can be moved to a cold frame very much sooner to provide more room in the greenhouse. It is important, however, to allow these plants to become well established in the greenhouse before placing them in a frame.

Planting out Summer bedding plants should, at all times, be protected from frosts and this is why they are not planted out in the garden until all danger of frost is over. The evening before the day they are to be planted, give the plants a thorough soaking so that at planting time the soil in the containers (and therefore the roots) is really moist.

Lift the plants very carefully from the seed trays to minimise root disturbance and plant immediately to avoid drying out of the roots. If you have the courage the best way to remove young plants from a tray is as follows. First gently tap the sides and ends of the tray on a hard surface to loosen the compost. Then, holding the tray very close to the ground, gently (that is the operative word) throw out the contents. The compost should be well permeated with roots and come out in a complete block. Now the plants can be gently teased apart. After planting, water the plants thoroughly if the soil is on the dry side.

Most of the plants listed in the table will provide colour from planting time, or soon after, right through to the first frosts of autumn. Plants are then pulled up and discarded, but remember that perennials can be propagated from cuttings in late summer and overwintered as young plants in a cool greenhouse. Examples include bedding calceolarias, gazanias, heliotrope and pelargoniums.

14   Bulbous and tuberous plants

Plants which grow from bulbs, corms, rhizomes and tubers form an important group for greenhouse decoration and a representative collection of such plants will ensure colour and interest all the year round. In the winter and spring one can have mainly hardy bulbs in flower like daffodils, hyacinths and tulips, while there is a big range of tender bulbs, corms and tubers which bloom in the summer and autumn.

Hardy bulbs for winter and spring flowering

The hyacinths, narcissi (daffodils), tulips and crocuses make superb displays in pots or bowls in the winter and spring, whether in a cool or intermediate greenhouse. For very early flowering – at Christmas time – one can plant specially prepared bulbs. Such bulbs are refrigerated by the suppliers before sale to have an early winter and must be planted immediately they are bought otherwise the effect wears off.

I like to display pots of bulbs with other seasonal flowering plants like cyclamen, primulas, senecio, solanums and ornamental capsicums. Bulbs also look superb when placed among foliage pot plants such as asparagus, abutilons with variegated foliage, chlorophytums, grevillea and hedera. Also, try some dwarf conifers in pots as a foil for bulbs.

Hyacinths These are among the most popular hardy bulbs for flowering in the greenhouse because of their delicious scent. Many cultivars are specially prepared for flowering at Christmas while unprepared bulbs will flower later in the winter or in early spring. When buying hyacinth bulbs, bear the following points in mind: they should feel hard and heavy in relation to their size, and size of bulb is important. Large-flowered prepared hyacinth bulbs should be 16 to 17 cm ($6\frac{1}{2}$ to $6\frac{3}{4}$ in) in circumference at the widest part, while Roman hyacinths should be 12 to 14 cm ($4\frac{3}{4}$ to $5\frac{1}{2}$ in). Unprepared bulbs of top-size hyacinths – those popularly known as exhibition hyacinths – should be 18 to 19 cm (7 to $7\frac{1}{2}$ in) in circumference.

Bulbs are planted in early autumn and details will be found under general cultivation. Let us, though, consider a few specific points. If you use a 15 cm (6 in) diameter bowl (a popular size) you will need three 16 or 17 cm bulbs or two 18 to 19 cm bulbs. To ensure that all the bulbs in the bowl flower at the same time, plant only one cultivar per container. The top third of each bulb should be left uncovered when planting. Each flower spike will need the support of a split cane.

Narcissi It is possible to buy prepared daffodil bulbs for flowering at Christmas. When buying bulbs remember that they should feel firm, dry and be free of cuts, bruises, dents and mildew. These comments apply, of course, to all bulbs. Daffodils are often sold according to size and the number of growing points on each bulb. 'Mother' bulbs are best for flowering under glass and each one should have two or three growing points. Such bulbs will produce up to six blooms each. Bulbs with only two growing points are generally slightly cheaper and are also suitable for cultivation under glass.

Planting time for daffodils is early or mid-autumn and the number of bulbs per container is as follows: a 15 cm (6 in) bowl will take one bulb, a 20 cm (8 in) container, three bulbs; a 25 cm (10 in) container, five bulbs; and a 30 cm (12 in) container, six bulbs.

Daffodils can be planted in two layers if desired to create a really spectacular display of flowers. In this instance use a well-crocked flower pot. Set the upper bulbs between the lower ones, the two layers being separated by a layer of compost. With normal planting the growing points of daffodils should be left uncovered. For further details of planting see general cultivation.

Tulips The early flowering tulips are excellent for pot or bowl culture under glass. One can again buy specially prepared bulbs for flowering at Christmas or early in the new year. Tulips are generally sold according to their circumference measurements around the widest part of the bulb. The size recommended for forcing is 12 to 14 cm ($4\frac{1}{2}$ to $5\frac{1}{2}$ in). The bulbs should be sound and healthy (see narcissi). It does not matter if the brown skin is peeling off, provided the actual bulb is not damaged in any way.

To ensure flowering by Christmas plant in early autumn. The tips of the bulbs should be exposed above the compost. A 15 cm (6 in diameter bowl will hold five bulbs and a 30 cm (12 in) container will take 10. For further details of planting see general cultivation.

Crocuses To be botanically correct the crocus is a corm, not a bulb, but this does not affect cultivation. Buy sound healthy bulbs and the largest available. The large-flowered Dutch crocuses are among the few small bulbs which are graded into sizes – buy corms which are 7 to 9 cm ($2\frac{3}{4}$ to $3\frac{1}{2}$in) in circumference. Each should produce at least three flowers.

Crocuses are planted in early or mid-autumn. They can be planted in a special crocus pot which has planting holes in the sides. This will take about eight corms around the sides and about four in the top. Or you could use a normal 15 cm (6 in) diameter bowl which will take about eight corms. The tops of the corms should be just covered with compost or bulb fibre. For further details of planting see general cultivation.

General cultivation There are several kinds of container suitable for bulbs, the most popular being bulb bowls. These do not have drainage holes in the base and therefore several small pieces of charcoal should be put in the bottom before you add the compost or bulb fibre to prevent stagnant conditions. Alternatively, and probably better for greenhouse cultivation, one could use clay or plastic pans or half pots, or even normal flower pots. As these have drainage holes in the base, first place a layer of crocks in the bottom before adding compost.

A suitable growing medium for bulbs is bulb fibre which is a mixture of sphagnum peat (or a peat alternative), broken charcoal and broken oyster shell; alternatively, a soilless compost would be just as good.

When planting, first place a layer of growing medium in the bottom of the container and firm it lightly. Stand the bulbs on it so that their tops are level with or slightly above the rim of the container. Add more growing medium between the bulbs and firm lightly. Allow a space of 12 mm ($\frac{1}{2}$in) between the compost surface and the rim of the container for watering.

Bulbs in bowls must be watered with great care, otherwise the growing medium can become saturated; after watering tilt the bowls on their sides to allow excess water to run out.

After planting, the bulbs need a period of complete darkness and cool conditions to encourage root development. Keep them in a temperature below 9° C (48° F). The bulbs could, for example, be put in a dark cellar. Alternatively, each container could be enclosed in a black polythene bag and placed in a cool shady place out of doors. The traditional method, however, is to bury the containers 10 to 15 cm (4 to 6 in) deep in a plunge bed of weathered ashes or sand in a cool shaded part of the garden. Ensure the growing medium is kept moist.

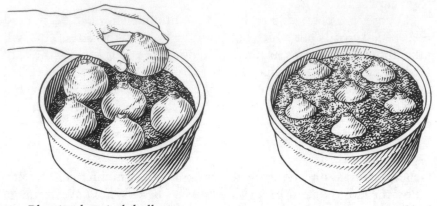

47 *Planting hyacinth bulbs*

After a period of five to eight weeks, when the bulbs have produced shoots, transfer to a place inside in subdued light for a period of seven to ten days. Then place in full daylight (they can go into the greenhouse now) at a temperature of 10°C (50°F). Do not force growth too much otherwise flowering may be affected. Only increase the temperature (if it is desired to speed up flowering) when the flower buds are well-formed, and then only to 15.5°C (60°F). Prepared tulips need a temperature of 20°C (68°F) to get them into bloom by Christmas. Most people do not maintain this sort of temperature in their greenhouse and therefore the tulips are taken into a warm room in the dwelling house. Remember that to maintain a succession of flowers over a long period bulbs can be planted over a period of several weeks and brought into the greenhouse in succession.

Of course, for unprepared bulbs the greenhouse can be maintained at a much lower temperature than recommended, but in this instance flowering will be even later. One can also flower unprepared bulbs in an unheated greenhouse but these will not be much more advanced than those in the garden. However, the blooms will be well protected from the weather.

After flowering, bulbs in their containers should be placed in a cold frame and given several liquid feeds to help build them up. The bulbs should be lifted when the leaves have died, dried off thoroughly and then stored in a cool dry airy place until planting time in the autumn. Do not force them again but plant in the garden.

Recommended cultivars

Name	Type	Colour

HYACINTHS

Name	Type	Colour
'Bismark'	Large-flowered	Pale Blue
'City of Haarlem'	Large-flowered	Yellow
'Delft Blue'	Large-flowered	Bright blue
'Jan Bos'	Large-flowered	Red
'King of the Blues'	Large-flowered	Indigo blue
'Lady Derby'	Large-flowered	Pale mauve-pink
'L'Innocence'	Large-flowered	White
'Myosotis'	Large-flowered	Sky blue
'Orange Boven'	Large-flowered	Apricot salmon
'Ostara'	Large-flowered	Dark blue
'Pink Pearl'	Large-flowered	Deep pink
'Princess Margaret'	Large-flowered	Pale pink
Roman hyacinth cultivars		White, pink or blue, fragrant and early flowering

NARCISSUS (DAFFODILS)

Name	Type	Colour
'Golden Harvest'	Trumpet type	Golden yellow
'Jack Snipe'	N. *cyclamineus* hybrid	White with orange-yellow cup
'Peeping Tom'	N. *cyclamineus* hybrid	Golden yellow with long trumpet
'Texas'	Double-flowered	Cream, yellow and orange
'Grand Soleil d'Or'	N. *tazetta* cultivar	Deep yellow with orange cup, fragrant, flowers in clusters
'Paper White'	N. *tazetta* cultivar	White, fragrant, flowers in clusters

TULIPS

Name	Type	Colour
'Bellona'	Early single-flowered	Yellow
'Brilliant Star'	Early single-flowered	Brilliant red
'Christmas Marvel'	Early single-flowered	Carmine
'Flair'	Early single-flowered	Yellow and vermilion
'Scarlet Cardinal'	Early double-flowered	Scarlet

Name	Type	Colour

CROCUSES

'Blue Pearl'	C. chrysanthus cultivar	Pale blue
'Cream Beauty'	C. chrysanthus cultivar	Ivory white inside, brownish base on outside
'E. A. Bowles'	C. chrysanthus cultivar	Bright yellow
'Ladykiller'	C. chrysanthus cultivar	Purple, white-edged petals
'Prinses Beatrix'	C. chrysanthus cultivar	Blue, with yellow base
'Snow Bunting'	C. chrysanthus cultivar	White
'Zwanenburg Bronze'	C. chrysanthus cultivar	Deep yellow with bronze shading on outside
'Flower Record'	Large-flowered Dutch crocus	Violet-blue
'Kathleen Parlow'	Large-flowered Dutch crocus	White
'Little Dorrit'	Large-flowered Dutch crocus	Silvery blue
'Paulus Potter'	Large-flowered Dutch crocus	Purple
'Pickwick'	Large-flowered Dutch crocus	Lilac with deeper stripes
'Remembrance'	Large-flowered Dutch crocus	Purple-blue

Tender bulbs, corms and tubers

The tender bulbs, corms and tubers flower mainly in the summer or autumn, but there are some which produce their blooms at other times of the year. All can be grown in pots and staged with other plants of seasonal interest, not forgetting a selection of foliage plants which thrive in the same conditions.

The following descriptive list includes mainly popular kinds and details their cultivation requirements, including minimum temperatures.

Achimenes These plants grow from scaly underground rhizomes and produce their trumpet-shaped or tubular flowers in summer and autumn. There are many hybrids available in a very wide range of colours and for a good selection one needs to buy from a specialist grower. Some have an upright habit but the rather weak stems need supports; others have a more spreading habit and are ideal for growing in hanging baskets.

Temperature: 15.5°C (60°F) minimum.

Cultivation: start rhizomes into growth from late winter to mid-spring by inserting them into moist peat or coconut fibre and placing them in a propagator, temperature at least 15.5°C (60°F). When shoots appear pot three to five in a 12.5 cm (5 in) pot, just covering with compost (use soilless or loam-based), or plant 10 to 15 in a hanging basket of average size. Try to maintain a minimum temperature of 15.5°C. Water generously in summer and provide a humid atmosphere. Provide twiggy sticks for supporting the upright growers. Lightly shade from strong sunshine. When the leaves begin to die down in autumn gradually reduce watering until the compost becomes dry. The rhizomes can be left in their pots and stored dry over the winter in a temperature of 7 to 10°C (45 to 50°F). When you wish to start the rhizomes into growth again in the following spring remove them from the old compost and proceed as outlined above.

Propagation: separate new rhizomes from the parents and start into growth as described.

Begonia The large double-flowered tuberous begonias are available in many colours and make a superb display in the greenhouse during summer. There are many named cultivars from which to choose (these are generally bought from a specialist grower) or one can buy mixed collections. There are also tuberous pendulous begonias which make superb displays in hanging baskets.

Temperature: minimum of 13°C (55°F).

Cultivation: start tubers into growth in late winter or early spring by pressing them into a tray of moist peat or coconut fibre, the hollow side facing upwards. Provide a temperature of 18°C (65°F). When shoots are starting to develop pot singly into 12.5 cm (5 in) pots, or plant several in a hanging basket. Use a loam-based or soilless compost. The top of each tuber should be level with the surface of the compost after planting. Provide split canes to support the stems as they grow. The flowers are usually produced in threes: a male which is a large spectacular double flower and two females on either side which are small and single. It is the male flowers which we want to keep and so the females are removed as early as possible in their development. Begin feeding when buds start to develop; shade from strong sunshine and water as required. When flowering is over reduce watering until eventually the compost becomes dry but do not stop watering until the foliage has completely died down. The tubers should be removed from the compost, cleaned off, have the dead top growth removed and then stored in dry peat or sand in a dry frost-proof place for the winter.

Propagation: tubers can be divided before starting them into growth. Tuberous begonias can also be raised from seeds sown in mid- or late winter.

Canna Commonly known as Indian shot lilies, the cannas have fleshy rhizomes and produce their spectacular heads of tubular flowers in the summer. Hybrids are generally grown, with flowers in shades of yellow, orange or red. Some cultivars are bicoloured. Height is 60 to 90 cm (24 to 36 in).

Temperature: minimum of 15.5° C (60° F).

Cultivation: start the rhizomes into growth in late winter or early spring in moist peat or coconut fibre (only just cover them), providing a temperature of 15.5° C (60° F). When shoots are produced pot individually into pots just large enough to take the rhizome comfortably. Provide a temperature of 15.5° C. When the pots are full of roots pot on into 15 to 22 cm (6 to 9 in) pots. John Innes potting compost No. 2 is recommended. Feed and water generously in the growing period and gradually reduce watering in the autumn. Cut down the top growth and store the plants for the winter in their pots in frost-free conditions. Make sure the compost does not become completely dry over the winter. In the following year remove rhizomes from the pots and start them into growth again as described.

Propagation: divide the rhizomes when they have started into growth – each piece must have at least one shoot.

Crinum These plants produce large bulbs, wide strap-like leaves and heads of lily-like flowers mainly in late summer and autumn. There are several species that are grown, such as *C. asiaticum*, white flowers; *C. macowanii*, white, flushed purple; and *C. moorei*, white, flushed red.

Temperature: minimum of 7 to 10° C (45 to 50° F).

Cultivation: pot in spring, using a large pot and John Innes potting compost No. 2. The neck and the upper third of the bulb should be above compost level. In the summer light shade and humidity are appreciated, together with regular feeding. The compost should be kept only slightly moist over the winter.

Propagation: divide clumps of bulbs or remove offsets in the spring.

Cyclamen The cyclamen, popular with florists, flower in the autumn and winter and grow from a tuber. They are hybrids of *C. persicum* and some of the newer ones have striking silver-marbled foliage. Colours include pink, red, purple, lilac, white and bicolours. Some flowers are scented while others may be frilled.

Temperature: minimum of 10° C (50° F).

Cultivation: cool well-ventilated conditions should be provided. Plants are generally raised from seeds sown in late summer. Seedlings are pricked out into 5 cm (2 in) pots and young plants are potted on until they are in a final size of 12.5 to 15 cm (5 to 6 in). Soilless composts are recommended. In the following summer the plants can be kept in a shaded cold frame and re-housed in early autumn. After flowering the leaves will eventually start to die down and this is the sign to reduce watering gradually until the compost is dry. Rest the plants in a cold frame and in late summer remove the tubers and repot into fresh compost. When potting ensure the upper part of the tuber remains above compost level. And when watering do not pour water into the centre of the plant.

Propagation: seeds, late summer, in a temperature of 18° C (65° F).

Cyrtanthus purpureus(syn. *Vallota speciosa*) is the Scarborough lily, a bulb which produces in summer or autumn large funnel-shaped scarlet flowers.

Temperature: minimum of 7° C (45° F).

Cultivation: pot bulbs singly in 12.5 cm (5 in) pots in late summer and ensure the neck of each protrudes above compost level. Water sparingly at first and gradually increase. When the foliage starts to die down in late spring or early summer dry off the bulbs to give them a rest. Resume watering when new growth appears. Repot every three years.

Propagation: detach bulblets when repotting and pot off.

Freesia The large-flowered freesia hybrids are usually grown for winter flowers and they come in a wide range of colours: white, cream, yellow, mauve, purple, pink and red. There are double-flowered freesias and many are scented.

Temperature: minimum of 7° C (45° F).

Cultivation: freesias are generally grown from corms which should be planted in late summer, seven or eight to a 15 cm (6 in) pot. Use John Innes potting compost No. 1 and cover with about 2.5 cm (1 in) of compost. Place in a cold frame and cover with peat or coconut fibre. After six weeks transfer to a greenhouse which should be kept well ventilated. Water moderately in autumn and winter. Use thin twiggy sticks to support the foliage and insert before it becomes too well developed. After flowering the foliage will eventually start to die down, so reduce watering and finally withhold it to give the corms a rest. Keep dry over the summer and in August remove the corms from the old compost and repot into fresh compost. Treatment is then as described above.

Many gardeners also like to raise freesias from seeds which can be sown in late winter or early spring for winter flowering. One can sow six to eight seeds directly into a 15 cm (6 in) pot. Germinate in a temperature of 18° C (65° F). Place in a cold frame for the summer, take into the greenhouse in early autumn, and treat as outlined above. Propagation: seeds late winter or early spring, 18° C (65° F). Or cormlets which should be potted in late summer.

Gloriosa These are tuberous-rooted climbers which produce superb lily-like flowers in the summer – indeed, they are in the lily family. The best-known species is *G. superba* with yellow and red flowers and reflexed wavy petals.

Temperature: minimum of 13° C (55° F).

Cultivation: pot tubers in spring and keep the compost only just moist – never overwater. Provide supports for the stems. Give plenty of ventilation and light shade from strong sun in summer, plus regular feeding. When leaves start to die, stop watering and store the dry tubers for the winter in a temperature of 7 to 10° C (45 to 50° F).

Propagation: seeds, mid-winter, or detach and pot small tubers in spring.

Haemanthus Bulbous plants which flower in spring, summer or autumn, often with strap-shaped leaves. Flowers in large umbels with long stamens, often surrounded by bracts. Commonly grown species include *H. albiflos*, white flowers and bracts; *H. coccineus*, flowers surrounded by red bracts; and *H. katherinae* (now correctly *Scadoxus multiflorus* ssp. *katherinae*) dark red flowers.

Temperature: minimum of 10 to 13° C (50 to 55° F).

Cultivation: pot bulbs in spring or when they are dormant, using John Innes potting compost No. 2, and make sure the neck of each bulb is above compost level. Provide plenty of ventilation in summer and allow the compost to dry out partially between waterings. Feed regularly when in full growth. In winter dry off species which lose their leaves. Repotting is carried out about every three years.

Propagation: bulblets when repotting.

Hippeastrum These bulbs produce huge trumpet-shaped flowers in various colours such as pink, crimson, scarlet and white, in winter or spring depending on the temperature maintained.

Temperature: minimum of 10° C (50° F) or 15.5° C (60° F).

Cultivation: grow a single bulb in a 15 cm (6 in) pot of John Innes potting compost No. 2, leaving the upper half of the bulb exposed. Repotting is needed only every three years and in the interim years a topdressing of fresh compost can be given when the bulbs are starting into growth – first scrape away some of the old compost. Bulbs can be started into growth in late winter but if you can provide a temperature of 15.5° C (60° F) you may start them off in early winter, when they will flower much earlier.

Be sparing with the water until growth is well under way. Specially prepared bulbs are now available which will flower in time for Christmas and these are planted in late autumn. You will, however, need to provide a steady temperature of 21° C (70° F) to ensure Christmas flowering – this is generally feasible only in the home.

The tall stems of hippeastrums need canes for support. After flowering feed weekly with a liquid fertiliser and in late summer, when the leaves start to die down, gradually reduce watering to give the bulbs a rest. Do not let the soil dry out completely during the rest period – keep it very slightly moist.

Propagation: bulblets detached when repotting.

Lachenalia The Cape cowslips are charming bulbs to grow in a cool or intermediate greenhouse, with their neat habit and tubular flowers. Several species are available such as *L. aloides*, yellow flowers in winter or spring; *L. a. aurea*, orange-yellow; *L. a.* 'Nelsonii', yellow; *L. contaminata*, white, spring; and *L. mutabilis*, pale blue, winter.

Temperature: minimum of 10° C (50° F).

Cultivation: pot in late summer or early autumn, using a loam-based compost, five to a 12.5 cm (5 in) pot. Place in shaded cold frame. Transfer to greenhouse when growth is under way. After flowering watering is gradually reduced until the compost is dry. The plants are then rested for the summer in a sunny place. Repot and start into growth again in late summer.

Propagation: bulblets detached when repotting.

Lilium Lilies are excellent for pot culture in the cool or intermediate greenhouse or even in an unheated greenhouse. Try the following: *L. auratum*, the golden-rayed lily of Japan, with gold and white flowers; *L.* 'Enchantment', orange-red; *L. longiflorum*, the white Easter lily; *L. regale*, the regal lily, with white and pinkish-purple flowers; *L. speciosum rubrum*, rose-pink and carmine; and *L. lancifolium splendens*, the orange tiger lily.

Temperature: try to keep the minimum below 10° C (50° F).

Cultivation: pot three bulbs to a 20 cm (8 in) pot in autumn, using John Innes potting compost No. 2 and crocking the pots well. When potting stem-rooting lilies like *longiflorum, regale, lancifolium splendens, speciosum rubrum* and *auratum*, only half fill the pots and plant the bulbs very shallowly. Later they will be topdressed with more compost. Place pots in a cold frame for the winter. As the stems of stem-rooting kinds develop, topdress with more compost until the level is 2.5 cm (1 in) below the pot rim. Transfer to the greenhouse no earlier than early or mid-spring, except for the early flowering *L. longiflorum*. Provide good ventilation.

The stems will start to die down in the autumn and the pots can then be put back in the cold frame. Remove dead top growth and keep the compost only slightly moist in the autumn and winter. The bulbs are, in fact, best planted in the garden while they are dormant as it is advisable not to force them again.

Propagation: bulblets in autumn, bulbils in spring, or scales in spring.

Nerine These bulbs produce their somewhat lily-like flowers in the autumn and are excellent subjects for a slightly heated greenhouse. Species include *N. bowdenii* which is almost hardy and, indeed, is grown outdoors in mild areas, flowers pink: *N. flexuosa*, a similar species; *N. sarniensis*, red or pink flowers; and *N. undulata*, pink. Named cultivars of *Nerine* are also available.

Temperature: minimum of 7° C (45° F).

Cultivation: pot bulbs in late summer, one per 9 cm ($3\frac{1}{2}$ in) pot, making sure the neck protrudes above the compost, which should be a loam-based type. Repotting is needed only every three years. Provide good ventilation and sunny conditions. Start to water when the flower stem and leaves appear. The compost should be allowed to become partially dry between waterings. Feed well-established bulbs regularly when in full growth. When the leaves start to turn yellow stop watering and recommence when growth starts again.

Propagation: detach and pot bulblets when repotting.

Polianthes *P. tuberosa*, commonly called the tuberose, grows from thick tuber-like rhizomes and produce funnel-shaped white flowers, which are highly fragrant, in summer or autumn. *P. t.* 'The Pearl' has double flowers.

Temperature: minimum of 15.5° C (60° F).

Cultivation: pot rhizomes singly into 12.5 cm (5 in) pots, 2.5 cm (1 in) deep, using a loam-based compost. Pot as soon as available, which is generally in late winter or early spring. Keep on the dry side until growth begins – then water regularly and also feed when growth is well under way. Provide sunny well-ventilated conditions. The tuberose does not generally flower well a second time, so it is the usual practice to buy new rhizomes each year.

Sinningia Tuberous plants, flowering in summer, and including the popular gloxinia. Species include *S. cardinalis* with bright scarlet tubular flowers and *S. leucotricha* with silvery white hairy leaves and orange-red tubular flowers. The hybrid cultivars of gloxinia have large showy bell-shaped flowers in shades of red, pink, purple or white.

Temperature: 15.5° C (60° F).

Cultivation: pot tubers in spring in loam-based or soilless compost and only just cover the tops. One tuber per 12.5 cm (5 in) pot. Start into growth in a temperature of 18–21° C (65–70° F). Do not overwater the plants and feed when in full growth. Ensure humidity in summer and shade from strong sun. When the foliage starts to turn yellow at the end of the season dry off the plants and store the tubers in a heated greenhouse. Repot and start into growth again the following spring.

Propagation: leaf cuttings, summer, 21° C (70° F).

Smithiantha Tubular foxglove-like flowers are produced in summer, the growth coming from fleshy tuber-like rhizomes. There are many hybrid cultivars with flowers in shades of yellow, orange, red and white. Species include *S. cinnabarina*, orange-red, and *S. zebrina* with yellow and scarlet flowers. All have attractive velvety leaves.

Temperature: 15.5° C (60° F) minimum.

Cultivation: this is the same as for *Achimenes* but it is better to provide a higher temperature for starting the rhizomes into growth. I start them off at 21° C (70° F).

Propagation: leaf cuttings in summer, 21° C (70° F).

Sprekelia The bulb *S. formosissima* produces striking crimson orchid-like flowers in summer.

Temperature: minimum of 10° C (50° F).

Cultivation: pot with the neck of the bulb protruding, in late winter, using a 12.5 cm (5 in) pot. Water sparingly at first and gradually increase as growth develops. In autumn allow the compost to become dry and store the bulbs over the winter in their pots.

Propagation: detach bulblets and pot off.

Tigridia Bulbs, of which *T. pavonia* is the one usually grown. This is the tiger flower with red and yellow flowers in summer. There are hybrids in shades of red, yellow or white.

Temperature: can be grown in an unheated or cool greenhouse.
Cultivation: pot bulbs in spring, using a loam-based compost, and ensure sunny conditions in the growing period. Do not be too heavy on watering. When the leaves start to die down in autumn stop watering and rest the bulbs in their pots over the winter in a heated greenhouse. Repot in spring and start into growth again.
Propagation: bulblets detached and potted off in spring.
Zantedeschia The arum lilies grow from thick rhizomes and in summer bear large inflorescences consisting of a spathe and spadix. Species include *Z. aethiopica*, white spathes; *Z. elliottiana*, bright yellow spathes; and *Z. rehmannii*, spathes pinkish purple.
Temperature: minimum of 10° C (50° F).
Cultivation: pot in early spring in a loam-based compost and be sparing with water until growth gets under way. Feed regularly when in full growth. With the exception of *Z. aethiopica* which should be kept moist at all times, arum lilies are dried off when the foliage starts to die down in autumn.
Propagation: division (offsets) in spring when repotting.

15   Pot plants for flowers

There is a tremendous range of plants which make good flowering pot plants and I have selected some of the most popular, splitting them into two groups: those which are regarded as temporary and discarded after flowering, and those which are kept for several or many years. In the first category are the annuals and biennials (or plants treated as such), and in the second the perennial plants.

There are flowering pot plants for all purposes, as will be seen in the alphabetical list which follows. For example, some of the trailing kinds can be grown in hanging baskets or other elevated containers; others may be grown up moss poles, like the anthuriums. Remember that any of the perennials or long-term plants could, if desired, be planted in a soil bed or border rather than grown in pots – they will then make better growth. Alternatively, pot-grown plants (including short-term subjects) could be plunged to the rims in a soil bed while they are in flower, and removed when the display is over. In this way one could maintain seasonal displays of plants in the soil bed, among the permanent subjects like shrubs and climbers.

Most amateur gardeners, however, probably grow their flowering pot plants on the greenhouse staging. This is fine but the effect will be much improved if you arrange them artistically, say with suitable foliage plants and other subjects. Just to give you an example: plants such as primulas, senecios and solanums look most attractive when arranged with spring bulbs and foliage plants like asparagus, abutilons and ferns. The most effective displays can be achieved with tiered staging. Failing this one could build up various levels for plants simply with some wooden planks supported on bricks. Remember to grow together only plants which need the same temperatures otherwise you will have trouble. For instance do not try to grow tropical subjects which need warmth and humidity with things like senecios and primulas which need cool well-ventilated conditions and a dry atmosphere.

There are flowering pot plants suited to the cold, cool, intermediate and warm greenhouse and in all of these environments one can have something in flower all the year round if plants are chosen with some thought.

Details of cultivation are given in the following list, but to prevent the need to repeat basic information, remember that unless otherwise stated plants can be grown in John Innes potting compost (No. 1 for first potting, No. 2 for potting on) or equivalent soilless types, and in clay or plastic pots. Most plants benefit from regular liquid feeding (say once a week or once a fortnight) during the growing season which, for most, is spring and summer.

Regarding propagation, I have given only brief details in the list; for full details of seed raising, taking and rooting cuttings, and the like, refer to Chapter 10 on Propagation.

Plants which are discarded after flowering

Annuals, hardy Some of these make excellent pot plants for the slightly heated or even cold greenhouse and if sown in late summer or early autumn will flower in the spring. Subjects include *Clarkia amoena*, *Centaurea cyanus* (cornflower), *Echium vulgare* and *Lavatera trimestris*. In May *Campanula medium* (Canterbury bell) and

Digitalis (foxglove) can be sown for flowering in the spring of the following year – they are treated as biennials.

Temperature: frost-free, cool or unheated greenhouse.

Cultivation: seedlings are pricked out individually into 9 cm (3½ in) pots and placed in a cold frame, where they should be given good ventilation on all suitable occasions. In early or mid-autumn pot on into 12.5 cm (5 in) pots. Return to the cold frame. By late autumn plants should be moved to final pots – generally 15 cm (6 in). Ensure plants are protected from hard frosts. In early winter plants can be moved into the greenhouse. During autumn and winter keep the compost only slightly moist and ensure adequate ventilation. Feed and water well when plants are in full growth. Larger plants will need staking and tying.

Canterbury bells and foxgloves are grown in the same way but the timing is a little different. They are sown in late spring and can be grown out of doors in their pots for the summer. They can be placed in a cold frame in early autumn and thereafter treated as for the other subjects.

Propagation: sow in late summer or early autumn (late spring for Canterbury bells and foxgloves). Germinate in a cold frame. Prick off as soon as seedlings are large enough to handle.

Browallia Free flowering low-growing plants. *B. speciosa* cultivars are usually grown and have blue or white flowers. *B. viscosa* has violet-blue flowers.

Temperature: 10° C (50° F); 13° C (55° F) for winter flowering.

Cultivation: prick out seedlings individually into 7.5 cm (3 in) pots, and eventually move into 12.5 cm (5 in) pots. Provide good light but shade from strong sun.

Propagation: sow in spring for summer flowering, or in late summer for winter blooms. Germination temperature: 18° C (65° F).

Calceolaria The large-flowered hybrid calceolarias, in a wide range of bright colours with attractively pouched flowers, are grown as biennials, being sown in early summer to flower in the spring of the following year.

Temperature: minimum of 7° C (45° F).

Cultivation: it is essential to grow calceolarias cool at all times. They certainly need no more than 7° C in the winter. Prick off the seedlings into trays and eventually transfer to 7.5 cm (3 in) pots. From the pricking-off stage grow in a cold frame with the lights off, except during inclement weather. Pot on into 12.5 cm (5 in) pots in mid-autumn and transfer to the greenhouse. Provide good ventilation on all favourable occasions. Keep the compost steadily moist in autumn and winter but not wet. In late winter pot on into 15 cm (6 in) pots. Propagation: sow in early summer and do not cover seeds with compost.

Germinate in greenhouse or cold frame.

Campanula There are two excellent bellflowers for the greenhouse – the trailing *C. isophylla* which can be grown in hanging baskets, and *C. pyramidalis*, the chimney bellflower, an upright grower to 1.2 m (4 ft). The first is a perennial (but it is best to replace plants regularly with young specimens) and the second a biennial. Both have blue flowers but there are also white forms, and they flower in summer.

Temperature: 10° C (50° F) minimum.

Cultivation: *C. isophylla* can be grown in 12.5 cm (5 in) pots or in hanging baskets, while *C. pyramidalis* will need a 15–25 cm (6–10 in) pot. Seedlings of *C. pyramidalis* are pricked off into individual 7.5 cm (3 in) pots and placed in a cold frame. In the summer they are placed out of doors and then overwintered in the frame. Take into the greenhouse when the flower spikes start to develop.

Propagation: *C. isophylla* – cuttings in spring or summer, or seeds in early spring (moderate heat for both). *C. pyramidalis* – seeds in early or mid-spring, in moderate heat.

Capsicum The ornamental peppers are grown not for their flowers but for colourful fruits produced in the autumn and winter. However, it is convenient to include them here. Generally the fruits are cone-shaped and come in shades of red, yellow or orange, according to cultivar. These dwarf plants are hybrids of *C. annuum*.

Temperature: minimum of 10° C (50° F).

Cultivation: seedlings are pricked out individually into 7.5 cm (3 in) pots, and when well rooted in these they are moved into 12.5 cm (5 in) pots. Grow on in a well-ventilated greenhouse and shade from strong sun. Spray overhead when in flower to encourage good pollination and therefore a good crop of fruits.

Propagation: seeds sown in mid-spring and germinated in a temperature of 18° C (65° F).

Celosia *C. cristata* Plumosa Group has a feather-like inflorescence. There are cultivars in various colours, such as brilliant reds and yellows, apricot and pink. Flowering is in the summer and lasts for many weeks.

Temperature: minimum of 10° C (50° F).

Cultivation: seedlings are pricked out individually into 7.5 cm (3 in) pots, in which they can be flowered, but larger plants will be obtained

48 *Ornamental capsicum*

by potting on into 12.5 cm (5 in) pots. Provide good light but shade from hot sun, and carry out normal watering.

Propagation: seeds, sown in early or mid-spring, and germinated in a temperature of 21° C (70° F).

Convolvulus The morning glory, *C. tricolor* is a popular climber with large funnel-shaped flowers, cultivars of which have blue, lavender or white blooms in summer.

Temperature: minimum of 10° C (50° F).

Cultivation: pot on until a final 20 cm (8 in) pot is reached. Provide good light but shade from strong sun. Ensure adequate ventilation. Train to suitable supports.

Propagation: seeds, sown in early or mid-spring (after soaking for 12 hours) and germinated in a temperature of 21° C (70° F). Sow one seed per 7.5 cm (3 in) pot.

Cuphea The cigar flower, *C. ignea*, from spring to autumn bears an abundance of small, deep red, white-tipped tubular flowers. A small compact sub-shrub, lasting for several years, which, however, is best replaced regularly with young specimens.

Temperature: minimum of 7° C (45° F).

Cultivation: provide well-ventilated conditions and cut hard back leggy specimens in the spring.

Propagation: softwood cuttings, early to mid-spring, or seeds mid- to late winter, moderate heat for both.

Exacum *E. affine* is a neat bushy annual smothering itself with bluish-purple flowers in summer and autumn.

Temperature: minimum of 13° C (55° F).

Cultivation: prick off seedlings into trays and then move on to 10 cm (4 in) pots in which they will flower. Good ventilation and shade from strong sun are necessary.

Propagation: seeds, sown in early or mid-spring, temperature 18° C (65° F).

Impatiens The well-known busy lizzies are hybrids developed from *I. walleriana*, and there are many named cultivars coming in a wide range of brilliant colours like shades of pink, red or orange, and also white. Modern ones are compact plants of low stature and flower continuously in summer and autumn. Best to raise new plants each year.

Temperature: minimum of 10° C (50° F).

Cultivation: prick off seedlings or move rooted cuttings into 9 cm (3½ in) pots, and pot on when necessary to 12.5 cm (5 in) pots. Provide light shade and humidity in summer and water freely (if plants are kept over the winter, keep the compost only slightly moist).

Propagation: seeds, early or mid-spring, cuttings mid-spring to late summer, temperature of 21° C (70° F) for seeds, and normal greenhouse conditions for cuttings.

Perennials, hardy There are various kinds of hardy perennial which can be potted and gently forced into early (spring) bloom in the cool or even unheated greenhouse. Examples include *Astilbe, Convallaria* (lily of the valley), *Dicentra spectabilis, Polygonatum multiflorum* (Solomon's seal), and wallflowers.

Temperature: the ideal temperature while plants are under glass is 7 to 10° C (45 to 50° F). An unheated greenhouse is also suitable.

Cultivation: pot young flowering-size plants (buy or lift from the garden) in the autumn. Keep them outside and house them from early winter onwards for a succession of flowers. Pots can effectively be plunged in an ornamental bed or border between, say, shrubs. After flowering plant out in the garden – do not force again.

Primula Ideal small pot plants for the cool or intermediate greenhouse, flowering in winter and spring. There are three kinds generally grown (apart from polyanthus, see below). *P. × kewensis* has yellow fragrant bell-shaped flowers and the young leaves and flower stalks are covered in white meal. The fairy primrose, *P. malacoides*, has fragrant star-shaped blooms in tiers. There are various colours: white, lilac, many shades of red and of mauve. *P. obconica* produces clusters of flowers in white, lilac, pink, red shades, orange, and shades of blue.

Temperature: 7–10° C (45–50° F) is ideal.

Cultivation: prick out seedlings into trays and then move into 9 cm ($3\frac{1}{2}$ in) pots. When well rooted in these provide a final size pot of 12.5 cm (5 in). Stand in a cold frame from early summer to early autumn and shade from strong sun. Keep the compost steadily moist. Re-house in early autumn and ensure good light and an airy atmosphere. Water carefully in autumn and winter – keep the compost moist but ensure the foliage does not become wet.

Propagation: sow *P. obconica* in early or mid spring, *P. malacoides* in late spring or early summer, and *P. × kewensis* in late winter or early spring. Germinate in a temperature of 15.5° C (60° F).

Primula × polyantha The polyanthus makes a superb pot plant for the cold, cool or intermediate greenhouse, and flowers in the winter and spring. Colours include shades of red, blue and yellow.

Temperature: ideally 4.5–7° C (40–45° F), but up to 10° C (50° F). Can also be grown without heat.

Cultivation: prick out seedlings into trays. Before overcrowding occurs pot off into 9 cm ($3\frac{1}{2}$ in) pots. Grow in well-ventilated cold frame for the summer and shade from sun. Keep compost steadily moist. Re-house in early autumn. Water with care in autumn and winter to keep the foliage dry. Maintain well-ventilated dry conditions in the greenhouse.

Propagation: sow seeds in early summer and germinate in cool moist conditions, such as a shaded cold frame.

Salpiglossis Commonly known as painted tongue, *S. sinuata* is an almost hardy annual with funnel-shaped flowers in summer and autumn. It comes in a wide range of colours and combinations of colours and there are several named strains available.

Temperature: artificial heat is not required for summer and autumn flowering.

Cultivation: seedlings should be pricked out either into trays or direct into 7.5 cm (3 in) pots. Move them on eventually into 12.5 cm (5 in) pots. Provide shade from strong sun in summer.

Propagation: seeds can be sown in early spring, temperature 18° C (65° F).

Schizanthus The poor man's orchid is a popular annual for the cool to intermediate greenhouse, generally grown to flower in winter or spring. The orchid-like flowers come in a wide range of colours, usually in striking combinations.

Temperature: 7–10° C (45–50° F) is ideal.

Cultivation: seedlings are pricked off into trays and before overcrowding occurs are potted into 9 cm (3½ in) pots. Provide canes for support. Seedlings and young plants can be grown in a cold frame and taken into the greenhouse when the weather starts to become cool in the autumn. In late winter pot on into 15 cm (6 in) pots. In the greenhouse ensure well-ventilated conditions.

Propagation: sow seeds in late summer and germinate in a cold frame.

Senecio The popular cinerarias are correctly *S. × hybridus*. They produce large heads of daisy flowers in late winter and spring and range in height from 30 to 60 cm (12 to 24 in). There are many strains and named cultivars available in a wide range of colours: shades of blue, purple, pink, red and white.

Temperature: ideally 7 to 10° C (45 to 50° F).

Cultivation: seedlings are pricked off into trays. Before overcrowding occurs pot into 9 cm (3½ in) pots and eventually into 12.5 cm (5 in) pots. Keep the plants in a cold frame for the summer, shading from strong sun and keeping the compost steadily moist. In early autumn move into the greenhouse, which should be well ventilated on all suitable occasions. Keep the foliage dry and do not allow the compost to become wet.

Propagation: seeds can be sown from mid-spring to early summer to provide a succession of flowers. Germinate in a cool greenhouse or cold frame.

Solanum Cultivars of *S. capsicastrum* and *S. pseudocapsicum* are popularly known as winter cherries because in autumn and winter they produce orange, red or orange-red berries.

Temperature: minimum of 7° C (45° F).

Cultivation: prick off seedlings into 7.5 cm (3 in) pots and eventually move into 12.5 cm (5 in) pots. Stop plants when a few inches tall and also pinch out the side shoots. Stand them out of doors from early summer to early autumn. Spray plants with water each day when in flower to ensure good pollination. Re-house in early autumn and ventilate on all suitable occasions.

Propagation: sow from late winter to early spring. Temperature 18° C (65° F).

Plants which are kept for some years

Anthurium These evergreen perennials have either a somewhat climbing habit and produce aerial roots, or a tufted habit of growth. The leathery leaves make a good background for the inflorescences, which consist of tiny insignificant flowers, a prominent spadix and a colourful spathe. The best known is *A. andreanum*, a tufted plant with scarlet or orange-red spathes. *A. crystallinum* is also tufted, with white-veined deep green leaves and green spathe. *A. scherzerianum* is a tufted plant with bright scarlet spathes, although these may be white or various shades of red in the cultivars.
Temperature: minimum of 15.5° C (60° F).
Cultivation: best growth achieved in warm humid atmosphere, with shade from sun. Keep compost moist but give less water in winter. There are various methods of growing these plants – pots, pans or orchid baskets. They can also be grown in a pillar or sphagnum moss and peat. A good compost consists of equal parts peat-based potting compost and sphagnum moss. Or use peat-based compost alone.
Propagation: division in mid-winter.
Begonia There are many begonias noted for their flowers and they often have attractive foliage (see begonias in Chapter 16). The tuberous-rooted 'Gloire de Lorraine' hybrids are winter flowering, producing mainly pink blooms but also shades of orange and yellow. The tuberous-rooted 'Elatior' hybrids produce double or semi-double flowers during winter, in shades of red, pink, peach and white. *B.* × *corallina* is one of the cane-stemmed begonias with 'angel-wing' leaves which are spotted with silver. There are also several hybrids. Pink flowers in large clusters are produced in spring, summer and well into autumn. *B. semperflorens* cultivars are popular for summer bedding but make superb pot plants capable of flowering the year round. There are many shades of pink and red, and also white, and the foliage may be green or bronzy.
Temperature: minimum of 13° C (55° F). Ideally a temperature of 15.5° C (60° F) in winter.
Cultivation: moderate humidity in high temperatures and good light throughout the year, but shade from strong sunshine. Allow compost to dry out partially between waterings. *B. semperflorens* and the

tuberous-rooted hybrids can be grown as annuals if desired.

Propagation: all can be raised from cuttings in spring or summer, temperature 21°C (70°F). *B. semperflorens* cultivars from seeds in early spring.

Clivia Evergreen perennials with strap-shaped leaves and umbels of funnel-shaped flowers in spring or summer. The best-known is *C. miniata* with orange or orange-red flowers.

Temperature: minimum of 7°C (45°F).

Cultivation: shade from strong sun and provide humidity in warm conditions. The plants have fleshy roots and do not like to be disturbed unless absolutely necessary. Really best grown in a soil bed, but pot cultivation is satisfactory.

Propagation: division after flowering.

Columnea Evergreen perennials, some being epiphytic, with climbing or trailing stems and tubular, often hooded flowers. *C. × banksii*, somewhat pendulous stems, scarlet flowers in winter; *C. gloriosa*, pendulous, brilliant red and yellow, autumn to spring; *C. microphylla*, small leaves, pendulous, red flowers, winter; and *C.* 'Stavanger', trailing, orange-red flowers.

Temperature: minimum of 15.5°C (60°F).

Cultivation: warmth and humidity for best results, plus shade from strong sunshine. Keep compost steadily moist but not wet. Grow trailing or pendulous kinds in hanging baskets, others in pans or pots. A good growing medium consists of an all-peat compost with extra grit added.

Propagation: soft or semi-ripe cuttings mid spring to late summer with strong bottom heat.

Crassula Rather succulent evergreen plants, of which *C. coccinea* is the one generally grown. A low compact plant producing heads of carmine flowers in autumn.

Temperature: minimum of 7°C (45°F).

Cultivation: ensure maximum light and plenty of sun, plus good ventilation. Older plants should have their stems cut back hard in early spring each year.

Propagation: cuttings in mid-spring, temperature 18°C (65°F).

Erica These are the heathers, all evergreen shrubs. *E. canaliculata* is a tall erect shrub with white flowers in spring. *E. gracilis* is a low grower with purplish flowers in autumn and winter and *E.g.* 'Alba' (syn. *E. nivalis*) is white. *E. × hyemalis* is also a low grower, but erect in habit, with pink and white flowers in autumn and winter – a very popular pot plant.

Temperature: minimum of 7° C (45° F).
Cultivation: cool well-ventilated conditions should be provided. Grow in an acid soilless compost. Stand outdoors in the summer, water and feed well, and return to the house in early autumn.
Propagation: softwood cuttings mid-spring to early summer, moderate heat.

Euphorbia *E. pulcherrima* is the popular winter-flowering poinsettia. It is not the flowers themselves which are showy but the leaf-like bracts, which are generally scarlet. There are cultivars, however, with pink or cream bracts.
Temperature: steady temperature of 15.5° C (60° F).
Cultivation: good light in winter but shade from strong sun in summer. Moderate humidity in warm conditions. Water freely in summer but allow compost to dry out partially between applications in winter. After flowering cut down the stems to 15 cm (6 in) and keep the plants virtually dry until late spring to give them a rest. Then repot, using fresh compost, and start into growth by increasing watering. When growth is well under way feed weekly with a liquid fertiliser. Poinsettias are short-day plants and will initiate flower buds only if (about eight weeks before you wish the plants to come into flower) you give them a daily programme of 14 hours of complete darkness followed by 10 hours of daylight.
Propagation: use new shoots as softwood cuttings and root in a temperature of 21° C (70° F).

Gerbera The Barberton daisy, *C. jamesonii*, is a clump-forming perennial producing in spring and summer large daisy-like flowers in yellow or orange-red. There are several named cultivars producing flowers in shades of yellow, orange, red, pink and also white.
Temperature: minimum of 7° C (45° F), or a few degrees lower.
Cultivation: provide plenty of ventilation on all suitable occasions and be sparing with water – keep the compost slightly moist and water less in winter. Provide light shade in summer from strong sun. A good pot plant but it will make excellent growth in a soil border.
Propagation: division in mid-spring, or cuttings spring and summer.

Hydrangea Cultivars of *H. macrophylla*, the garden hydrangea, make superb pot plants for flowering in the spring. The large mop-like blooms are blue if plants are grown in a lime-free soil, but pink in alkaline soils.
Temperature: minimum of 7° C (45° F) while in the greenhouse.
Cultivation: plants can be raised from softwood cuttings in mid- or late spring. Pot rooted cuttings into 7.5 cm (3 in) pots, using an acid

John Innes potting compost if blue flowers are required. A special blueing compound can be added to the compost. Pot on into 12.5 cm (5 in) pots, using acid JIP2, again adding blueing compound. Stop plants when well established in these pots, but before mid-summer. At this stage move plants to a cold frame for the summer, re-housing them in early or mid-autumn. By this time a further move into 15 cm (6 in) pots will probably be necessary. When in the greenhouse maintain a temperature of 7° C (45° F). Water far less in winter – keep the compost only just moist. The temperature can be increased at the turn of the year to speed up growth, but this is not essential. After flowering remove the dead blooms plus a little of the stem to maintain compact well-branched plants. Plants will benefit from repotting, with fresh compost. They can be stood out of doors or in a cold frame for the summer. Many gardeners like to raise new plants each year rather than save the older ones.

Propagation: softwood cuttings in mid- or late spring, temperature 18° C (65° F).

Pelargonium Erroneously called geraniums, the pelargoniums are among the most popular pot plants for the greenhouse. All are tender and are mainly perennials, although some are classed as shrubs. There are three kinds which are commonly grown: *P. × hortorum*, the zonal pelargonium; *P. domesticum*, the regal pelargonium; and *P. peltatum*, the ivy-leaf pelargonium. There are many cultivars in each group which in summer produce flowers in shades of red, pink, orange, purple and mauve, to mention the basic colours, and also white. The zonals and regals make reasonably compact bushy plants while the ivy-leaf cultivars have a trailing habit and are good subjects for hanging baskets.

The zonal and ivy-leaf cultivars are used extensively in summer bedding schemes but also make good greenhouse plants.

As well as cultivars of the three groups so far mentioned, there are many available species of pelargonium, often with scented foliage, and these are well worth growing in the greenhouse to add further interest. Examples are *P. capitatum*, the rose-scented geranium; *P. crispum*, the lemon-scented geranium; the variegated *P.c.* 'Variegatum'; *P. graveolens*, the rose geranium; *P. quercifolium*, the oak-leaved geranium with aromatic foliage; and *P. tomentosum*, the peppermint geranium.

Temperature: minimum of 10° C (50° F) for most, but resting plants of zonals will be satisfactory with a minimum of 7° C (45° F).

Cultivation: ensure good light and plenty of sun but shade from very strong sunshine in summer. A dry atmosphere is needed all year round plus good ventilation. Water regularly in the growing season but sparingly in the winter – give just enough water to prevent the compost from completely drying out. Rooted cuttings are potted off into 9 cm (3½ in) pots and overwintered in these. Pot them on into 12.5 cm (5 in) pots in early spring. One can raise new plants each year and discard the old ones, or keep plants for several years. In this instance cut back the stems by half before growth begins in the spring and repot, using fresh compost. Remove most of the old compost from around the roots. Older plants should be rested in winter by keeping them cool and on the dry side.

Propagation: semi-ripe cuttings in late summer, temperature 18° C (65° F).

Saintpaulia This is the well-known African violet and it is mainly cultivars of *S. ionantha* which are grown, with single or double flowers in many shades of blue, violet, purple, pink and red. African violet enthusiasts sometimes grow species such as *S. confusa* (deep violet-blue); *S. grandiflora* (deep violet); *S. intermedia* (medium blue); *S. nitida* (deep blue-purple); *S. orbicularis* (pale lilac); *S. pendula* (lavender blue); *S. pusilla* (mauve and white); and *S. velutina* (deep violet and white); as well as *S. ionantha* (light blue to deep violet-blue).

Temperature: ideally maintain within the range 18–24° C (65–75° F).

Cultivation: shade from strong sunshine in summer but allow some sun. Provide plenty of humidity in warm conditions. Take care with watering as overwet compost will cause root rot. Keep the compost moist at all times and do not allow it to dry out completely. Use a soilless compost and half pots or pans – allow plants to become slightly pot-bound.

Propagation: leaf cuttings early to late summer, 21° C (70° F), or division mid to late spring.

Spathiphyllum Evergreen perennials bearing large white or green spathes which form a backcloth for the prominent yellow spadix. There are several species grown like *S. floribundum*, *S.* 'Mauna Loa' (a hybrid) and *S. wallisii*.

Temperature: minimum of 13° C (55° F).

Cultivation: provide humidity in warm conditions and shade from strong sunshine. Water regularly in growing season but less in winter if the minimum temperature is being maintained.

Propagation: division of clumps in mid-spring.

Strelitzia This is the bird of paradise flower and the species generally grown is *S. reginae* with striking blue and orange flowers resembling the head of a bird. The large broad evergreen leaves are reminiscent of those of a banana. Height is about 1.5 m (5 ft).

Temperature: minimum of 7° C (45° F).

Cultivation: plenty of sun and good ventilation in summer. Grow in a large pot or tub, or in the greenhouse border. Water normally but less in the minimum winter temperature.

Propagation: division in mid-spring.

Streptocarpus The ones generally grown are clump-forming evergreen perennials which are very popular as pot plants. Tubular or funnel-shaped flowers are produced in summer. These plants are hybrids and available in various colours. The cultivar 'Constant Nymph' is very well known and has purple-blue flowers.

Temperature: minimum of 7 to 10° C (45 to 50° F).

Cultivation: provide humidity in summer and shade from strong sunshine. Give the plants a rest in winter by providing the minimum temperature. Water regularly in growing season but allow the compost to dry out partially between applications. Keep on the dry side while resting.

Propagation: leaf cuttings (sections) early to late summer, temperature 21° C (70° F).

16 Foliage plants

Plants with colourful or otherwise attractive foliage should always be included in decorative plant displays, where they act as a contrast for flowering plants and create additional interest.

All of those recommended here are suited to pot culture and unless otherwise stated can be grown in John Innes potting compost (No. 1 for initial potting, No. 2 for potting on) or equivalent soilless types. Generally potting should be carried out during early or mid-spring.

If you have a soil bed or border in the greenhouse devoted to decorative plants, you may wish to plant some foliage plants in this, say around and between larger plants such as shrubs and climbers. Many of the low-growing kinds make excellent ground cover and all will make far better growth as their roots will not be restricted.

The following list includes mainly popular kinds, and specific cultural requirements, temperatures and propagation methods are given for each.

Popular plants with notable foliage

Acalypha The 2 m (6 ft) tall shrub *A. wilkesiana* has large leaves, basically copper-green but boldly marked with red. There are several hybrids with equally attractive leaves.
Temperature: minimum of 15.5°C (60°F), but better in a higher temperature.
Cultivation: warmth and high humidity, plus shade from strong sun, ensure excellent growth.
Propagation: softwood cuttings, mid-spring, 21°C (70°F).
Aglaonema Evergreen perennials, generally low growing, with large leaves. Recommended species: *A. commutatum*, green leaves flecked silver-grey; cultivars 'Pseudobracteatum' (syn. 'White Rajah') and 'Silver Queen', with bold white markings; *A. costatum*, ivory midribs; and *A. modestum*, plain mid-green leaves
Temperature: minimum of 13°C (55°F).
Cultivation: these plants like really warm humid conditions, a daytime temperature of 18–21°C (65–70°F) being ideal. Water freely in spring and summer but keep on the dry side during autumn and winter. These are shade lovers and must not be subjected to strong sunshine. Feed regularly in summer.
Propagation: division, mid-spring; cuttings of stem sections, summer.
Asparagus Evergreen perennials grown for their ferny green foliage. *A. setaceus* has very fine foliage; *A. densiflorus* 'Sprengeri' produces needle-like leaves on pendulous stems; and *A. asparagoides*, smilax, has long bright green zig-zag shoots. *A. densiflorus* 'Sprengeri' is ideal for a hanging basket or for trailing over the edge of the staging, while the other two can have their stems trained to supports.
Temperature: minimum of 10°C (50°F).
Cultivation: no particular requirements – a humid atmosphere in summer is appreciated.
Propagation: division mid-spring, seeds mid-winter to mid-spring.
Aspidistra The well-known evergreen perennial, *A. elatior*, has large deep green leaves, while the cultivar, *A. e.* 'Variegata', has white and green striped foliage.

Temperature: minimum of 7° C (45° F).

Cultivation: shade from direct sun – very tolerant of shady situations.

Propagation: division, mid-spring.

Begonia The following begonias are recommended for their attractive foliage: *B.* 'Cleopatra', maple-like leaves marbled bronze; *B.* × *erythrophylla*, leaves dark green above, red beneath; *B. luxurians*, hand-like leaves, red-flushed, and cane-like stems; *B. masoniana* (iron cross), deep green leaves with dark purple cross in centre; *B. rex*, many cultivars with various leaf patterns, colours including cream, silver, pink, purple, red and maroon; and *B. serratipetala*, lobed and toothed leaves, pinkish or reddish. All are evergreen perennials.

Temperature: minimum of 10° C (50° F), but better if minimum of 15.5° C (60° F) can be maintained.

Cultivation: good growth in soilless composts. Shade from direct sun, provide a humid atmosphere in summer, water only when the compost feels dry, water even less in winter, and feed regularly in summer.

Propagation: *masoniana* and *rex* types, leaf cuttings in spring; others, soft cuttings, spring, or division if possible. Strong bottom heat advisable.

Caladium *C. bicolor* is a perennial with tuber-like rhizomes and large thin leaves which die down in autumn. There are many cultivars with strikingly patterned leaves in various colours.

Temperature: minimum of 18° C (65° F) in growing season.

Cultivation: start tubers into growth in spring – place in trays of peat or coconut fibre in propagator with basal temperature of 21° C (70° F). When shoots have been produced pot individually into 15 cm (6 in) pots. Shade from direct sun, water normally when in full growth and feed regularly. Ensure high humidity. When leaves start to die down in autumn stop watering and store the dry tubers in a temperature of 13° C (55° F).

Propagation: offsets planted in spring.

Calathea Clump-forming evergreens. Recommended species: *C. lancifolia* (syn. *insignis*), long narrow wavy leaves with olive-green marks, purple beneath; *C. makoyana*, ovate leaves with thin bright green veins and dark green ovals on a silvery base; *C. ornata*, oval leaves, dark green with fine white or pink stripes; and *C. zebrina*, large leaves, deep velvety green above with mid-rib and veins banded yellow-green, undersides purple.

Temperature: minimum of 10° C (50° F). 18–21° C (65–70° F) during day for good growth.

Cultivation: plenty of warmth and humidity and shade from direct sun. Normal watering and feeding in summer.

Propagation: division in mid-spring.

Chlorophytum *C. comosum* 'Variegatum', the spider plant, is a common evergreen perennial with grassy green and white striped leaves. New plants form on the ends of the arching flower stems and can be left to form a 'cascade' of growth.

Temperature: minimum of 7° C (45° F).

Cultivation: very easy going but due to rapid growth needs regular potting on. Keep well watered in summer and feed occasionally. Shade from very strong sun. Warmth and humidity appreciated.

Propagation: division, spring, or root plantlets in small pots.

Cissus Evergreen climbers, of which *C. antarctica* is well known. Dark shiny green toothed leaves. *C. rhombifolia* is very common and has bright green lobed leaves.

Temperature: minimum of 4.5° C (40° F).

Cultivation: provide supports for the stems. Shade from strong sun – tolerant of shady situation. Humidity appreciated in summer. Allow compost to become fairly dry between waterings. Feed regularly in summer.

Propagation: soft cuttings, spring, moderate heat.

Codiaeum Evergreen shrubs, popularly called crotons. *C. variegatum pictum* has given us many cultivars, with leaves in various sizes, shapes and colours. Many have richly coloured foliage – colours include shades of red, yellow, orange, pink and copper. Often a cultivar will have a combination of several colours.

Temperature: minimum of 15.5° C (60° F).

Cultivation: warmth coupled with high humidity will result in luxuriant growth. Provide good light but shade from strong sun. Water freely in summer, far less in winter, and feed fortnightly during growing season.

Propagation: soft or semi-ripe cuttings mid-spring to late summer with strong bottom heat.

Coleus One of the most popular short-term foliage plants, now correctly known as *Solenostemon*, available in a wide range of colours. Some cultivars have leaves of one colour only, such as red or yellow, but most have multicoloured leaves, splashed or edged with contrasting colours.

Temperature: minimum of 10° C (50° F).

Cultivation: seedling or rooted cuttings are potted off into 7.5 cm (3 in) pots, and eventually moved on to 12.5 cm (5 in) pots. Provide good light and a humid atmosphere when temperatures are high. Stop young plants and also pinch out the lateral shoots to ensure bushy specimens. Feed regularly in summer. Old plants are not generally overwintered, so discard in late autumn.

Propagation: seeds sown in spring, soft cuttings from mid-spring to late summer. Temperature of 15.5° C (60° F) for both.

Cordyline Large-leaved plants, the most popular being *C. fruticosa* with bronzy-red or purplish mature leaves, the young ones generally being cream edged with pink. There are several cultivars such as *C. t.* 'Tricolor' with leaves attractively marked with cream, pink and red, and the reddish-purple and green 'Red Edge'.

Temperature: minimum of 15.5° C (60° F), or a few degrees lower.

Cultivation: provide humidity and light shade in summer.

Propagation: cuttings (stem sections), late spring to early summer, temperature of 21° C (70° F).

Ctenanthe Evergreen perennials, of which *C. oppenheimiana* 'Tricolor' is the best known, with lanceolate leaves splashed with white, pink below.

Temperature: minimum of 10° C (50° F). 18–21° C (65–70° F) during day for good growth.

Cultivation: plenty of warmth and humidity and shade from direct sun. Normal watering and feeding in summer.

Propagation: division in mid-spring.

Dieffenbachia Evergreen perennials with attractive bold foliage. The following are worth growing: *D. seguine* 'Amoena', pale green leaves, patterned with white and pale yellow; *D. maculata*, deep green, blotched with white; and *D. seguine* 'Exotica' with cream-yellow leaves.

Temperature: minimum of 15.5° C (60° F).

Cultivation: good light but shade from strong sun. Provide plenty of humidity when temperatures are high. Water normally all year round. Feed established plants regularly in the growing season.

Propagation: cuttings (stem sections) in early summer, temperature 21° C (70° F).

Dracaena Evergreen shrubs, very variable in leaf shape and colour. Good species include *D. deremensis*, dark green silver-striped sword-shaped leaves; *D. d.* 'Bausei', leaves with white centre; *D. d.* 'Warneckei', grey-green leaves with thin white stripes; *D. fragrans* 'Massangeana', broad arching leaves, deep green with gold centre; *D. godseffiana*, rounded leaves spotted with pale yellow or cream; *D. marginata*, a palm-like plant with long thin green leaves; *D. m.*

'Tricolor', striped pink and cream; and *D. sanderiana*, green silver-edged leaves.

Temperature: minimum of 10° C (50° F); 13° C (55° F) for *deremensis* and *fragrans*.

Cultivation: provide plenty of humidity and light shade in summer.

Propagation: cuttings (stem sections), late spring to early summer, temperature of 21° C (70° F).

Epipremnum Evergreen climbers which are similar to philodendrons. *E. aureum* bears ovate leaves marbled yellow; *E. a.* 'Marble Queen' has cream, green and grey-green leaves; *E. a.* 'Tricolor' possesses green leaves marbled with pale green, cream and yellow; and *E. pictum* 'Argyraeus' has silver-grey spotted leaves.

Temperature: minimum of 21° C (70° F).

Cultivation: as for *Philodendron*

Propagation: cuttings (stem sections or tips) early to late summer; leaf-bud cuttings, early to late summer.

Ficus This genus includes the rubber plants and figs; trees and shrubs, climbers and trailing plants. The best-known species are *F. benjamina*, the weeping fig, a small tree with pendulous branches and rich green glossy ovate leaves; *F. deltoidea*, the mistletoe fig, shrubby, oblong deep green leaves, yellow berries; *F. elastica* 'Decora', the well-known rubber plant, with broad, leathery, glossy deep green leaves; *F. e.* 'Tricolor', green, with pink and cream patches; *F. lyrata*, the fiddle-back fig, with huge deep green glossy spoon-shaped leaves; *F. pumila*, climbing or trailing, small green heart-shaped leaves; and *F. sagittata* 'Variegata', climbing or trailing, cream-edged pointed leaves.

Temperature: minimum of 15.5° C (60° F) but *F. deltoidea* and *F. pumila* will survive with a minimum of 10° C (50° F).

Cultivation: good light but shade from strong sun. Warm humid atmosphere for best results. Keep compost steadily moist but allow to become almost dry between waterings in winter. Feed regularly in spring and summer.

Propagation: soft or semi-ripe cuttings or leaf-bud cuttings, mid-spring to mid-summer, temperature of 21° C (70° F).

Fittonia Evergreen perennials, low growing. *F. verschaffeltii* has green leaves with red veins, and *F. v. argyroneura* has silver veins.

Temperature: minimum of 15.5° C (60° F).

Cultivation: provide a warm humid atmosphere and light shade. Keep compost moist all year round but avoid saturated conditions.

Propagation: division, mid-spring; cuttings early to late summer in strong bottom heat.

Grevillea The silk oak, *G. robusta,* is a tree in the wild but a popular pot plant under glass, with its pinnate fern-like green leaves with silky undersides.

Temperature: minimum of 4.5° C (40° F).

Cultivation: provide ventilation on all suitable occasions, and good light, but shade from very hot sun. Normal watering. Slightly acid compost.

Propagation: easily raised from seeds, sown in spring, moderate heat.

Hedera Ivies are climbing plants but they have other uses apart from being trained upwards on suitable supports. They make good trailing specimens, especially the small-leaved kinds, and can therefore be grown in hanging containers or allowed to cascade over the edge of the staging. Ivies also make good ground cover between larger plants in a bed or border. There are many good cultivars of the common ivy, *H. helix,* such as the green-leaved 'Chicago' and 'Sagittaefolia', and the variegated 'Adam', 'Little Diamond', 'Glacier', 'Oro di', 'Bogliasco' and 'Luzii'. 'Buttercup' is plain yellow. The large-leaved Canary Island ivy, *H. algeriensis,* is well worth growing, together with its variegated cultivar 'Gloire de Marengo'.

Temperature: minimum of 4.5° C (40° F).

Cultivation: shade from direct sun but try to give variegated ivies good light to maintain leaf colours. Green-leaved kinds are ideal for shady places in the greenhouse, such as under the staging. Provide humidity when temperatures are high. Water sparingly in winter but normally in spring and summer. Feed regularly in growing season.

Propagation: soft or semi-ripe cuttings, or leaf-bud cuttings, spring or summer, moderate heat.

Hypoestes A charming small perennial with red-spotted leaves. *H. phyllostachya* makes a good pot plant and is popularly known as the polka dot plant.

Temperature: minimum of 15.5° C (60° F).

Cultivation: try to provide a warm humid atmosphere and shade from direct sun. Keep the compost steadily moist. Shoots can be pinched back to encourage compact specimens.

Propagation: seeds, mid-winter to mid-spring 21° C (70° F).

Maranta Very striking evergreen perennials. The following are generally available: *M. leuconeura,* whose leaves have bluish-green veins and purple undersides; *M. l. erythroneura,* dark green leaves with red veins and red-purple undersides; *M. l. kerchoviana,* greyish-green leaves spotted with red-brown; and *M. l. massangeana,* dark green leaves with silvery veins.

Temperature: 10° C (50° F) minimum.

Cultivation: warm humid conditions for best growth. Shade from direct sun but maximum light in winter. Normal watering in growing season but less in winter. Liquid feed in summer.

Propagation: division, mid-spring; cuttings, mid-spring, 21° C (70° F).

Monstera Evergreen climbers, of which *M. deliciosa*, the Swiss cheese plant, is the one normally grown. Large green leaves, deeply cut, and perforated as they age. The stems produce aerial roots.

Temperature: minimum of 15.5° C (60° F) or slightly lower.

Cultivation: provide shade and humidity when temperatures are high. Best grown up a pole thickly covered with sphagnum moss so that the stems can root into it. Or a wire cylinder filled with moss and supported internally with a pole or stake. Keep moss moist.

Propagation: stem cuttings or leaf-bud cuttings, early to late summer, temperature 21° C (70° F).

Palms There are quite a few palms available that make good greenhouse foliage plants, such as *Howea forsteriana*, *Chamaedorea elegans*, *Phoenix canariensis* (Canary Island date palm) and *Chamaerops humilis*.

Temperature: minimum of 10° C (50° F) but preferably 13° C (55° F).

Cultivation: provide shade from direct sun and a humid atmosphere in warm conditions. Water freely in summer but give far less in winter. Feeding established plants in summer promotes good growth.

Propagation: seeds in spring, strong bottom heat; or rooted suckers if produced in spring.

Peperomia Low-growing evergreen perennials, varying widely in leaf shapes and colours. Popular ones include *P. argyreia*, with silver and green banded leaves; *P. caperata*, dark green, rounded, deeply crinkled leaves; *P. griseoargentea*, similar to *caperata* but leaves larger; and *P. obtusifolia*, thick fleshy leaves, green, but edged cream in the cultivar 'Greengold' and cream variegated in 'Variegata'.

Temperature: 13–15.5° C (55–60° F) minimum.

Cultivation: they relish soilless composts and should be restricted to small pots. Shade from sun but provide good light in winter. A humid atmosphere is essential. Allow compost almost to dry out between waterings. Feed regularly in spring and summer.

Propagation: leaf cuttings mid-spring to late summer, 21° C (70° F), or division in spring.

Philodendron Shrubs and climbing plants with large handsome leaves and aerial roots produced from the stems. Available species include *P. bipinnatifidum*, shrub, dark green and deeply cut leaves; *P. augu-*

stisectum, climbing, deep green foliage, deeply cut; *P. erubescens*, climbing, leaves green flushed with copper; *P. domesticum*, climbing, glossy green leaves; *P. pedatum*, climbing, deep green lobed leaves; and *P. scandens*, climbing, heart-shaped deep green leaves. Attractive named cultivars include 'Burgundy', climbing, red-flushed leaves, and *P. tuxtlanum* 'Tuxla', climbing, glossy green leaves.

Temperature: 15.5° C (60° F) minimum.

Cultivation: the climbing kinds can be grown as for *Monstera* (see this entry). Or grow up trellis or other suitable supports. *P. scandens* is suitable for a hanging container. Shade from strong sun (will take a position in light shade) but full light in winter. Provide high humidity. Normal watering, but reduce in winter. Feed regularly in spring and summer.

Propagation: cuttings (stem sections or tips), or leaf-bud cuttings, early to late summer, 21° C (70° F).

Pilea Low-growing evergreen perennials. Try *P. cadierei*, the aluminium plant, with silver-grey and green leaves, or the more compact *P. c. nana*. *P. involucrata* 'Moon Valley' produces green-gold leaves with reddish veins. The artillary plant, *P. microphylla*, has minute light green leaves which create a mossy appearance.

Temperature: minimum of 13–15.5° C (55–60° F).

Cultivation: shade from strong sun but provide good light in winter. Humidity encourages better growth and stopping young plants results in bushy specimens. Water normally but in winter allow compost almost to dry out between waterings.

Propagation: soft or semi-ripe cuttings mid-spring to late summer, moderate heat, or division in mid-spring if feasible.

Sansevieria Evergreen perennials with rather succulent leaves, either erect and sword-like or in flattish rosettes. *S. trifasciata* is the well-known mother-in-law's tongue with sword-like erect leaves in clumps, deep green with transverse bands of lighter green. *S. t.* 'Hahnii' is a dwarf plant forming a rosette of leaves, and *S. t.* 'Golden Hahnii' has broadly yellow-edged leaves. The best-known cultivar, however, is *S. t.* 'Laurentii', virtually the same as the species except that the leaves are edged with yellow.

Temperature: minimum of 10° C (50° F).

Cultivation: although good light is enjoyed, provide shade from very strong sun. Be careful with watering – allow compost to dry out partially between applications. Dry atmosphere appreciated. Do not grow in too large a pot and pot on only when present pot is full of roots.

Propagation: division (rooted suckers), mid-spring; leaf cuttings (sections), early to late summer. 'Laurentii', however, will lose its yellow edge if propagated from leaf cuttings.

Tradescantia Very popular trailing evergreens, often planted in hanging containers or allowed to cascade over the edge of the staging. *T. fluminensis* is the wandering Jew with elliptic glossy green leaves; *T. f.* 'Albovittata' has white-striped leaves; *T. f.* 'Variegata', white and green striped leaves; and *T. f.* 'Quicksilver' has white and green stripes. *T. zebrina* has silver-banded leaves, purple below. It has some attractive cultivars: *T. z.* 'Purpusii' with deep green leaves blushed purple, and *T. z.* 'Quadricolor' whose leaves are banded pink, red and white.

Temperature: minimum of 7° C (45° F).

Cultivation: light shade in summer plus normal watering and feeding. Keep on the dry side in low temperatures.

Propagation: cuttings mid-spring to early autumn – can be rooted without artificial heat in summer.

17   Fuchsias

Because of their versatility and ease of culture fuchsias are very popular. They make a superb show of colour in the greenhouse during the summer and can also be used outdoors in summer bedding schemes. Not only are they grown as bush plants but fuchsias can also be trained to various shapes, the most popular being the standard, with a tall clear stem and a head of branches at the top. Those kinds with a pendulous or semi-pendulous habit of growth are ideal for hanging baskets, either in the greenhouse or outdoors for summer display. Fuchsias are also used in window boxes and in garden containers of all kinds.

The plants flower freely throughout the summer and they do not demand a great deal of heat; a cool or intermediate greenhouse providing satisfactory conditions. Indeed, fuchsias can be kept in a greenhouse which is only just frost free during the winter.

Fuchsias can, if desired, be kept for many years, when they will form large specimens; or, as most people prefer, new plants can be raised each year and the older ones discarded.

Propagation Fuchsias are easily raised from softwood cuttings which can be rooted any time from spring to late summer. Probably the most popular time is late spring or early summer – cuttings rooted then will result in large plants for flowering the following summer.

If you wish to produce standard fuchsias, take cuttings in early summer to ensure tall flowering-size specimens by the summer of the following year.

Prepare cuttings from the soft tips of side shoots, ideally without flower buds. However, if you cannot find any shoots free of buds, then use what is available and nip off the buds while preparing the cuttings. Cut the base of each shoot immediately below a node or leaf joint, strip the lower leaves and dip the base of the prepared cutting in a hormone rooting powder formulated for softwood cuttings. Prepared cuttings are ideally about 7.5 cm (3 in) long.

Large quantities of cuttings are best inserted in seed trays, but as most people want to root only a few of each cultivar, I would recommend 9 cm ($3\frac{1}{2}$ in) pots, using a separate pot for each cultivar. This size of pot will take up to eight cuttings. The rooting medium can be either equal parts peat and coarse sand, or equal parts peat and Perlite (or use a peat alternative). Insert the cuttings almost to their lower leaves, firm them in lightly and water in with a rosed can.

A temperature of 18°C (65°F) is recommended for rooting the cuttings and rooting time is about four weeks. Cuttings need humidity, so root them either in a closed propagating case or insert each pot in a clear polythene bag and tie at the top. It is necessary with both methods to ventilate several times a week to allow excess condensation to disperse and to prevent a stagnant atmosphere – conditions which quickly lead to rotting of the cuttings.

General cultivation When the cuttings have rooted pot them off into 9 cm ($3\frac{1}{2}$ in) pots, using John Innes potting compost No. 1 or a soilless type. Fuchsias grow particularly well in the proprietary soilless composts. Water the newly potted young plants and place on the staging in a cool greenhouse.

Provide plenty of ventilation but avoid draughts and violent fluctuations in temperature. Shade the young plants from strong sunshine to prevent scorching of the foliage. Keep the compost steadily moist –

do not allow it to dry out completely and do not create saturated conditions.

In winter a steady temperature of 10°C (50°F) will enable the young plants to make slow but steady growth. Plants raised from cuttings in late summer will certainly need this temperature in order to reach a reasonable size by the following summer. Plants can be given a minimum winter temperature of 4.5°C (40°F) but they will make virtually no growth until the weather warms up in the spring.

When the initial pots are full of roots, but before the plants become pot bound, pot on to 12.5 cm (5 in) pots, using John Innes potting compost No. 2 or an equivalent soilless type. Plants raised in late summer are often kept in their initial pots over the winter and potted on in early spring. It is important not to overwater in the winter when temperatures are low.

Young plants to be grown as bushes – the usual way of growing fuchsias – and those intended for hanging baskets, need to be stopped. Pinch out the tip of each plant when 15 cm (6 in) high. This will result in side or lateral shoots being produced. When the laterals are about 10 cm (4 in) long pinch out their tips. This treatment will result in really bushy or well-branched plants with tremendous flowering potential.

If the fuchsias are to be used for greenhouse display they should, ideally, be potted on to 15 cm (6 in) pots in which they will flower. Again use JIP2 or an equivalent soilless compost. This potting on will result in larger plants.

Plants which are well established in their final pots can be fed weekly from late spring to early autumn with any good liquid fertiliser. Again, keep the compost steadily moist throughout the spring and summer and at all costs do not let it dry out during flower-bud development as it invariably results in bud drop. During the flowering period regularly remove dead flowers and seed pods.

Plants intended for display in the garden during the summer must be well hardened in a cold frame two to three weeks before setting them outside. Do not plant out until all danger of frost is over – it should be safe enough in early summer in all parts of the country.

If you wish to keep older plants for several years they need to be rested over the winter. You will certainly need to keep some plants over the winter for the production of cutting material in the spring. From mid-autumn onwards, therefore, gradually reduce watering of the plants which have flowered to encourage them to shed their leaves. When the leaves have fallen and throughout the winter keep the compost only barely moist. The resting plants need only frost-free conditions.

Fuchsias which were planted outdoors for the summer should be lifted in early autumn before the frosts begin. Shake off all the garden soil and pot them into 15 cm (6 in) pots, first doing some root pruning if the roots are too long for the pots. Overwinter as described above.

In the spring the plants are started into growth again, but first repot them into the same size of pot, using fresh compost, having removed all the old compost from around the roots. In early or mid-spring gradually increase watering and the temperature – try to provide at least 10° C (50° F) – to start the plants into growth. Before growth starts, however, prune back all shoots to within two or three buds of their base. Alternatively, pruning can be carried out just after leaf fall – plants will then take up far less room in the greenhouse over the winter.

Growing standard fuchsias Choose strong-growing cultivars with an upright habit of growth, as indicated in the table. A standard fuchsia has a tall straight clear (unbranching) stem and a head of branches at the top. Standards give height to a display of fuchsias whether in the greenhouse or out of doors in summer bedding schemes.

To train a plant into a standard, the main shoot or stem is allowed to grow until the required stem height is reached. A stem 1 m (3 ft 3 in) in height is generally acceptable, while a half-standard has a stem half this height. Provide a bamboo cane of the appropriate stem height from an early stage in the plant's development and tie in the stem regularly as it grows, using either raffia or soft garden string. When the desired height has been reached pinch out the top of the stem. Side shoots will then develop near the top to form the head. When these are 10 cm (4 in) long pinch out their tips also. Throughout this training period side shoots lower down the stem should be removed as soon as they appear. Leave the foliage on the stem as this encourages stem thickening.

Fuchsias for hanging baskets Choose cultivars of lax or pendulous habit (see accompanying table). Young plants in 9 cm (3½ in) pots can be planted in baskets during early spring. Use either traditional wire baskets lined with sphagnum moss or black polythene, or the modern moulded plastic types.

A selection of fuchsias Fuchsias are available in many colours and combinations of colours; some cultivars have single flowers while others sport semi-double or fully double blooms. In very simple terms a fuchsia flower is generally pendulous and bell-like in shape, and it is made up as follows:

a. There is a cylindrical part which is attached to the flower stalk or petiole and this is known as the 'tube'.

b. Attached to the tube are the 'sepals' which look like petals. Very often the tube and sepals are of the same colour.

c. The bell-shaped part of the flower is known as the 'corolla'. This is often of a different colour from the tube and sepals (generally a contrasting colour) but in some cultivars it is the same colour.

There are many hundreds of hybrid fuchsias available and the cultivars listed in the accompanying table are well known, reliable and easily obtained from a specialist grower. I have also included a few well-known species which make a nice change from the hybrids and give additional interest to a collection. They are grown in the same way and trained as bush plants.

Fuchsias for various purposes

Name	Flowers	For Bush Form	For Standards	For Hanging Baskets
HYBRIDS				
'Caroline'	Single, cream flushed pink tube and sepals, bright pink corolla	√	√	
'Cascade'	Single, white flushed carmine tube and sepals, carmine corolla			√
'Citation'	Single, rose-pink tube and sepals, white corolla	√		
'Flirtation Waltz'	Double, white flushed pink tube and sepals, light rose corolla	√		
'Golden Marinka'	Single, red tube and sepals, corolla of a deeper red. Foliage golden-yellow			√

Name	Flowers	For Bush Form	For Standards	For Hanging Baskets
'Jack Acland'	Single, pink tube and sepals, rose-pink corolla	√	√	
'La Campanella'	Semi-double, white flushed pink tube and sepals, violet corolla			√
'Lady Isobel Barnett'	Single, rose-red tube and sepals, rose-purple corolla	√		
'Leonora'	Single, tube, sepals and corolla a pleasing shade of pink	√		
'Marinka'	Single, red tube and sepals, corolla deeper red			√
'Melody'	Single, rose-pink tube and sepals, purple corolla	√	√	
'Mission Bells'	Single, scarlet tube and sepals, purple corolla	√		
'Mme Cornelissen'	Semi-double, scarlet tube and sepals, white corolla with cerise veining	√		
'Mrs Marshall'	Single, white tube and sepals flushed pink, rose-cerise corolla	√	√	
'Sleigh Bells'	Single, white tube and sepals, white corolla	√	√	
'Swanley Gem'	Single, scarlet tube and sepals, deep violet corolla	√		
'Swingtime'	Double, red tube and sepals, white corolla veined pink at base	√	√	
'Tennessee Waltz'	Semi-double, rose-pink tube and sepals, lilac-lavender corolla flushed rose pink	√	√	
'Thalia'	All parts orange-scarlet	√		
'Ting-a-Ling'	Single tube, sepals and corolla are white	√		

SPECIES

fulgens	Scarlet, long tube, green-tipped sepals	√		
microphylla	Deep red	√		

Name	Flowers	For Bush Form	For Standards	For Hanging Baskets
procumbens	Pale orange-yellow tube, sepals green, tipped purple	prostrate habit		√
triphylla	Orange-scarlet	√		

18   Flowering shrubs and climbing plants

Visit the greenhouses of any botanic or large private garden and you will come across a very wide range of shrubs and climbers which are grown primarily for their flowers. There are, in fact, shrubs and climbers suited to any size of greenhouse, from the largest to the smallest, and to any temperature range, from the unheated house to the warm greenhouse.

Shrubs and climbing plants are very worthwhile additions to a greenhouse or conservatory; they live for many years and flower regularly each year, very often over a long period. Generally speaking they are trouble-free and easy to grow, requiring minimum attention.

There is no doubt that the most attractive way of displaying shrubs is to plant them in a soil bed or border, especially if you have a fairly large greenhouse or conservatory. Here they will make excellent growth due to the unrestricted root run. The bed can be mulched with bark chippings to create an attractive finish and to help conserve moisture.

Climbers are best grown in the same way, but should be planted against the back wall of a conservatory, for example, or against the side or end walls of a free-standing greenhouse, so that they can be tied in to horizontal wires. There are special fixings available to attach training wires to the glazing bars of aluminium houses. Wires should be spaced about 30 to 45 cm (12 to 18 in) apart and can even be fixed in the roof area right up to the ridge so that the plants can be encouraged to grow in this otherwise wasted space. As an alternative to horizontal wires you may wish to train climbers on ornamental trellis, either timber or plastic-coated wire types. Trellis is particularly recommended for the back wall of a lean-to or conservatory.

Of course, not all gardeners are able to grow shrubs and climbers in soil beds, but fortunately they can equally well be grown in pots or tubs. You will buy shrubs and climbers as young plants in 10 to 15 cm (4 to 6 in) pots, and they should be potted on as necessary – that is, when the present pot is full of roots but before the plant becomes pot bound. Always pot on into the next size of pot. For most shrubs a 30 cm (12 in) pot is a suitable final size although for some of the more vigorous and larger growing plants you may consider it necessary to progress to a tub of suitable size – up to 45 cm (18 in) diameter. Potting generally takes place in early or mid-spring. I am very traditional when it comes to composts for shrubs; I consider you cannot do better than to use a loam-based type for most of them – John Innes potting compost No. 2 or 3. The soilless composts do not, in my opinion, hold most shrubs firmly enough and with many kinds the nutrients are quickly used up by the plants.

Many shrubs require no regular pruning, only the removal of dead or dying wood, and the removal of dead flowers and leaves.

Specific cultural requirements are given in the following descriptive list of shrubs and climbing plants.

Shrubs and climbers

Abutilon Evergreen shrubs with hanging bell-shaped flowers and maple-like foliage. Some of the hybrids are well worth growing such as 'Ashford Red', crimson; 'Boule de Neige', white; 'Canary Bird', yellow; 'Fireball', reddish orange; *A.* × *hybridum* 'Golden Fleece', yellow; and *A.* × *hybridum* 'Savitzii', grown only for its white and green variegated leaves. This one is a low grower but the others can reach up to 1.8 m (6 ft). *A. pictum* has red flowers and can attain 3 m (10 ft), while *A. p.* 'Thompsonii' has most attractive yellow-mottled foliage. Temperature: minimum of 10° C (50° F), or a few degrees lower. Cultivation: good ventilation in summer. Cut plants hard back in early spring. Feed established plants weekly in summer. Propagation: semi-ripe cuttings, mid-summer to early autumn. **Acacia** Evergreen shrubs with fluffy yellow flowers mainly in spring. Many have attractive bipinnate foliage. The most popular are *A. baileyana*, the Cootamunda wattle, with blue-grey leaves, and *A.*

dealbata, the silver wattle, with silvery leaves (the mimosa of florists).
Temperature: minimum of 10° C (50° F) or a few degrees lower.

Cultivation: good ventilation in summer and also on all favourable occasions in the winter. It is not necessary to prune, although
pruning can be undertaken after flowering if you wish to keep
plants to a manageable height. Normally these species are tall
growing.

Propagation: seeds when ripe or semi-ripe cuttings in mid- or late
summer.

Acalypha Shrubs with long catkin-like flowers. *A. hispida* is the one
usually grown, a 3 m (10 ft) high species with crimson flowers.

Temperature: minimum of 15.5° C (60° F).

Cultivation: keep well shaded from strong sun. Excellent in large pots
of soilless potting compost. To keep plants to a manageable height
prune back in spring. Or you could replace plants every couple of
years or so with young specimens raised from cuttings.

Propagation: softwood cuttings in mid-spring, rooted with strong
bottom heat.

Allamanda The evergreen climber *A. cathartica* is a vigorous plant
with sumptuous bright yellow trumpet-shaped flowers in summer and
autumn. *A. c.* 'Grandiflora' is pale yellow, while *A. c.* 'Hendersonii' is
deep golden-yellow.

Temperature: 15.5° C (60° F) minimum.

Cultivation: shade from strong sun and provide plenty of humidity
in the summer. Ideally grow in a soil bed, alternatively in a large pot.
As they develop, train growths to suitable supports. Pruning can be
carried out in early spring: cut back the previous year's growth to
within two nodes (leaf joints) of its base. This will keep the plant to
a manageable size.

Propagation: softwood cuttings in mid-spring, rooted with strong
bottom heat.

Aphelandra Evergreen shrubs, the best known being *A. squarrosa*
'Louisae', often called the zebra plant because of its white-striped
leaves. More compact is 'Dania'. It produces a pyramid-shaped
inflorescence consisting of bright yellow bracts and flowers. Altogether a most striking greenhouse plant.

Temperature: minimum of 10° C (50° F), but a few degrees higher if
possible.

Cultivation: straightforward, but provide shade in summer plus
plenty of humidity when temperatures are high. Prune back the stems
after flowering to maintain a compact well-branched specimen.

Propagation: softwood cuttings mid-spring to mid-summer, or leaf-bud cuttings. Provide strong bottom heat.

Boronia Australian evergreen shrubs, of which *B. megastigma* is probably the best known, a 60 cm (2 ft) high shrub with purple-brown and yellow fragrant flowers in spring.

Temperature: minimum of 7° C (45° F).

Cultivation: an acid compost required, ideally a soilless type. Feed regularly in the summer, and after flowering prune back fairly hard.

Propagation: semi-ripe cuttings late summer or early autumn.

Bougainvillea Among the most popular greenhouse climbers, the flowers being surrounded by highly colourful bracts. *B. glabra* has purple bracts; *B. spectabilis* is purple or reddish. There are many named hybrids like 'Mrs Butt', crimson to magenta; 'Orange King' and 'Golden Glow', orange; and 'Brilliant', copper-orange.

Temperature: minimum of 10° C (50° F).

Cultivation: plenty of sun and ventilation needed in the growing season together with plenty of humidity. Provide a humus-rich soil or compost and train stems to wires or trellis. Keep on the dry side in winter. In early spring increase watering and prune by cutting out weak shoots to leave strong stems. These can be cut back by a third if desired.

Propagation: semi-ripe cuttings in mid- or late summer, with heat.

Bouvardia Of these shrubs, the named cultivars of *B. × domestica* are generally grown, like the scarlet-flowered 'President Cleveland' and the rose-pink 'Rosea'. They flower in the summer and through into autumn.

Temperature: minimum of 10° C (50° F).

Cultivation: provide light shade in summer and well-ventilated conditions. Young plants need stopping several times to ensure well-branched specimens. They make good small compact shrubs for limited space. After flowering, and throughout the winter keep the soil or compost on the dry side; in late winter prune the plants by cutting back shoots to within one leaf joint. In early spring increase watering, and the temperature if possible. Old plants are best replaced with young ones propagated as detailed below.

Propagation: softwood cuttings as soon as available in spring, rooted with strong bottom heat.

Brugmansia Shrubs with large trumpet-shaped flowers in summer and autumn. Species generally available include *B. cornigera*, 3 m (10 ft), white or cream fragrant flowers; *B. c.* 'Knightii', double

flowers; *B. sanguinea*, 2 m (6 ft) tall, orange-red flowers; and *B. suaveolens*, up to 5 m (16 ft) tall, with white fragrant flowers.
Temperature: minimum of 10° C (50° F).
Cultivation: give plenty of ventilation and light shade in summer. Ideally plant in a border, or grow eventually in large pots or tubs. To restrict height prune in late winter by cutting back the previous year's stems to within 15 cm (6 in) of the soil. Feed well in the summer.
Propagation: soft or semi-ripe cuttings from late spring to early autumn, in heat.
Brunfelsia Superb evergreen shrubs which remain at a suitable height for the average greenhouse. *B. pauciflora* is the one generally grown, and it produces masses of fragrant blue-purple flowers in summer. *B. p.* 'Floribunda' is of a darker shade, and *B.p.* 'Macrantha' has larger blooms. *B. latifolia* sports pale violet blooms which are scented, and *B. undulata* bears wavy, scented white flowers.
Temperature: minimum of 10° C (50° F).
Cultivation: shade from sun from spring to early autumn. Young plants should be stopped several times to create bushy shapely specimens.
Propagation: semi-ripe cuttings from early to late summer. Provide strong bottom heat.
Callistemon Evergreen shrubs from Australia with bottlebrush-like flowers in summer. Suitable for the small to medium greenhouse. The flowers, or rather the long stamens which produce the brush-like effect, generally come in shades of red. There are several species grown, such as *C. citrinus*, *C. glaucus*, *C. linearis*, *C. rigidus*, and *C. subulatus*.
Temperature: minimum of 4.5° C (40° F).
Cultivation: provide good ventilation and allow plenty of sun. An acid compost or soil, well drained, should be provided. Plants in pots or tubs may, with advantage, be stood in a sunny sheltered spot out of doors for the summer.
Propagation: semi-ripe cuttings from early to late summer; also easily raised from seeds.
Camellia Evergreen shrubs with attractive glossy deep green foliage, making excellent pot or tub plants. There are many hundreds of cultivars of *C. japonica*, with flowers in all shades of red and pink, and also white. *C. reticulata* cultivars can also be recommended, together with cultivars of *C.* × *williamsii*. Choose those which particularly appeal to you, as there are so many – it is best to buy flowering plants from a garden centre.

Temperature: while under glass provide a temperature of 4.5 to 10° C (40 to 50° F). Or they could be flowered in a cold greenhouse.

Cultivation: grow in large pots or tubs, using an acid compost consisting mainly of peat and leafmould, with the addition of coarse sand and, if available, acid loam. Place the plants in the greenhouse in autumn, where they will flower in winter and spring. Provide good ventilation and keep the compost steadily moist, but not wet. After flowering place the plants outside, preferably in a plunge bed, in a sheltered, semi-shaded situation and keep steadily moist throughout the growing season. Feed every two weeks while in full growth with a liquid fertiliser. Avoid using 'hard' water.

Propagation: semi-ripe cuttings or leaf-bud cuttings in late summer with strong bottom heat.

Carissa Evergreen spiny shrubs with tubular fragrant flowers in spring. *C. grandiflora*, popularly known as the Natal plum, is the most commonly available species. It grows to a height of 2 m (6 ft) and bears 12 mm ($\frac{1}{2}$ in) long white scented flowers.

Temperature: minimum of 10° C (50° F).

Cultivation: needs very little attention and grows particularly well in a soilless compost with extra sand or grit added to ensure good drainage and aeration.

Propagation: seeds in spring or heel cuttings in summer, providing a temperature of 18–21° C (65–70° F).

Cassia Leguminous shrubs, many species, but *C. corymbosa* is the one generally available. It grows to 2 m (6 ft) in height and bears deep yellow flowers in late summer.

Temperature: minimum of 4.5° C (40° F).

Cultivation: plenty of ventilation should be provided in spring and summer but otherwise no special requirements.

Propagation: seeds sown mid-winter or mid-spring, or semi-ripe cuttings late summer or early autumn.

Cestrum Shrubs, most of which are evergreen. Clusters of tubular flowers produced in summer or autumn. Recommended species include *C. aurantiacum*, height 3 m (10 ft), semi-evergreen, brilliant orange flowers; *C. elegans*, of the same height, reddish-purple flowers; *C.* 'Newellii', crimson flowers; and *C. roseum*, 2 m (6 ft) tall, with bright pink flowers.

Temperature: minimum of 7–10° C (45–50° F).

Cultivation: provide shade from hot sun in summer, and feed established plants regularly in the growing season. Best grown in a soil bed, or large pot or tub, in a soil or compost rich in humus. Train to horizontal wires and allow the plants to grow into the roof area. Pruning can consist of removing all three-year-old stems, allowing the rest to remain. The old flowered tops of the stems can also be cut out. Prune in late winter.

Propagation: seeds sown mid-winter to mid-spring, and semi-ripe cuttings taken in late summer or early autumn. Provide heat for both.

Chorizema Evergreen leguminous shrubs with pea-like flowers. *C. ilicifolium*, the one generally offered, grows to about 60 cm (2 ft) in height and flowers in spring and summer, the blooms being orange to red, and purple and yellow.

Temperature: minimum of 7–10° C (45–50° F).

Cultivation: these shrubs like plenty of sun and good ventilation. An acid compost is required, and the soilless types are particularly good, especially if extra sand or grit is added. Allow compost to dry out partially between waterings. Prune after flowering by cutting back stems by about half their length. The rather lax stems will need canes for support.

Propagation: softwood cuttings in early spring or seeds mid-winter to mid-spring. Provide heat for both.

Clerodendrum Under glass *C. thomsoniae* is the species usually grown; an evergreen climber to about 4 m (13 ft), producing, in summer, crimson flowers surrounded by a white calyx.

Temperature: minimum of 15.5° C (60° F).

Cultivation: provide light shade and a humid atmosphere in summer. Train to horizontal wires or other supports.

Propagation: softwood or semi-ripe cuttings mid-spring to late summer, or seeds sown between mid-winter and mid-spring, both with heat.

Clianthus Evergreen leguminous shrubs with pinnate foliage and large pea-like flowers. Species include *C. formosus*, prostrate in habit, bearing, in summer, brilliant red flowers with a black blotch, and *C. puniceus*, popularly known as parrot's bill, growing to about 2 m (6 ft) in height and producing red flowers in spring and summer. There is a white cultivar called *C. p.* 'Albus'.

Temperature: minimum of 7 to 10° C (45 to 50° F).

Cultivation: grow *C. puniceus* in a large pot or tub, or in a border. *C. formosus* is generally grown in a hanging basket. Water this species very carefully – allow the compost almost to dry out between applications and allow to become almost dry in the winter. These shrubs like good light but shade from very strong sun.

Propagation: seeds in spring or semi-ripe cuttings in late summer or early autumn. Provide good bottom heat for both.

Crossandra Evergreen shrubs, of which *C. infundibuliformis* is the best known with striking orange-red flowers in summer. It grows to 91 cm (3 ft) in height.

Temperature: minimum of 15.5° C (60° F).

Cultivation: provide humidity and light shading during summer and feed established plants regularly during growing period. In early spring stems can be pruned back by about half to maintain a compact shape.

Propagation: soft or semi-ripe cuttings from mid-spring to late summer, or seeds from mid-winter to mid-spring. Provide bottom heat.

Erythrina Shrubs and trees with trifoliate leaves and handsome pea-like flowers in summer. The species generally available is the coral tree, *E. crista-galli*, with spiny stems up to 2 m (6 ft) tall and heads of scarlet flowers.

Temperature: needs only a frost-free greenhouse, say a minimum of 4.5° C (40° F).

Cultivation: ensure good light and plenty of ventilation, water normally in summer but keep the soil or compost almost dry over the winter when the plant is resting. In spring the previous year's stems should be cut back to within a few centimetres of their base where new shoots will appear.

Propagation: softwood cuttings from mid-spring to early summer or seeds from mid-winter to mid-spring. Bottom heat temperature of 21° C (70° F).

Gardenia Evergreen shrubs, of which *G. augusta* is the best known. It grows up to 2 m (6 ft) in height if planted in a soil border, but will be far shorter when pot grown. The deep green leaves make a good background for the very fragrant white flowers which appear in summer and autumn.

Temperature: minimum of 15.5° C (60° F).

Cultivation: provide shade and humidity in summer and feed regularly with a liquid fertiliser. Grows well in soilless composts. Young plants should be stopped to ensure bushy specimens. After flowering prune the plants by cutting back by half the old flowered stems.

Propagation: softwood or semi-ripe cuttings from mid-spring to late summer, rooted with strong bottom heat.

Hardy shrubs Some hardy shrubs can be gently forced into early flower in the greenhouse, like *Daphne mezereum, Forsythia, Ham-*

amelis mollis, Magnolia stellata, Prunus × subhirtella 'Autumnalis', *Prunus tenella* 'Fire Hill', *Ribes sanguineum, Spiraea* 'Arguta', *Spiraea thunbergii* and *Syringa*.

Temperature: slightly heated or cold greenhouse. Ideal temperature to provide is 7–10° C (45–50° F).

Cultivation: pot young flowering-size plants (buy them, or lift from the garden) in the autumn, using pots of suitable size. Stand them outside and take them into the greenhouse from early winter onwards – ideally in stages to ensure a succession of flowers in late winter and spring. After flowering plant them in the garden as they should not be forced a second time.

Hibiscus Shrubs with large flamboyant colourful flowers in the summer. *H. rosa-sinensis* is the species generally grown in greenhouses, reaching a height of about 2 m (6 ft), and bearing deep red flowers. There are many cultivars and more and more of these are now becoming available in Britain. Many of them have been raised in the USA. Colours include red, pink, yellow, orange and white as well as combinations, and there are cultivars with double flowers. A well-known cultivar is *H. rosa-sinensis* 'Cooperi' with white and green variegated leaves.

Temperature: minimum 10° C (50° F).

Cultivation: in summer provide light shade and humidity. Best grown in a soil border if a good large specimen is required, but equally happy in a large pot or tub eventually.

Propagation: softwood cuttings from mid-spring to early summer, rooting them with strong bottom heat.

Hoya Evergreen climbers with pendulous clusters of flowers from late spring to autumn. *H. carnosa*, the wax flower, is the best known and bears white flowers which take on a pinkish tinge as they age. A climber ideally suited to the small greenhouse.

Temperature: minimum of 7° C (45° F).

Cultivation: provide light shade and humidity in summer, water normally but keep the soil or compost almost dry in the winter if maintaining the minimum temperature. Feed with a liquid fertiliser in the summer. Supports need to be provided.

Propagation: semi-ripe cuttings early to late summer with strong bottom heat.

Jacaranda Trees and shrubs, of which *J. mimosifolia* is generally grown. It is a deciduous tree, but unlikely to exceed about 2 m (6 ft) in height when grown in a pot. It has attractive ferny bipinnate leaves and blue flowers. Although blooms are not produced by small pot-grown specimens this plant is worth growing for its foliage alone.

Temperature: minimum of 10° C (50° F).

Cultivation: likes light airy conditions in the summer and normal watering. Keep drier in the winter when dormant.

Propagation: semi-ripe cuttings in early or mid-summer, or seeds early to mid-spring. Provide a temperature of 21° C (70° F) for both.

Jasminum Climbers with sweetly scented flowers. *J. polyanthum* is the species generally grown under glass and it bears masses of white flowers in spring and summer. *J. mesnyi* has yellow flowers.

Temperature: only frost-free conditions needed, say a minimum of 4.5° C (40° F).

Cultivation: very easy going with no special requirements. Provide plenty of ventilation in the summer and give very light shade. Watering is regular throughout the year. Train the climbing stems to suitable supports. Pruning can consist of thinning out growth in late winter if it becomes congested, leaving plenty of young stems. Height can be reduced slightly if necessary.

Propagation: semi-ripe cuttings in late summer or early autumn, rooted in moderate heat.

Justicia Evergreen shrubs, of which *J. brandegeeana* is the one generally grown, and popularly known as the shrimp plant. Growing to about 90 cm (3 ft) in height, it produces, for most of the year, a succession of inflorescences consisting of shrimp-pink bracts and white flowers. There are also forms with yellowish bracts.

Temperature: minimum of 10° C (50° F) or slightly lower.

Cultivation: easy to grow, needing shade from strong sun and regular liquid feeding in the summer. Young plants should be stopped several times to ensure well-branched specimens. Prune in late winter to maintain a compact bushy habit – growths may be cut back by half their length.

Propagation: soft or semi-ripe cuttings in summer.

Lantana Small shrubs which flower freely in summer and into autumn. *L. camara* is the one generally seen under glass and it bears heads of yellow flowers. There are numerous forms and cultivars with yellow, pink, red or white flowers.

Temperature: minimum of 7° C (45° F).

Cultivation: lantanas like plenty of sun and good ventilation, and make large specimens if grown in a border or large pots. One can maintain a succession of small plants in small pots by taking cuttings each year. In early spring the plants can have their stems pruned back to about 15 cm (6 in). Young plants should be stopped to encourage a bushy habit.

Propagation: softwood cuttings between mid-spring and early summer, rooted in moderate heat. Seeds in the spring.

Lapageria Considered by many people to be one of the most beautiful greenhouse climbers, *L. rosea* produces in late summer and autumn large pendulous tubular waxy flowers in crimson. This evergreen climber, which can attain 3 m (10 ft) in height, is popularly known as the Chilean bellflower. There is also a white variety available.

Temperature: needs only a frost-free greenhouse, a suitable minimum being 4.5–7° C (40–45° F).

Cultivation: grows well in soilless compost with some coarse sand added. Best planted in a soil border but also successfully grown in (eventually) a large pot. Provide supports for the stems and give good ventilation and light shading in the summer.

Propagation: simple layering mid-spring to early summer, or seeds when ripe.

Mandevilla Evergreen climbers with trumpet-shaped lobed flowers mainly in summer. Species include *M. boliviensis*, 4 m (13 ft) high, white flowers with orange throat; *M. sanderi*, up to 5 m (16 ft), pink with yellow throat; *M. splendens*, up to 3 m (10 ft), white flushed with pink; *M. s. profusa*, deep carmine; and *M. s. williamsii*, same as the species but with deep pink throat.

Temperature: minimum of 15.5° C (60° F) minimum.

Cultivation: in the summer provide humidity and light shade from strong sun. They grow best in a soil border or in large pots or tubs. The stems will need supports.

Propagation: softwood cuttings from mid-spring to early summer, in strong bottom heat.

Nerium This is one of the most popular evergreen shrubs, the species grown being *N. oleander*, better known simply as oleander. On average it attains 2 m (6 ft) in height and in summer and autumn produces funnel-shaped lobed flowers in shades of pink, red or purplish red. There are several cultivars, like *N. o.* 'Album Plenum', double white; *N. o.* 'Roseum Plenum', double pink; and *N. o.* 'Variegatum', pink, leaves edged with cream.

Temperature: minimum of 7° C (45° F).

Cultivation: oleander likes plenty of sun and well ventilated conditions. In fact, plants can be placed outside from early summer to early autumn. Water as required in growing season but keep plants

on the dry side in winter. Feed regularly in the growing season. Best results are obtained if eventually plants are given large pots or tubs.
Propagation: semi-ripe cuttings late summer or early autumn. Seeds in spring, moderate heat.

Pachystachys An attractive small shrub is *P. lutea* which produces spikes of bright yellow bracts through which poke white tubular flowers. These appear in summer and autumn.
Temperature: minimum of 13° C (55° F).
Cultivation: in the summer provide light shade, humidity; water plants normally and feed at fortnightly intervals. The plants can be cut hard back after flowering and should be kept on the dry side in winter. Increase watering as plants come into new growth.
Propagation: softwood cuttings in spring, rooting in a temperature of 21° C (70° F).

Passiflora Most gardeners want to grow a passion flower in the greenhouse and fortunately their cultivation is easy. There are several of these climbers which can be recommended, like the common blue passion flower, *P. caerulea*; *P. × caeruleoracemosa*, purple; *P. × exoniensis*, deep pink; and *P. quadrangularis*, pale violet or pink. All are tall vigorous plants.
Temperature: minimum of 10° C (50° F).
Cultivation: provide light shade and humidity in summer. Best grown in a bed or large pot or tub. Provide wires or similar for support. Pruning consists of thinning out the stems when plants become congested, removing the oldest and leaving young growth. Lateral shoots on the remaining stems should be shortened to within 15 cm (6 in).
Propagation: leaf-bud cuttings in late spring or early summer, seeds in spring. Provide moderate heat.

Plumbago *P. auriculata* is a clambering shrub to about 3 m (10 ft) in height and bears masses of sky-blue flowers throughout summer and autumn. There is a white variety, *P. a.* var. *alba. P. indica rosea* is a semi-climber but can be grown as a shrub if it is cut back each year. It bears scarlet flowers in summer.
Temperature: minimum of 7° C (45° F) for *P. auriculata*, and 15.5° C (60° F) for *P. indica rosea*.
Cultivation: best grown in a border but can be successfully pot grown. In summer provide light shade, feed regularly and water normally, but ensure the soil remains only slightly moist in winter. Pruning consists of cutting back *P. indica rosea* to within 15 cm (6 in) of the soil in winter, while *P. auriculata* has its side shoots cut back to within

a few centimetres of their bases, and its main stems shortened by about one-third, in late winter

Propagation: soft or semi-ripe cuttings rooted with strong bottom heat from late spring to mid-summer.

Rhododendron The tender rhododendrons are ideally suited to a cool greenhouse and there are three groups from which to choose. The best known is the Indian azalea, *R. simsii*, or rather its many cultivars which are seen in a wide range of colours in florist shops in the autumn and winter. They are low-growing evergreen shrubs which flower freely given suitable conditions. There are also many cultivars of *R. indicum*, a very similar species.

There are many interesting half-hardy evergreen species, growing to about 3 m (10 ft) in height, such as *R. lindleyi* with white waxy flowers, highly fragrant; *R. lyi*, again with white scented blooms; and *R. veitchianum* with large funnel-shaped flowers.

Finally there are the Malesian (Malaysian) species from Malaya and other parts of South-east Asia. Like the half-hardy evergreen species, they are not very easy to obtain. Recommended species include *R. lochiae* with scarlet flowers on 90 cm (3 ft) tall bushes; *R. brookeanum* with orange-pink or orange-yellow flowers on low compact bushes; and *R. jasminiflorum* with scented white flowers.

Temperature: all are grown in a cool greenhouse, with a minimum temperature of around 7° C (45° F).

Cultivation: all kinds can be grown either in a soil bed or border or in pots of suitable size. Compost must be lime-free or acid. A good compost is peat and leafmould in equal parts, plus some coarse sand, or simply peat with some coarse sand added. A base fertiliser should be included in the mix. Alternatively purchase an acid peat-based potting compost. Pot on in late winter. Liquid feed during the growing season and provide good ventilation as well as humidity. Water regularly so that the compost does not dry out. Provide light shade from strong sun. Indian azaleas are best placed out of doors for the summer, in a semi-shaded sheltered spot.

The Malesian species are mainly epiphytes and are best grown in a compost consisting of equal parts live sphagnum moss and acid leafmould. Do not firm the compost around the roots and use pans or orchid baskets as containers. However, they are also seen growing in beds and borders.

Propagation: *R. simsii*, semi-ripe cuttings in early or mid-summer, with bottom heat; other types – seeds in early or mid-spring, or simple layering from mid-spring to late summer.

Sparmannia *S. africana* is a tall large-leaved shrub with white flowers in spring and early summer.

Temperature: minimum of 7° C (45° F).

Cultivation: good ventilation and light shade in summer; feed regularly and water normally, but keep dryish in winter. Pot culture keeps plants small.

Propagation: softwood cuttings from mid-spring to early summer, moderate heat, or seeds in early or mid-spring in heat.

Stephanotis The Madagascar jasmine, *S. floribunda*, is a strong climber producing waxy white highly fragrant flowers from spring to autumn.

Temperature: minimum of 13° C (55° F).

Cultivation: best grown in a border, alternatively a large pot or tub eventually. Climbing stems need adequate support. Feed regularly in the summer; normal watering required, plus light shade and some humidity.

Propagation: semi-ripe cuttings mid- to late summer with strong bottom heat.

Streptosolen *S. jamesonii*, commonly called the marmalade bush, is a scrambling evergreen shrub to about 2 m (6 ft), bearing bright orange flowers in spring and summer.

Temperature: minimum of 7° C (45° F).

Cultivation: light shade in summer and good ventilation; normal watering but keep dryish in winter. Provide supports for the lax stems. Can be pruned fairly hard back in late winter.

Propagation: softwood cuttings in spring, moderate heat. Pinch out tips of young plants.

Tibouchina The glory bush, *T. urvilleana*, is an evergreen shrub about 3 m (10 ft) tall, bearing bluish purple flowers in summer and autumn.

Temperature: minimum of 10° C (50° F).

Cultivation: provide light shade in summer, water normally but give less in winter, and feed regularly when in growth. Stems can be cut back hard in late winter if you wish to maintain a small specimen.

Propagation: soft or semi-ripe cuttings mid-spring to late summer, with strong bottom heat.

19 Alpines and dwarf bulbs

Alpines and dwarf bulbs are among the finest plants for providing colour and interest during the winter and spring in the unheated greenhouse and, what is more, they are very easily grown. Even the smallest greenhouse has room for a few pots or pans or alpines and bulbs, and some gardeners become so enthusiastic about growing them that they may devote an entire greenhouse to their cultivation. This is then properly known as an alpine house.

A greenhouse which is to be entirely devoted to alpines should ideally have brick walls to staging height and plenty of ventilators. Ideally there should be continuous roof vents on either side of the ridge and continuous vents along the sides, just above the bench. Box vents in the walls just above ground level are also to be recommended. Good solid staging all round the house is necessary to hold pea shingle in which to plunge pots or pans to their rims. There are some greenhouse manufacturers who will supply and build an alpine house to specific requirements.

I am not, however, going deeply into the subject of alpine cultivation but merely outlining the basics for obtaining a good display in the mixed, unheated greenhouse. The accompanying tables list a selection of easy alpines and dwarf bulbs which will provide colour and interest over a long period. Most of these should be readily available from local garden centres, or you may wish to visit a specialist alpine nursery or even buy your plants and bulbs by mail order from specialist nurserymen. Many of them produce very informative catalogues.

Alpine cultivation

Let us first consider the year-round cultivation of alpines, or rock plants as some people prefer to call them. You will initially buy young plants in small pots, generally 7.5 cm (3 in) in diameter. A good time to buy, for flowering the following year, is in early autumn.

49 Sempervivum *species*

Containers and planting Suitable containers for displaying alpines are clay or plastic pans or half pots, 15–22 cm (6–9 in) in diameter and 12.5 cm (5 in) deep. I would not recommend normal flower pots as these are too deep for most alpines – they look out of proportion to the low-growing plants.

To prepare the containers for planting, place a piece of perforated zinc over the drainage holes to prevent worms from entering the pans. This should be followed by a 2.5 cm (1 in) layer of crocks (broken clay flower pots) and then a thin layer of rough peat or coconut fibre.

It is essential to use a well-drained compost for alpines. I generally use, for the easy plants with no special fads, John Innes potting compost No. 1 to which has been added one-third extra of coarse horticultural sand or grit. If, eventually, you progress to the more choice and fussy alpines, then you will need special compost mixes. But there is no need to worry about these for the plants recommended here.

The number of alpines you plant in each container depends on the diameter of the pan or half pot and the size of the plants. You will need sufficient plants of each species to make a good display in each container, but you must allow some space between plants, and between plants and the edge of the container, for subsequent growth.

Carefully knock the plants out of their small pots and plant them in the pans to the same depth. Firm them in moderately with your fingers and try to avoid getting compost into the centres of the plants – this applies particularly to cushion, mat and rosette-forming kinds – as it is difficult to remove. Cover the plants with one hand as you are adding compost with the other.

After planting, cover the surface of the compost with a thin layer of grit, shingle or stone chipping. This not only provides an attractive appearance but helps to prevent rapid drying out of the compost and germination of weed seeds.

As the plants outgrow their pans they should be moved on to larger containers. This can be done either in the spring after flowering, or in late summer/early autumn. There is no reason why you should not use pans up to 30 cm (12 in) in diameter. When alpines have obviously outgrown large containers they should be divided into smaller portions and replanted. The mat and cushion-forming alpines are very easy to divide.

Cultural needs For most of the year pans of alpines are best kept in a cold frame. Take the plants into the greenhouse when they are coming into flower and return them to the frame when their display is over. An alpine frame should be positioned in an open sunny part of the garden and the containers are best plunged to their rims in well-weathered ashes to prevent rapid drying out during warm weather and frost damage in winter. It is not only the plants' roots which benefit from frost protection but also clay pans – hard frosts can cause these to crack and flake.

The frame lights or glass covers should be put on the frame (it is best to have removable ones for alpines) in early autumn. They should be removed again in mid- or late spring. Their sole purpose is to protect plants from excessive rain (alpines detest wet soil, especially in the winter), frost and fog. It is important, however, not to coddle alpines, so throughout the winter ventilate freely, except during very hard frosts, fog or snowstorms. Remember that alpines are very hardy plants.

During the winter be very careful with watering – keep the compost only slightly moist and do not wet the plants. In the spring, summer and early autumn carry out normal watering – that is, check the compost daily and apply water if it is starting to dry out on the surface.

When alpines are in the greenhouse they should also be given good ventilation at all times, except during very hard frosts, fog or snow-storms. Maximum light is needed throughout the winter, so keep the glass clean and have your display in the lightest part of the greenhouse. From mid-spring onwards the plants may need shading during periods of very strong sunshine. Roller blinds are therefore recommended.

Displaying plants For a small collection of alpines a bench along one side of the greenhouse, or even a section of bench, should be adequate. You may wish to modify this to take pea shingle or gravel, as the most pleasing effect is obtained by plunging the pans to their rims. Pans do tend to detract from the flower display.

The most pleasing display is achieved by mixing pans of dwarf bulbs with the alpines. You could also have a 'framework' of con-trasting woody foliage plants – I can particularly recommend dwarf conifers in pots, such as *Juniperus communis* 'Compressa', *Picea glauca* var. *albertiana* 'Conica' and *Pinus parviflora* 'Brevifolia'. To give you ideas on displaying alpines and dwarf bulbs I recommend a visit to the alpine houses in botanical and other gardens during winter and spring.

Growing dwarf bulbs

Dwarf bulbs are the ideal companions for alpines because they need the same conditions in the greenhouse. Their flowering period, again, is winter and spring. All of the bulbs listed in the accompanying table are readily available from garden centres or specialist bulb growers.

Containers and planting Suitable containers are pans or half pots, either clay or plastic, with a diameter of 15–30 cm (6–12 in). Use a well-drained compost such as John Innes potting compost No. 1. The best time to pot dwarf bulbs is in early autumn, with the exception of tulips which should be planted mid- to late autumn.

Most of the bulbs in the accompanying table are quite small and can be spaced close together in the pans – 2.5–4 cm (1–1½ in) apart each way. However, the tulips make somewhat larger bulbs and therefore need a spacing of 5–6 cm (2–2½ in) apart each way. Approximately half fill the container with compost, make it moderately firm and then gently press the bulbs on to it. Cover them with a layer of compost which is equal to at least their length. Firm the compost moderately around and over the bulbs and then water them in.

Plunge the containers to their rims in weathered ashes in a well-ventilated cold frame set in a cool, shady part of the garden. The compost should always be kept slightly moist.

Flowering and aftercare When the bulbs have produced shoots about 12 mm (½ in) long, in mid- or late autumn, they can be taken into the unheated greenhouse and placed on the staging. In due course they will flower – and the blooms will be at their best, for they will not be damaged by weather. Watering and ventilation are the same as for alpines.

When flowering is over, return the pans of bulbs to the cold frame and water normally until the foliage starts to become yellow and dies down. This is the sign to cease watering.

The pans of bulbs should be stored in a cool dry place for the summer, with the exception of tulips which are best kept in a warm situation such as a greenhouse.

For most bulbs the compost should remain dry during the resting period but it is best not to allow *Narcissus* and *Galanthus* to become dust dry. Give them an occasional watering. Repot the bulbs annually in early autumn (mid-autumn for tulips), using fresh compost.

A *choice of alpines*

Botanical Name	Common Name	Flowering Time	Colour	Height cm	in
Androsace sarmentosa	Rock rose	Late spring to early summer	Deep pink	10	4
Arabis alpina	Rock cress	Late spring to early summer	White	15	6

Botanical Name	Common Name	Flowering Time	Colour	Height cm	in
Campanula cochlearifolia	Bellflower	Early summer to early autumn	Blue	10	4
Dianthus alpinus	Alpine pink	Early summer	Deep pink	10	4
Draba aizoides	Whitlow grass	Late spring to early summer	Yellow	7.5	3
Dryas octopetala	Mountain avens	Early to mid summer	White	7.5	3
Erodium reichardii	Heron's bill	Early summer	Pink	7.5	3
Gentiana verna	Gentian	Mid- to late spring	Blue	7.5	3
Geranium cinereum var. *subcaulescens*	Crane's bill	Early to mid-summer	Rose-pink	12.5	5
Iberis sempervirens	Evergreen candytuft	Late spring to early summer	White	15	6
Lewisia cotyledon	Bitter-wort	Late spring to early summer	Pink shades	10	4
Morisia monanthos	Mediterranean cress	Mid-spring to early summer	Yellow	7.5	3
Phlox subulata	Moss pink	Mid-spring to mid-summer	Pink	10	4
Primula allionii	Primrose	Early to mid-spring	Pink	7.5	3
rosea	Primrose	Early to mid-spring	Pink	15	6
Ranunculus calandrinioides	Buttercup	Early to late spring	White	15	6
Raoulia australis	Tasmanian moss	–	Silvery leaves	2.5	1
Rhodohypoxis baurii	–	Late spring to early summer	Pink	5	2
Saxifraga burseriana	Saxifrage	Early to	White	10	4

Botanical Name	Common Name	Flowering Time	Colour	Height cm	in
		mid-spring			
'Carmen'	Saxifrage	Early to mid-spring	Yellow	10	4
'Gregor Mendel'	Saxifrage	Early to mid-spring	Yellow	10	4
'Jenkinsiae'	Saxifrage	Late spring to early summer	White	10	4
'Southside Seedling'	Saxifrage	Late spring to early summer	White and red	15	6
Sedum spathulifolium 'Purpureum'	Stonecrop	–	Purple and grey leaves	7.5	3
Sempervivum (many species)	Houseleek	–	Foliage often red or purple	5	2
Silene acaulis	Moss campion	Early to late summer	Pink	5	2

A selection of dwarf bulbs

Botanical Name	Common Name	Flowering Time	Colour	Height cm	in
Anemone blanda	Windflower	Late winter to mid-spring	White, pink, purple, blue	10	4
Chionodoxa luciliae	Glory of the snow	Early spring	Blue	7.5	3
Crocus ancyrensis	–	Mid- to late winter	Orange-yellow	10	4
chrysanthus cvs.	–	Mid- to late winter	Yellow shades, orange, white, blue shades	7.5	3
imperati	–	Early to mid-winter	Buff and purple	7.5– 15	3– 6

Botanical Name	Common Name	Flowering Time	Colour	Height cm	in
laevigatus	–	Mid-autumn to early winter	White and purple	15	6
Cyclamen coum	–	Late winter to early spring	Red shades, white	7.5	3
Eranthis hyemalis	Winter aconite	Late winter	Yellow	7.5–10	3–4
hyemalis Tubergenii Group	Winter aconite	Late winter	Yellow	7.5–10	3–4
Galanthus plicatus ssp. *byzantinus*	Snowdrop	Late autumn to mid-winter	White	15	6
reginae olgae	Snowdrop	Early winter	White	7.5	3
ikariae ssp. *ikariae*	Snowdrop	Late winter to mid-spring	White	20	8
nivalis	Snowdrop	Late winter to early spring	White	7.5–15	3–6
Iris danfordiae	–	Mid- to late winter	Yellow	15	6
histrioides 'Major'	–	Mid-winter	Purple-blue	10	4
reticulata	–	Late winter to early spring	Blue-mauve, purple	15	6
Muscari armeniacum	Grape hyacinth	Mid-spring	Blue	15	6
Narcissus asturiensis	Daffodil	Mid- to late winter	Yellow	7.5	3
assoanus	Daffodil	Early to mid-spring	Yellow	15	6
bulbocodium	Hoop-petticoat daffodil	Mid-winter to early spring	Yellow shades	7.5–10	3–4
cyclamineus	Daffodil	Late winter to early spring	Yellow	7.5–10	3–4
Scilla bifolia	Squill	Late winter	Mauve-blue	10	4
siberica	Squill	Late winter	Brilliant	10	4

Botanical Name	Common Name	Flowering Time	Colour	Height cm	in
mischtschen koana	Squill	Late winter to early spring	blue Pale and dark blue	15	6
Tulipa humilis	Tulip	Mid-spring	Pink-purple	10	4
humilis pulchella	Tulip	Early spring	Violet-purple	15	6
kaufmanniana cvs.	Tulip	Early to mid-spring	Many	15	6
tarda	Tulip	Late spring	Yellow and white	15	6

20   Bromeliads

The *Bromeliaceae* family contains about 2,000 species but undoubtedly the best-known member, and of the greatest economic importance, is the pineapple. The ornamental species, however, are of the greatest interest to greenhouse owners and many rank among the most colourful and striking foliage and flowering plants.

Members of the *Bromeliaceae* are popularly referred to as bromeliads. They are tropical plants, found in Central and South America and also the West Indies. Many species are epiphytic, living on trees and rocks in the warm, humid rain forests, but others are terrestrial, growing on open savannas in conditions which can become exceedingly dry at times.

Although most bromeliads can be grown in pots there is no doubt that the epiphytic ones are displayed to best advantage on a 'plant tree'. (See section on displaying bromeliads, pp. 173.)

Most species have stiff, hard leaves, often with sharp spines along the edges, a good example again being the pineapple or *Ananas*. Often the leaves are highly coloured, and in many species are tightly folded at their base, forming a watertight vase. In the plants' natural habitats this vase catches rainwater, acting as a storage reservoir.

Aechmea is a good example of a bromeliad with this habit of growth.

Many of the bromeliads have a striking flower head or inflorescence, with brightly coloured bracts which last for a considerable time – several months. After flowering, the rosette of leaves dies but is replaced by one or more new rosettes, which will in turn flower provided the plants are grown in a very warm and humid greenhouse. Most people cannot provide such conditions and therefore grow bromeliads in lower temperatures purely as foliage plants.

Growing conditions As already indicated, bromeliads like a moist humid atmosphere but this should be created only in warm conditions. In cool conditions the atmosphere should be kept very much drier. So in warm conditions, particularly during the summer, damp down the floor and staging of the greenhouse and syringe the plants with tepid water twice a day.

Although bromeliads are tropical plants they will tolerate a minimum temperature of 12°C (55°F), or even 10°C (50°F), but the ideal minimum is 15.5°C (60°F). Normal daytime temperatures in summer in cool temperate climates will not be too high for bromeliads: in their natural habitats they experience temperatures over 32°C (90°F).

Good bright light is recommended but the plants will take some shade provided it is not too dark. During the summer it may be necessary to shade from extremely strong sunshine, particularly if there are other kinds of plants in the greenhouse. Ensure maximum light in winter – if available one could even use artificial illumination during dull days in winter.

Watering and feeding The compost must on no account remain saturated, otherwise the plants' roots may rot, especially in winter. It is best to allow the compost to dry out partially between waterings and then soak it right through. Of course, the higher the temperature the more water that will be required. Plants which are grown on trees may be watered with a hosepipe or a coarse sprayer.

If plants have leaf vases these should be kept filled with water – rainwater is ideal. Replace with fresh water every four to six weeks to prevent stagnant conditions. Remember that one should still water the compost as described above. The water in the leaf vases attracts insects which pollinate the flowers. The flowers often rise straight through the water.

Very little feeding is required – an occasional foliar feed can be

Some well-known bromeliads

Botanical Name	Common	Foliage
Aechmea fasciata	Urn plant	Broad, recurved, grey-green banded
fulgens	Urn plant	Recurved wavy green leaves, purple below
Ananas comosus var. *variegatus*	Pineapple (ornamental)	Narrow, spiney, green, wide cream margin
Bilbergia 'Fantasia'	–	Deep green, marked with cream
horrida	–	Deep green, banded with grey
nutans	Queen's tears	Deep green, narrow
× *windii*	–	Green, covered with grey scales
Cryptanthus beuckeri	Earth star	Green, pink and white
bivittatus	Earth star	Deep and light green stripes, suffused with rose-pink
bromelioides 'Tricolor'	Earth Star	Cream, green, white and pink stripes
fosterianus	Earth star	Deep copper, crossbanded with grey stripes
zonatus	Earth star	Coppery, banded grey
Guzmannia lingulata	–	Green, shiny, finely striped purple
lingulata 'Splendens'	–	Red above and purple-red below, shiny
monostachia	–	Light green, shiny
Neoregelia carolinae b. tricolor	Painted fingernail plant	Striped green, cream and pink, red centre to plant
spectabilis	Painted fingernail plant	Deep green red-tipped leaves
Nidularium fulgens	–	Shiny, green, mottled deeper green, bright red centre to plant
innocentii	–	Brown-red above and red-purple below, red centre to plant
Tillandsia cyanea	Pink quill	Narrow, pointed, green
lindeniana (*lindeni*)	Blue-flowered torch	Narrow, pointed, purple at base
usneoides	Spanish moss	Greyish green

Inflorescence	Habitat
Blue or lilac flowers, pink bracts	Tall leaf-vase rosettes, epiphytic
Bright red flowers	Tall leaf-vase rosettes, epiphytic
Forms a reddish fruit after flowering	Wide-spreading rosette, terrestrial
Purple and red flowers, red bracts	Forms a tubular shape, epiphytic
Green, blue-tipped flowers, pink bracts	Urn shaped, epiphytic
Green, pink and blue flowers, pink bracts	Clump of arching leaves, epiphytic
Green, pink and blue flowers, pink bracts	Clump of arching leaves, epiphytic
White flowers	Small loose rosette, terrestrial
White flowers	Low flattish rosette, terrestrial
White flowers	Fairly upright rosette, terrestrial
White flowers	Flat spreading rosette, terrestrial
White flowers	Star-shaped rosette, terrestrial
Orange or red bracts	Spreading rosettes, epiphytic
Purple-red bracts	Spreading rosettes, epiphytic
Scarlet flower head, pale green bracts striped deep brown	Spreading rosettes, epiphytic
Small white flowers	Large flattish rosettes, epiphytic
Small white flowers	Large flattish rosettes, epiphytic
Violet-blue flowers, red bracts	Low spreading leaf-vase rosettes, epiphytic
White flowers, red bracts	Low spreading leaf-vase rosettes, epiphytic
Blue flowers, pink bracts	Arching rosette, epiphytic
Blue flowers, pink bracts	Arching rosette, epiphytic
Small yellow-green flowers	Pendulous 'ferny' growth, no roots, epiphytic

Botanical Name	Common Name	Foliage
Vriesia fenestralis	–	Light green, deeper veins
hieroglyphica	–	Light green, transverse bands of deeper green and purple
splendens	Flaming sword	Deep green, brown bands

given in the spring and summer. If plants are being grown in soil beds or borders, then topdress annually with a 2.5 cm (1 in) deep layer of leafmould or peat (or a substitute). These will provide very little in the way of nutrients but add essential humus to the soil and create an attractive appearance.

Potting and composts Bromeliads have shallow root systems and can be grown in relatively small pots. These will keep the plants small – an important point if space is limited. It is only necessary to pot on every two or three years, into the next size of pot. The most appropriate time to pot on is when the pot is obviously restricting the growth of offsets.

A well-drained compost is essential and it must be rich in humus and slightly on the acid side. There are quite a few compost mixes suitable for bromeliads but I can recommend the following:

2 parts sphagnum moss, peat and/or leafmould
1 part fibrous loam (slightly acid) } parts by volume
1 part coarse sand

Alternatively:
equal parts by volume of loam and leafmould
Or:
equal parts by volume of peat and leafmould

Whatever mix you use, always add a few pieces of charcoal to keep it 'sweet'.

Use clay or plastic pots and always put plenty of drainage material in the base before adding compost. Pot moderately firmly.

Propagation The main method of propagation is vegetative – removing and rooting offsets. When the offsets are well formed (in spring or summer) cut them off and pot into small pots. Root them in a mixture of equal parts (by volume) of peat and sand. Place the offsets

Inflorescence	Habit
Yellow flowers, green bracts	Rosette of broad arching leaves, epiphytic
Yellow flowers, green bracts	Rosette of broad arching leaves, epiphytic
Yellow flowers, scarlet bracts	Leaf-vase rosette, epiphytic

in a humid place with strong bottom heat (such as a propagating case). When rooted transfer to small pots, using one of the compost mixes recommended earlier.

Bromeliads can be raised from seeds but this is a slow process. Sow in a soilless seed compost and germinate in warm humid conditions. Prick out the seedlings into individual small pots.

Displaying bromeliads Many large 'architectural' plants and their shapes need to be shown to advantage. Bromeliads are therefore best displayed alone, apart from other kinds of plant. I mentioned pot culture earlier, but plants can also be grown in soil beds and borders. A raised bed, perhaps terraced and edged with logs, makes a superb setting. It can be built up with any of the composts recommended for potting. In such conditions bromeliads will form larger plants than if pot grown, and will flower well, due to the unrestricted root run. However, if you wish small plants then they must be pot grown.

There is no better way to display the epiphytic bromeliads than to grow them on a dead tree – or at least part of a tree or a large branch. It should be quite thick, well branched and inserted firmly into the greenhouse border or bed. Ideally use the smaller bromeliads on a tree, like *Tillandsia* species and *Vriesia*. To plant, pack some compost around the roots, surround with sphagnum moss to retain it, and secure to the tree with either thin nylon string or thin plastic-coated wire. Alternatively, secure each plant to a separate piece of bark and hang on the tree. This will allow you to move plants around.

Large 'broms' like *Nidularium* and *Neoregelia* are better planted in a 'pocket' on the tree; for example it can be made with pieces of bark and filled with compost. This will give the plants a more substantial roothold.

The pendulous Spanish moss, *Tillandsia usneoides*, is simply fixed to a tree or piece of wood (gently held in place with nylon string or plastic-coated wire). Keep it well syringed with tepid water.

21   Cacti and succulents

Cacti are in the family *Cactaceae*, one of the many families of succulent plants. Generally they have swollen stems which store water and come in a great diversity of shapes and sizes. Most do not have leaves, although an exception is the genus *Pereskia*, species of which have thin stems and normal leaves.

An important characteristic of cacti, which distinguishes them from other plants, is the areole. This bears spines and often wool, bristles, felt or hairs. Areoles are formed on the rib edges of the plants and flowers often arise from them.

Some cacti have large and spectacular flowers – particular kinds flower very freely, like species of *Rebutia*, while others are shy such as the *Opuntia*.

There are many other succulent plants, apart from cacti, coming from many plant families. Some again have swollen stems while others have fleshy water-holding leaves. The majority of other succulents are not spiny as with cacti, but there are exceptions; for example, some species of *Euphorbia*.

The majority of succulent plants, including cacti, are found in hot dry areas, like semi-deserts and mountain-sides, hence the need to store water in the stems and leaves.

Some cacti, however, are epiphytic, living on trees in their natural habitats, and these are popularly called forest cacti. Examples are *Epiphyllum*, *Schlumbergera* and *Rhipsalis*. They have flattened, or cylindrical, leafless stems and are generally pendulous in habit. Flamboyant flowers are a characteristic of this group.

Cultivation of desert cacti These plants need really good light, especially in the winter. They like the sun so there is no need to provide shade in the summer.

Most cacti survive with a minimum night temperature of 4.5° C (40° F). Once the temperatures reaches 21° C (70° F) start ventilating. In fact, good ventilation is necessary at all times, even in the winter if the weather is fine. In hot weather leave all the vents and the door open. Cacti need a dry atmosphere and this is particularly important during the winter.

50 Opuntia *species*

I grow cacti in a loam-based potting compost, generally John Innes potting compost No. 2 to which has been added one-third extra of coarse sand or grit. The compost must be well drained and aerated, and you should put plenty of drainage material in the bottom of the pots.

Clay or plastic pots can be used and the pot size should equal the diameter of the plant (including the spines) plus an extra 12 mm ($\frac{1}{2}$ in) all round. Pot on as necessary in the spring.

There is a lot of misunderstanding about watering, but really this is straightforward. From late autumn to spring keep the compost dry, but give the occasional watering to prevent undue shrivelling of the plants. When the weather warms up in the spring start watering again. Give a thorough soaking and do not water again until the compost is dry. When growth gets under way water regularly, but allow the compost almost to dry out between applications. Continue like this throughout the summer and when autumn arrives reduce watering – allow the compost to dry out completely between applications. Try not to wet the plants as the sun, playing on the droplets of water, can cause scorching.

There are various ways of propagating cacti. Offsets, if produced, can be removed and potted in the spring and summer, or stem cuttings can often be taken, either the tops of stems or sections. Seeds can be sown in the spring.

Finally let us consider ways of displaying the plants. If they are grown in pots it is best to stand them on slatted benches in the greenhouse for good air circulation. However, this is the least attractive way of displaying cacti. A much more effective method is to construct a 15 cm (6 in) deep bench and fill with potting compost. Find some attractive rocks and place these at random over the bench, partly sinking them into the compost. Then plant your cacti in pleasing groups and finally topdress the compost with a layer of shingle, crushed rock, or very coarse sand or gravel.

If you have the space, cacti could be planted in a bed or border in the greenhouse or conservatory. Make the bed interesting by contouring it, or terrace it with rocks. The bed can be made up with the compost recommended for potting. Again some interesting rocks should be 'scattered' over the bed, finishing with a mineral topdressing as described above.

Cultivation of forest cacti These plants need light shading from the sun from spring to autumn, otherwise brown scorch marks appear on the stems. Provide maximum light in winter.

The ideal minimum winter temperature is 10° C (50° F). Fresh air is essential, so provide good ventilation consistent with maintaining the minimum temperature. Unlike desert cacti, the forest types need a humid atmosphere, so damp down the floor and staging when the weather is warm, and also spray the plants with water. Obviously far less humidity is needed when the winter minimum temperature is being maintained.

Although forest cacti like a well-drained compost it should be rich in humus. Soilless potting composts can be recommended, with one-third extra of coarse sand or Perlite added. A slightly acid compost is desirable. Pots and potting are as discussed under desert cacti – again pot on as necessary in the spring, using a final pot size of about 15 cm (6 in).

Water the plants throughout the year but allow the compost almost to dry out between applications. But do not allow it to become dust dry. It is advantageous to apply dilute liquid fertilisers on a regular basis in the spring and summer.

Avoid fluctuations in greenhouse conditions – temperature, light etc. – because this can result in flower-bud drop.

Propagation is from cuttings – stem sections – in the summer and from seeds sown in spring.

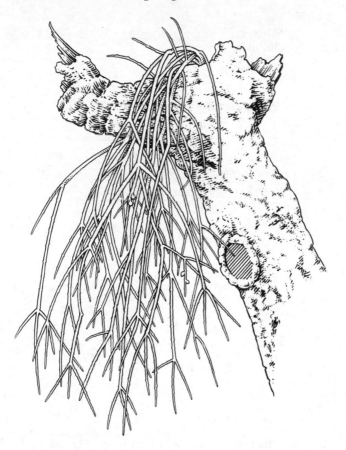

51 Rhipsalis baccifera

Because of their pendulous stems the forest cacti need vertical space to develop. Being epiphytic they can most effectively be displayed on a 'plant tree' (a dead tree), planted in pockets of compost. For further details see the chapter on bromeliads (p. 173).

Many people grow the forest cacti in hanging pots to give the often long stems space to develop. Hang these from the greenhouse roof. The pots can be hung out of doors in the summer if desired, where the plants will make splendid growth. Use a light-weight compost, such as soilless with Perlite added, if planting in hanging pots.

Cacti and succulents worth growing

Botanical Name	Common Name
DESERT CACTI	
Astrophytum	Star cacti
Cephalocereus senilis	Old man
Cereus	
Chamaecereus sylvestrii	Peanut cactus
Cleistocactus strausii	
Coryphantha	
Echinocactus	
Echinocereus	
Echinopsis	
Ferocactus	
Gymnocalycium	
Heliocereus	Sun cacti
Lobivia	
Mammillaria	
Notocactus	
Opuntia	Prickly pear
Parodia	
Pereskia	
Rebutia	
Selenicereus	Moon cacti
grandiflorus	Queen of the Night

Habit	Flowers
Globular, sometimes flattish	Yellow, large
Columnar, covered with long white hairs	Red and white
Large columnar stems, often greyish	White, nocturnal
Low clump of branching light green stems	Scarlet, freely produced
Columnar, covered with white bristles	Red
Globular or cylindrical, prominent tubercles	Mainly yellow
Globular to cylindrical, very spiny	Small, generally yellow, not usually produced in pots
Stems upright or prostrate, some species spiny, others not	Large, white, yellow, red or purple
Globular or cylindrical stems	Freely produced, trumpet shaped, white or pink
Rounded or cylindrical stems, heavily spined	Smallish, red, yellow or violet
Globular, prominent ribs, spines sparse	Freely produced, white, pink or red
Thin trailing stems	Large, scented, red
Globular	White, yellow or red
Generally globular but some are cylindrical, with tubercles, very spiny, often woolly	Small, often freely produced, white, yellow or red
Mainly globular, flat on top, very spiny	Generally yellow, also red
Usually well branched; jointed stems – flattened, cylindrical or rounded. Prominent areoles packed with barbed bristles (glochids)	Large, but not often produced in pots; yellow, orange or red
Globular or cylindrical, very spiny	Flowers freely produced, red or yellow
Very spiny woody stems, large shiny leaves which may fall in rest period	White, yellow or pink, sometimes fragrant
Mainly globular, small, quite spiny, with tubercles	Generally very freely produced, many colours
Long thin stems, trailing or climbing	Large, white, often tinged with another colour, fragrant, generally nocturnal
Long thin stems, trailing or climbing	White within, yellowish to tawny without, fragrant, nocturnal

FOREST CACTI

Botanical Name	Common Name
Aporocactus flagelliformis	Rat's tail cactus
Epiphyllum hybrids	Orchid cacti
species	
Hylocereus	
Rhipsalidopsis gaertneri	Easter cactus
rosea	
Rhipsalis	
Schlumbergera bridgesii	Christmas cactus
truncata	Crab or lobster cactus
(syn. *Zygocactus truncatus*)	

OTHER SUCCULENTS

Adromischus (*Crassulaceae*)

Aeonium (*Crassulaceae*)
Agave (*Agavaceae*)   Century plant

Aloe (*Liliaceae*)
Ceropegia (*Asclepiadaceae*)
Ceropegia woodii   Hearts entangled
Conophytum (*Aizoaceae*)

Crassula (*Crassulaceae*)

Echeveria (*Crassulaceae*)

Euphorbia (*Euphorbiaceae*)   Succulent spurges

Faucaria (*Aizoaceae*)   Tiger's jaw

Gasteria (*Liliaceae*)

Habit	Flowers
Long trailing stems	Crimson-pink
Stems flat, leaf like, jointed	Large flowers in many colours
Stems flat, leaf like, jointed	Flowers usually smaller and nocturnal
Long-jointed angular or winged stems with aerial roots	Flowers often nocturnal and scented, large, white
Pendulous stems, jointed, flat, leaf-like	Scarlet
Pendulous stems, jointed, flat, leaf-like	Pink
Flat, cylindrical or angular stems, trailing	Small, white, pink or red
Pendulous, flat, leaf-like jointed stems	Magenta or deep pink; hybrids and varieties in white, red and violet
Pendulous, flat, leaf-like jointed stems	Rose-pink
Low, leaves vary in shape: spoon shaped, rounded, etc., often mottled	Small, white or pink
Rosettes, die after flowering	White, yellow, pink, red
Tough sword-shaped leaves, spiny edges in rosette which dies after flowering	Generally only after many years
Generally rosette forming	Yellow, orange or red
Twiners or upright habit	Tubular, often odd shapes
Creeper, heart-shaped leaves	
Small, clump-forming, rounded, cylindrical, conical or ovate	Daisy-like, yellow, cream, white, red
Various forms: e.g. branching and shrubby, trailing, low growing, etc., leaves generally opposite	Small, in clusters, white, yellow, pink
Rosette-forming, leaves generally waxy or grey-green	White, yellow, orange, red
Various forms, from shrubby and woody to cactus-like; poisonous latex (sap)	Insignificant in most species but brilliant red in *E. splendens*, the crown of thorns
Forms clumps of thick triangular leaves, spines on edges	Large, yellow
Thick fleshy leaves in two ranks of rosettes, may be covered with white tubercles	Red

Botanical Name	Common Name
Glottiphyllum (*Aizoaceae*)	Tongue leaf
Haworthia (*Liliaceae*)	
Kalanchae (*Crassulaceae*)	
Lamphranthus (*Aizoaceae*)	
Lithops (*Aizoaceae*)	Living stones
Pachyphytum (*Crassulaceae*)	
Sedum (*Crassulaceae*)	Stonecrop
Senecio (*Compositae*)	
Stapelia (*Asclepiadaceae*)	Carrion flower

Cultivation of other succulents This is really the same as for desert cacti, but remember that some succulents rest in the summer and grow in the winter and so need to be watered accordingly. Make sure you can find out their requirements when buying – a specialist grower will tell you. Propagation may be from leaf cuttings, stem cuttings or offsets in the summer. Seeds are sown in the spring.

Habit

Thick fleshy leaves, soft and waxy

Generally rosette-forming, some having tubercles on leaves

Tall, shrubby, some with plantlets along edges of leaves, which may be flat or cylindrical

Somewhat shrubby, long narrow leaves

Plant bodies of various shapes – many resemble stones or pebbles

Thick leaves and stems, leaves of various shapes

Tallish to prostrate plants, fleshy stems and leaves, leaves of various shapes and colours

Variable, e.g. clumps of short stems, or rosettes, etc., leaves often glaucous

Low, branching, fleshy stems, often leafless

Flowers

Free flowering, yellow

Insignificant, on long stalks

Red, pink, yellow, orange

Free flowering, daisy-like, pink, red, purplish, mauve, yellow, orange

Yellow or white

Flowers similar to *Echeveria*

White, yellow, pink, etc.

Daisy-like flowers, often yellow

Bizarre flowers, often yellowish with bold brown, purplish or reddish markings. Most smell of carrion and attract blowflies which pollinate them

22 Perpetual-flowering carnations

The flowers of perpetual-flowering carnations are excellent for cutting and, indeed, are to be seen in every florist shop. As their name implies, they flower over a long period – all the year round if suitable conditions are provided. These carnations are freely available from several specialist growers and they come in a wide range of colours. The cultivars with Sim in the name are very popular and are among the easiest to grow.

Conditions required Perpetual-flowering carnations need maximum light all the year round, but light shading from strong sunshine is recommended during the flowering period to prevent scorching of the blooms. Good ventilation is also needed at all times of the year and a dry atmosphere is necessary in the winter.

To ensure flower production in the winter a minimum temperature of 10–15.5° C (50–60° F) is necessary. However, many people will find this too expensive to maintain and therefore a minimum winter temperature of 4.5° C (40° F) is suggested. Although the plants will not then flower in the winter, blooms will nevertheless be produced during the rest of the year. The plants will rest over the winter in these cool conditions.

Cultivation Start by buying plants from a specialist grower, preferably in early spring. Ideally buy plants that have been stopped and have produced, or are starting to produce, side shoots. Such plants will have been grown in pots – generally 7.5 cm (3 in) pots – and may be supplied with or without these. Sometimes they are supplied in peat pots.

These young plants should be potted on receipt into 12.5 cm (5 in) clay or plastic pots. Crock the pots well as good drainage is needed, and use a soil-based compost such as John Innes potting compost No. 2. Insert canes and tie in the shoots as they develop, using either soft garden string or the wire rings known as carnation rings. Newly potted plants should be kept on the dry side until they are growing well and then normal watering can be carried out.

Pot on into 15 or 17 cm (6 or 7 in) pots before the plants become pot bound. Again use a soil-based compost like JIP2. By this time 1.5 m (5 ft) canes will be needed for support.

In the summer, feed the plants once a fortnight with a liquid fertiliser – ideally one which is formulated for carnations. A fertiliser suitable for carnations is one equally balanced with nitrogen and potash.

Flowering will start in the summer and to ensure large blooms it will be necessary to disbud. At the top of each stem a large main flower bud will be produced, known as the crown bud, and it will be surrounded by several smaller buds which should be removed by carefully snapping them out, to leave the crown bud.

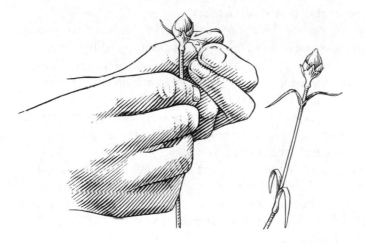

52 *Disbudding a carnation*

To prevent the calyx from splitting, and so ruining the shape of the flower, place a calyx ring or small elastic band around each bud before it opens.

Plenty of ventilation is needed in the summer, and at other times when the weather is favourable, consistent with maintaining the minimum temperature. If you cannot provide enough heat for winter flowering, remove all flower buds from mid-autumn onwards and let the plants have a rest. Buds often rot in low temperatures in the autumn and winter so it is not worth retaining them.

Keep the compost only slightly moist in the autumn and winter, especially in low temperatures, and increase watering again in the spring when the plants will start their second flowering season. At all costs avoid keeping the compost very wet, otherwise the plants may rot.

It is best to discard plants at the end of their second year (in autumn or late winter) and replace with young plants that you have raised from cuttings. In the second year from buying you can propagate – between mid-winter and early spring. Use side shoots about 7.5 cm (3 in) long and remove them by giving a sharp pull so that they snap out cleanly. Remove the lower pair of leaves to facilitate insertion. Dip the cuttings in hormone rooting powder and insert in trays of equal parts peat and coarse sand, or peat and Perlite. Place in a heated propagator to root.

The cuttings should be well rooted within three or four weeks, at which stage they should be lifted and potted into 7.5 cm (3 in) pots with John Innes potting compost No. 1.

When the young plants are about 15 cm (6 in) high, or have developed about 10 pairs of leaves, they should be stopped by snapping out the top of each to leave about six pairs of leaves. This encourages the production of side shoots – like the plants which you originally bought. From now onwards cultivation is as outlined earlier.

Do not neglect to control pests and diseases. The main ones to watch out for are red spider mites, greenfly, thrips, caterpillars (including tortrix), rust, mildew and botrytis.

Finally a word about where to keep the plants in the greenhouse. Young plants can be placed on the staging, but as they grow they will probably run out of headroom and therefore should be placed on low staging, or failing this on the floor. Many of the cultivars will eventually grow as tall as you!

This, then, is basic cultural advice to produce acceptable flowers for cutting. Exhibitors lavish a lot more care and attention on their plants to achieve the superb, perfectly shaped blooms that one sees at carnation shows.

Cultivars There are many cultivars available but I have made a personal selection (see accompanying table) which should please most gardeners. I have found these easy to grow and the colours are pleasing. I should mention also the American spray carnations. These are also perpetual flowering and are grown in the same way as ordinary perpetual-flowering carnations, except that disbudding is different. Remove only the large terminal or crown bud so that a spray of blooms is produced. Spray carnations do not grow as tall as the ordinary kinds and are ideally suited to growing on the staging.

Recommended cultivars

Name	Colour	Height
'Arthur Sim'	White, pencilled scarlet	T
'Dusty Sim'	Pastel pink	T
'Fragrant Ann'	Pure white	D
'Harvest Moon'	Golden-yellow	T
'Joker'	Crimson	M
'Lena'	Salmon pink	T
'Shocking Pink Sim'	Bright pink	T
'Skyliner'	Yellow, finely striped scarlet	M
'Tangerine Sim'	Tangerine	T
'White Sim'	White	T
'William Sim'	Scarlet	T
'Yellow Dusty'	Sulphur yellow	T

Key: T = tall   M = medium height   D = dwarf or low growing

23   Carnivorous plants

Carnivorous plants are those which have become specially adapted to trap insects and other small creatures and digest them as an additional source of food. The natural habitats of the majority are acid peat or sphagnum bogs – wet areas which are generally low in plant foods. Most of the temperate species are found in such areas and because they are mainly easy to grow and need little artificial heat they are undoubtedly the most popular with amateur greenhouse owners. There are, however, tropical carnivorous plants, the *Nepenthes*, which inhabit damp humid forests, but far fewer amateurs grow these because they need very warm humid conditions. Nevertheless, I shall deal with these also for those who are able to provide the necessary conditions.

Temperate species

General cultivation These are cool-greenhouse plants and need a minimum winter temperature of 4.5° C (40° F). The plants become dormant in the winter and at this time the plants must be kept only just moist, because wet conditions lead to rotting.

The plants start into growth again in the spring as the weather becomes warmer and this is when cultural requirements change. In the warmer conditions of spring and summer constant humidity is essential and this is ensured by damping down the floor of the greenhouse and spraying the plants. Alternatively, you could place the pots in a 5 cm (2 in) deep plastic gravel tray (without the gravel) and keep it half filled with water. This results in a humid atmosphere around the plants and also keeps the compost wet. On no account, though, have water in the tray during winter – the plants must then be kept only barely moist. Although the compost must be kept wet in the summer, this does not mean that it should be waterlogged; using the right kind of compost will prevent this.

It is best to use only rainwater for spraying and watering the plants; alternatively, distilled water could be used. Tap water, especially in 'hard-water' areas, can kill plants through the chemicals it contains.

Adequate ventilation should be coupled with high humidity, and most plants need good light. Although plenty of sunlight is enjoyed it will be necessary to shade the plants from strong sunshine to prevent scorching – slatted blinds are ideal for shading.

You can use a dilute foliar feed in the summer, giving the plants a light spraying.

Coming now to pots and composts, I recommend plastic pots rather than clay: potting is generally carried out in spring. A useful potting medium for some plants is pure live sphagnum moss, especially for the larger, more vigorous plants like *Sarracenia*. This retains water well yet does not become waterlogged. Or you can make up a compost of granulated moss peat and Perlite for many plants. This is a good open compost yet retains moisture. After potting it can be topped with live sphagnum moss which will then grow on top.

A mixture of granulated moss peat and silver sand is recommended for small species like *Dionaea* and *Drosera*. Fertilisers should not be added to any composts. (See under genera for more specific compost requirements.)

Selected genera The following are considered easy plants and ideal for beginners, although they are no less exciting for that.

Darlingtonia californica Cobra lily. Closely related to *Sarracenia*. The pitchers (the part of the plant that catches insects) resemble cobras poised to strike and are yellow-green in colour. Insects fall into the pitchers and drown in water in the bottom, where they are digested. Flowers are crimson with pale green sepals.

Pure live sphagnum moss is a suitable potting medium plus a 15 cm (6 in) pot with crocks in the bottom. Repot every three years. *Darlingtonia* needs to have cool roots; instead of standing in a tray of water, water from the top with cool water several times a day in warm weather.

Dionaea muscipula Venus fly trap. Probably the best known carnivorous plant, with leaves like jaw-like traps which snap together when insects alight on them. White flowers.

It can be grown in a mixture of moss peat and Perlite, moss peat

53 Darlingtonia californica

and silver sand (50 : 50) or moss peat alone. Top with live sphagnum moss. A 15 cm (6 in) pot will take three plants.

Drosera Sundews. Easy species are listed below. The leaves are covered with sticky tentacles: insects stick to these and are trapped. Plants can be grown in a peat and Perlite mixture topped with sphagnum moss, a peat/silver sand mix or pure sphagnum moss. Use 10 cm (4 in) half pots. Shade from very strong sunshine.

Two good species are *D. binata* with forked leaves, green, deep red tentacles, white flowers; and *D. capensis*, linear leaves, green, bright red tentacles, purple flowers.

Sarracenia Trumpet pitchers. These plants have funnel- or trumpet-shaped pitchers with 'lids' (these do not move) giving a hooded effect. Insects fall into the pitchers and drown in the liquid at the bottom. They are generally very colourful plants.

Grow either in pure live sphagnum moss or a granulated moss peat/Perlite mix. Use 12.5 cm (5 in) pots and divide and repot every two to three years in the spring. Shade from very hot sun.

Some species I can recommend include *S. × catesbyi*, a natural hybrid, greenish/pinkish pitchers, brick-red flowers; *S. flava*, tall pale green pitchers, large yellow flowers; *S. leucophylla*, tall white pitchers with green/red veining, red flowers; and *S. purpurea*, low grower, short fat red pitchers.

Tropical species

Here I shall deal with the genus *Nepenthes*, the pitcher plant, which is everybody's idea of a 'jungle plant'. These plants are mainly climbers and are found in warm 'steamy' forests or jungles. They have pendent lidded pitchers (the lids do not move) carried at the tips of leaf tendrils, blotched or marbled red or purple. Insects fall into these and are drowned in the liquid at the bottom, where they are digested. The small insignificant flowers are green or bronzy.

Recommended species *N. ampullaria* has green pitchers, often blotched red; *N. hookeriana* has pale green pitchers mottled with purple; *N. khasiana*, generally considered the easiest species to grow, has green or red-flushed pitchers; and *N. rafflesiana* has pale green pitchers which are attractively marked with deep brown or deep red.

General cultivation High temperatures and humidity are needed for best growth. This means a minimum winter night temperature of

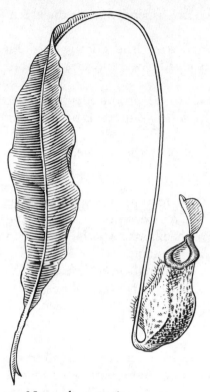

54 Nepenthes *species*

15.5°C (60°F) and a minimum winter day temperature of 21°C (70°F). In the summer maintain a minimum night temperature of 21°C (70°F) and a minimum day temperature of 24–27°C (75–80°F). The hardiest (if that is the right word) is N. *khasiana,* so if you cannot maintain such high temperatures this is the one to grow.

To maintain the necessary high humidity you will have to damp down several times a day or install an automatic overhead misting system if you are out all day. No ventilation is needed, though shading will be necessary from very strong sunshine. But remember that plants need some sunshine for the pitchers to form – slatted blinds provide the ideal shading.

Start off young plants in 15 cm (6 in) pots and move on to 20 cm (8 in) pots, or orchid baskets of the same size, when necessary. A well-drained open compost is needed – 50:50 broken sphagnum moss and orchid bark, or live sphagnum moss alone. Crock the pots for good drainage and do not firm the potting medium too much. The pots can be placed on a slatted bench or suspended from the green-house roof.

Water the plants from the top and keep the potting medium wet. Use tepid water, which should ideally be rainwater or 'soft' water.

Feed the plants when pitchers start to be produced; during the summer and autumn apply a liquid fertiliser at intervals of about six weeks.

Prune the plants in early spring – cut back the old stems to leave young growths.

Microclimates obviously it would cost a fortune to heat a large or even medium-sized greenhouse to the temperatures required and therefore most people will have to give the plants a special small area in which the required temperatures can be maintained.

For instance one could devote a very small greenhouse to the cultivation of *Nepenthes*, or section off a larger greenhouse with a permanent glass partition and an access door. Some greenhouse manufacturers are able to provide internal partitioning for their models.

If you are a handy person you may be able to construct a tall frame or glass case in a warm greenhouse to accommodate your plants, with additional heating facilities within. Traditional Wardian cases or terrariums are not really suitable as they do not have sufficient height for *Nepenthes*.

24   Chrysanthemums

There are certain plants that are widely grown by greenhouse gar-deners. Tomatoes almost certainly come at the top of the list, closely followed by chrysanthemums. In fact, chrysanthemums literally follow tomatoes, for when this utility crop is cleared out at the end of the season chrysanthemums in pots are moved into the greenhouse.

The florists' chrysanthemums – the ones considered here – are now correctly *Dendranthema*, although I feel it will be some years before this becomes a household name, if ever. So in the meantime I will continue to call these plants chrysanthemums.

I consider there is no better plant for creating colour in the greenhouse from mid-autumn until well after Christmas than the chrysanthemum, and it is one of the finest subjects for cutting. Many gardeners become great enthusiasts of this flower and grow superb blooms for exhibiting at the autumn shows. However, in this book I shall deal only with basic cultivation to produce good blooms for decoration and cutting.

The mid-autumn-flowering cultivars are the first to bloom and these are followed by the late-flowering kinds; flowering can, however, overlap. Chrysanthemums are among the easiest plants to grow but a reasonable amount of attention will be needed throughout the growing season.

Cultivation

Growing on young plants Start off with rooted cuttings early in the year. Initially these are bought from a specialist chrysanthemum grower and subsequently propagated from your own stock of plants (see Chapter 10 for propagation).

Pot rooted cuttings singly into 9 cm ($3\frac{1}{2}$ in) pots, using John Innes potting compost No. 1. Transfer to 12.5 cm (5 in) pots before the plants become pot-bound (about mid-spring), using JIP2. When well established in these move into final pots, 20 cm (8 in) being large enough, and use JIP3. Final potting is carried out in late spring or early summer.

Always crock pots and pot really firmly for final potting, using a wooden potting stick. Leave a space of 5 cm (2 in) between the compost surface and the pot rim for a topdressing of the same compost in late summer. Use plastic or clay pots for each stage.

At no time should you give the plants too high a temperature because it leads to soft weak growth. Young plants growing on in the greenhouse should be given a temperature of 4.5 to 7° C (40 to 45° F).

Provide maximum light and keep plants well spaced out on the staging. This results in good light and air circulation all round the plants and ensures that they do not become 'leggy' and devoid of leaves at the base. Gradually increase ventilation after initial potting of rooted cuttings and give plenty of ventilation when established in their pots on all favourable occasions.

Young plants should be transferred to a cold frame as soon as possible to encourage 'hard' growth. Start moving them out of the greenhouse in early spring. Harden them off further in the frame by gradually increasing ventilation.

Young plants should be stopped. This results in the formation of shoots and flowers (and more of them) earlier than would occur naturally. Stopping is carried out between early and late spring, with a second stopping (for the majority of cultivars) in early or mid-summer. The timing of this depends on several factors: the time the cuttings were taken, the cultivar, and the part of the country in which they are being grown. The optimum times are gained through experience. Some chrysanthemum catalogues give stopping dates for cultivars but these should be taken only as a rough guide. The time of stopping, of course, determines the time at which the plants will flower, and this is very important if you intend exhibiting.

Stopping simply involves pinching out the growing tip of each plant before it naturally forms a 'break bud', after which lateral or side shoots will be produced near the top of the plant. Each will produce a 'first crown bud'. The second stopping (if needed) involves pinching out the tips of the lateral shoots before the first crown buds appear. More shoots are then produced near the top and are known as the sub-laterals. These will eventually produce flower buds at their tips which are known as the 'second crown buds'. These are the buds that will produce the flowers.

Without stopping, plants will form these shoots naturally but they will flower later. Generally allow about six good shoots per plant, which means six blooms – one per shoot. Surplus shoots are removed at an early stage of their development.

Provide supports for the plants from an early stage. A thin bamboo cane can be used for plants in their first and second pots. After final potting use a 1.2 to 1.5 m (4 to 5 ft) stout bamboo cane in each pot, the length depending on the eventual height of the cultivar. Some gardeners use one cane for each shoot, but this is really only necessary if you are growing for exhibition, when only two or three blooms are allowed to develop on each plant. Tie in the shoots regularly with raffia or soft garden string, but not too tightly.

Summer care of plants Remove the plants from the cold frame in early summer, by which time they should be well hardened off and in

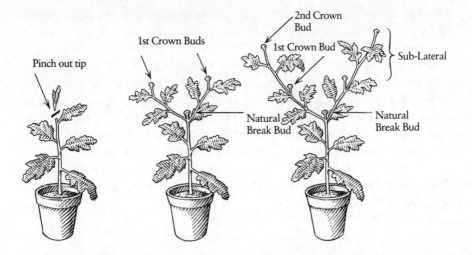

1st Crown Buds

Pinch out tip

2nd Crown Bud

1st Crown Bud

Sub-Lateral

Natural Break Bud

Natural Break Bud

55 Stopping a chrysanthemum

their final pots. Put them on a suitable standing ground for the summer.

Any convenient area can be used provided it is in an open, sunny situation, sheltered from winds. Either stand the pots on a layer of well-weathered ashes, or on tiles or pieces of slate. This is to prevent earthworms from entering the pots through the drainage holes. Alternatively, stand the pots along the edge of a path or on a patio.

On a standing ground the pots are traditionally placed in double rows, 45 cm (18 in) between the plants and 91 cm (3 ft) between each double row. You will need to support the plants to prevent them being blown over. Insert a wooden stake at each end of each row and stretch galvanised wire between them, at the top and half-way down. Then securely tie the canes to these wires.

Watering will have to be attended to regularly – certainly each day. In very warm weather the pots may need to be watered two or three times a day.

From late summer start feeding; initially every two weeks and gradually increase to once a week. When the colours of the flowers show, feeding should stop. Use a proprietary chrysanthemum fertiliser as this is correctly balanced in nitrogen, phosphorus and potash. In late summer or early autumn give a topdressing of John Innes potting compost No. 3.

Do not forget that a second stopping will probably be needed in early or mid-summer. Remove surplus side shoots as they appear in the leaf axils and cut out any shoots which form around the base of the stems.

Disbudding (removal of surplus flower buds) will start in late summer and continue into the autumn. It is necessary if you want large blooms on long stems for cutting. A cluster of flower buds is produced at the tip of each shoot. The one in the centre is the 'crown bud'. Retain this and rub out all the others; each shoot should bear only one flower. However, sometimes we may want smaller flowers in sprays (useful for flower arrangements); in this instance rub out the crown bud and leave the others. Disbud as soon as the buds are large enough to handle easily.

Flowering the plants The plants are flowered in the greenhouse where the blooms will be well protected from the elements. The pots are stood on the floor and this may necessitate removing some staging. Before taking the plants inside, clean the house thoroughly.

House the plants before frosts start – one normally gets them inside in early autumn. First spray them to kill any pests and diseases. Use gamma-HCH to control pests and benomyl for fungal diseases. Also clean the pots by scrubbing them well. Carry the plants into the greenhouse horizontally, pot first to prevent damage to buds and shoots. If you are setting the pots on a soil border place a slate or tile under each one to prevent worms from entering.

Provide just enough heat to prevent a damp atmosphere (cool or intermediate conditions) which results in 'damping' of the blooms. Mildew and greymould can ruin foliage and blooms. Ventilation must be given on all favourable occasions – good air circulation is essential to prevent diseases.

Feeding can continue until the colour of the flowers shows. As to watering, keep the compost steadily moist but not saturated.

Three to four weeks after flowering the stems are cut down to within 22 cm (9 in) of the compost. Remove the plants from the pots (label each one first) and remove all soil. It is best to remove any new shoots at the base of the stem. Then box the 'stools', as they are now called, into deep wooden boxes. A suitable compost is equal parts loam, peat (or a substitute) and sand, without fertiliser. Place a thin layer in the bottom of the box, pack the stools close together and cover the roots with compost. Keep them in a cold frame with the compost only just moist.

Raising new plants New plants are raised each year from cuttings; generally between late winter and early spring. The stools are started into growth early in the year, in a little heat – 7° C (45° F) at night and 12° C (55° F) by day. Good light and air should be provided.

The stools produce shoots at their base and these are used as cuttings. Remove shoots as close as possible to their base with a sharp knife when 5 to 7.5 cm (2 to 3 in) high. Trim just below a node and cut off the lower leaves. Dip the bases in a hormone rooting powder formulated for softwood cuttings.

56 Chrysanthemum cuttings

Insert cuttings in a 9 cm (3½ in) pot, up to half a dozen around the edge, or in a tray, using a compost of equal parts peat and coarse sand, equal parts peat and Perlite, or 'straight' Perlite or vermiculite. Water in and root in a heated propagating case – a temperature of 10–15° C (50–60° F) is sufficient. Wean off the rooted cuttings before potting individually into their first (9 cm) pots, as described at the beginning of this chapter. Pot off as soon as rooted for there are no nutrients in the above rooting media.

The old stools are discarded when a crop of new plants has been secured. If any of your plants are infected with viruses or eelworm they are best discarded and a new clean batch of rooted cuttings bought in from a specialist grower.

A personal choice of greenhouse chrysanthemums

There is such a large range of cultivars available that all one can do, when recommending a selection, is to give a personal choice. So here are the ones I can recommend – I hope you enjoy them as much as I do, and remember that all of the cultivars mentioned are completely reliable and have a high reputation among growers.

Intermediate Very popular, with double flowers and incurving or reflexed florets ('petals'). A range of cultivars will provide flowers from mid-autumn to Christmas. Allow about six blooms per plant. Some of my favourites are: 'Balcombe Perfection', amber-bronze; 'Fred Shoesmith', white; 'Red Balcombe Perfection', bright red; and 'Yellow Fred Shoesmith', yellow.

Incurved Much used for exhibition. Allow up to six blooms per plant. Ball-shaped blooms with incurving florets, produced in late autumn. My favourites include: 'John Hughes', white; 'Lilian Shoesmith', orange-bronze; 'Red Shirley Model', red and copper; and 'Yellow John Hughes', yellow.

Large exhibition Formerly known as Japanese. Huge blooms, much used for exhibition, in which case allow only one or two blooms per plant. Flowering time is late autumn. Good cultivars are: 'Cossack', crimson; 'Duke of Kent', white; 'Green Goddess', pale green; 'Harry Gee', silvery pink; 'Jessie Habgood', white; 'Shirley Primrose', pale yellow; and 'Yellow Duke', a deep yellow.

Singles Single daisy-like flowers. Can either be grown as sprays (remove the crown bud from each shoot) or disbudded to leave one flower per stem. Flowering period late autumn and early winter.

Sprays Excellent for cutting. Masses of small flowers from late mid-autumn until early winter. There are available single- and double-flowered and quill-petalled cultivars.

Anemones Daisy-like flowers with cushion-like centres. Good for cutting. Come in a range of bright colours. Grown as for the singles.

Spiders Very popular for flower-arranging is 'Rayonnante' with long quilled florets. Colours include white, yellow, pink and bronze.

Charms These make excellent pot plants, about 45 cm (18 in) in height and very bushy. They smother themselves with small single flowers, in a wide range of colours, from mid-autumn to early winter. Plants can be raised from seeds sown in mid-winter in a minimum temperature of 10°C (50°F). They can also be grown from cuttings in the normal way. Stop the plants when 7.5 to 10 cm (3 to 4 in) tall, and then allow to branch and grow naturally.

Cascades These are raised from seeds as for the charms, or from cuttings. They make excellent pot plants and have a pendulous habit of growth. The shoots, however, need training to suitable supports to make them hang down. Pots of cascades need to be elevated both while growing and while flowering in the greenhouse. Small flowers are produced in a wide range of colours.

25   Ferns

The ferns are primitive, non-flowering spore-bearing plants (spores are the reproductive bodies) and a selection from the many kinds should be in every greenhouse collection for they have beautiful foliage. I like to place ferns among flowering plants; the fresh green foliage makes a good contrast for bright colours. Because ferns do not like direct sunlight another good place to grow them is under the greenhouse bench, but near the front, a position in the greenhouse which is not often fully utilised.

There are ferns suited to the cool, intermediate and warm house, and some even to the hot, humid 'stove' house; but it is the easier cool and intermediate kinds that I feel most gardeners will want to grow, so I have devoted this chapter to these. However, there are one or two in the accompanying table which grow best in a warm greenhouse.

General cultivation Suitable minimum temperatures for each genus are recommended in the accompanying table. It is important to shade ferns from direct sunlight from spring to autumn because sun through glass can cause the fronds (leaves) to shrivel and turn brown. Ferns

Ferns which are easy to grow

Botanical Name	Common Name
Adiantum	Maidenhair fern
Asplenium bulbiferum	Spleenwort
nidus	Bird's nest fern
Davallia canariensis	Hare's foot fern
Dicksonia antarctica	Tree fern
Nephrolepis exaltata	Sword fern
Pellaea rotundifolia	Cliffbrake

Platycerium bifurcatum
    lemoinei
    vassei
	Staghorn fern

Pteris cretica *tremula*	Table ferns
Polystichum falcatum	Holly fern

Habit of Growth	General Comments Plus Minimum Temperature
Blackish leaf stalks, compound leaves, pinnate, bi-pinnate or multi-pinnate, generally light or bright green – very dainty appearance	Popular ferns, 10° C (50° F)
Bi- or tri-pinnate fronds, plantlets borne on upper surface	Propagate from plantlets, 10° C (50° F)
Epiphytic. Long, broad, bright green fronds in shuttlecock formation	Generally pot grown, 15.5° C (60° F)
Epiphytic. Long-stalked fronds, multi-pinnate.	Excellent for hanging baskets or plant tree, 10° C (50° F)
Tall, stout stem topped by rosette of long tri-pinnate fronds	Grow in large pot or tub, or greenhouse border, 10° C (50° F)
Lanceolate pinnate fronds, bright green	Makes an excellent specimen if grown in a hanging basket; 10–15.5° C (50–60° F)
Arching fronds, pinnate, the pinnae (leaflets) being almost circular, deep green	Can be recommended for growing in hanging baskets; 4.5° C (40° F)
Epiphytic. Two types of fronds: flattish shield fronds (often chestnut brown) and fertile spore-bearing fronds, antler-like in appearance and erect or pendulous	Can be grown in pots, but better for older plants to be grown on a board suspended from the greenhouse structure, or in hanging wooden lattice baskets; 10–15.5° C (50–60° F)
Long-stalked fronds, pinnate or bi-pinnate	10° C (50° F)
Deep green shiny pinnate fronds	4.5–10° C (40–50° F)

like a humid atmosphere, the amount being determined by the greenhouse temperature. When it is very warm in the summer frequent damping down and spraying of the foliage will create the conditions in which ferns will thrive. In lower temperatures far less humidity will be needed but remember that ferns do not like a dry atmosphere which should be avoided at all costs. Good ventilation is also necessary, especially during very warm weather.

Any good potting compost is suitable for ferns but I prefer to use one of the soilless types; the plants seem to grow particularly well in this. The time to pot on is the spring just before new growth commences. At this time the clump-forming ferns can be divided if you feel that they are becoming too large. This is the easiest way to propagate most ferns, although *Asplenium bulbiferum* can be increased in summer from the plantlets which form on the upper surface of the leaves. Simply detach and 'prick them out' into a seed tray to root.

Although ferns like moisture they should not have their roots in wet compost. Therefore aim to keep the compost steadily moist. Feed every two weeks in the summer with a general-purpose liquid fertiliser. Remember that some ferns will die down in the winter, but most are evergreen. Remove dead fronds to maintain hygienic conditions.

Epiphytic ferns So far I have been dealing with terrestrial ferns (those that grow in the ground) but there are some epiphytic kinds which grow naturally on trees and rocks. *Platycerium* is the best-known example, and indeed is a very popular fern.

Let us deal first of all with composts for *Platycerium*. For young plants, a mixture of coarse moss peat and bark chippings can be recommended, or even moss peat alone. For older plants a more suitable mixture is one-third each of moss peat, coarse bark chippings and sphagnum moss.

Young plants can be started off in pots but eventually it is better to suspend plants of *Platycerium* from the greenhouse structure because of their spreading or pendulous habit which makes them top-heavy. Each plant can be mounted on a board, or planted in a wooden lattice basket – the type often used for epiphytic orchids. If mounting on a board, use plastic-covered wire to secure the plant and to hold in the compost. A pot-grown plant will have a ball of compost around its roots, so it is not as difficult as it seems to mount a plant on a board.

To water, thoroughly soak the root area and then leave until it is fairly dry before watering again. The entire root area can be immersed in a container of water, especially if the plants are being grown on a board or in baskets. When plants are well established and in full growth feed with a balanced liquid fertiliser; use a weak dilution rate and apply about once a month.

Asplenium nidus is also an epiphytic fern but is generally pot grown. It will appreciate sphagnum moss being added to the compost (a peat-based type) when potting. Another epiphyte is *Davallia* and this can be grown in hanging baskets, on a 'plant tree' (see the chapter on bromeliads, page 173) or on a rock partially sunk in the greenhouse border. Make sure it has some compost around the roots to get it established.

26 Orchids

Many people fight shy of orchid growing because they think that these plants are difficult to grow and need high temperatures. In fact, there are many as easy to grow as any other greenhouse plant, thriving in cool or intermediate conditions. I will concentrate mainly on these kinds, but also include one or two that need warm conditions to satisfy gardeners who can provide high temperatures.

Types of growth Most orchids are epiphytic plants, growing on trees and rocks in their natural habitats, and many form abundant aerial roots. There are two distinct types of growth in orchids:

a. Sympodial growth. The plants in this group produce pseudo-bulbs, swollen above-ground stems which act as storage organs. These are joined by rhizomes under the soil and they carry the leaves and flowers. One can propagate orchids by detaching the older leafless pseudobulbs and potting them off. These are called 'back bulbs'.

b. Monopodial growth. Plants in this group produce a single stem which grows upright, bearing leaves all the way up. Growth and new leaves are produced at the top.

Temperatures There are three temperature ranges for orchids and you will notice that they are slightly higher than the three general ranges given earlier in this book. Choose only those orchids which are suited to the temperatures you are able to provide.

1. Cool conditions. Minimum winter night temperature of 10°C (50°F). Day temperature in winter of 15.5°C (60°F) recommended. Maximum temperature in summer 18–21°C (65–70°F).

2. Intermediate conditions. Minimum winter night temperature of 13°C (55°F). Day temperature in winter of 18°C (65°F) recommended. Maximum temperature in summer 27°C (80°F).

3. Warm conditions. Minimum winter night temperature of 18°C (65°F). Day temperature in winter of 24°C (75°F) recommended. Maximum temperature in summer 27°C (80°F).

The minimum night temperatures should be somewhat higher in summer.

Humidity All orchids need humidity, which can be achieved by damping down the floor and staging as necessary. Provide a suitable amount of humidity for the prevailing temperature; for example, the higher the temperature the higher the humidity, the cooler the conditions the less humidity required.

Ventilation and shading Orchids need fresh air so pay attention to ventilation which should be consistent with maintaining the required temperature. At all costs avoid subjecting orchids to draughts. Orchids will need shading during the spring and summer to prevent scorching of the foliage, but remember that good light is also necessary. Ideally, try to create dappled shade when the sun is shining, achieved by the use of lath roller blinds.

Watering and feeding The aim of watering is to keep the compost steadily moist – do not subject the plants to extremes of wetness or dryness. Good drainage is needed and this is discussed under composts. In winter many orchids become dormant and at this time very little or no water is needed. Watering is resumed in the spring with the commencement of new growth. It is not essential to feed orchids, but if you wish to do so apply liquid fertiliser in the summer in the way you would feed any other greenhouse plant.

Composts and potting Spring is the time to pot on and repot orchids, but not while they are in flower. As a rough guide, plants can be repotted or potted on every two years. Certainly pot on when the pseudobulbs have no further room to develop.

The compost must be well drained and you will find that many mixes are recommended for orchids. No doubt all are good, but it may be very confusing to the beginner to be presented with half a dozen different compost mixes, so here I have simplified things. In my opinion, a good general compost (one that will suit all the orchids mentioned here) consists of pine-bark chippings (generally sold as 'orchid bark'), some sphagnum-moss peat (to retain moisture), and a small amount of charcoal (to keep the compost 'sweet'). Fertilisers should not be included. More specific details on composts are given in the list of genera which follows.

Orchids can be grown in either plastic or clay pots, which should be well crocked. When repotting, or potting on, remove any dead roots and other growth; in the case of older established plants tease away most of the old compost. Orchids can also be grown in special orchid baskets hung from the greenhouse roof. These are square openwork containers made of slatted wood. Both drainage and air circulation around the root area are very good .

Some of the epiphytic orchids can be grown on vertical slabs of wood, again hung from the greenhouse roof, especially those kinds with long creeping rhizomes or plants with pendulous or semi-pendulous flowers. One can also use cork bark, or real bark, for the same purpose. The roots of the plant should be free of compost and they are laid on the wood or bark on a layer of live sphagnum moss. Cover with a little more moss and hold in place with thin nylon thread, making sure it does not come into contact with stems or roots.

Epiphytic orchids can also be grown on a plant tree (see the chapter on bromeliads, p. 173), especially those kinds with a pendulous habit of growth. Again use the 'sphagnum moss and nylon-thread technique' for securing the plants to the tree.

The author's choice of genera

Cattleya Temperature range: Intermediate.
Habit of growth: Epiphytic. Produces pseudobulbs. Large flamboyant flowers in a wide colour range. Autumn or spring flowering.
Cultural hints: Ventilate whenever possible and provide high humidity. Spray overhead in summer. Reduce watering in resting period, or apply no water, but do not let the pseudobulbs shrivel unduly. Shade from spring to autumn. Use a compost mix with a high proportion of bark as well-drained compost is essential.

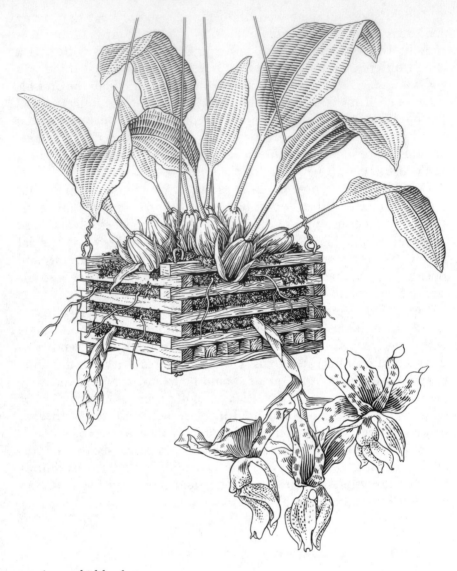

57 *An orchid basket*

Coelogyne Temperature range: Cool for the majority.
Habit of growth: Epiphytic. Produces pseudobulbs. Flowers spring
or summer, main colour being white. *C. cristata* is a very popular and
easy species with white wavy flowers.
Cultural hints: Easy to grow. Keep dry during the winter rest period

and provide full light. Repot only when essential – can be grown in pans. Use a bark/moss/charcoal compost.

Cymbidium Temperature range: Cool.

Habit of growth: Terrestrial or epiphytic. Produces pseudobulbs. Undoubtedly the most popular orchids, especially the hybrids. Easily grown and flowered; good for cutting. Winter and spring flowering, many colours. Miniatures ideal for small greenhouse.

Cultural hints: Plenty of ventilation in summer, even at night – need cool conditions at night during the summer. It can be an advantage to place plants out of doors for the summer, but protect from very hot sun and re-house before frosts commence. Spray overhead and liquid feed during the summer. Use a compost of equal parts bark and peat, plus some charcoal.

Dendrobium Temperature range: Cool, although some species need warm conditions.

Habit of growth: Epiphytic. Cane like pseudobulbs. *D. nobile* is the most popular species and the most easily obtained; spring flowering.

Cultural hints: Keep dry in winter during rest period, and provide good light. When flower buds are visible resume watering. Likes warmth and humidity in summer, plus plenty of moisture. Use a compost of equal parts bark and peat, plus some charcoal.

Lycaste Temperature range: Cool and intermediate.

Habit of growth: Mainly epiphytic, some terrestrial. Produces pseudobulbs. Winter and spring flowering, mainly during rest period. Flowers generally yellow or white.

Cultural hints: Shade well in summer and do not allow compost to dry out. Keep dry during winter rest period and provide maximum light. Use a bark/peat compost, to which can be added a little loam if desired to make a more substantial compost.

Miltonia Temperature range: Cool.

Habit of growth: Epiphytic. Produces pseudobulbs. Known as the pansy orchid. Free flowering, at various times of the year, the most frequent colours being reds, pale pinks, whites and light yellows. Not the easiest genus to grow.

Cultural hints: Keep steadily moist all year round. Shade as necessary, provide good ventilation, and do not maintain too high a level of humidity. Compost of equal parts bark and peat plus a little charcoal.

Odontoglossum Temperature range: Cool.

Habit of growth: Mainly epiphytic. Produces pseudobulbs. Probably as popular as *Cymbidium*. In a wide range of colours, many attractively marked. Flowering season is throughout the year.

Cultural hints: An open compost needed – two-thirds bark and one-third peat, plus some charcoal. Plenty of air and light essential but lightly shade from hot sun. Keep cool at night in the summer. Can place plants out of doors in summer, at which time they like plenty of humidity and liquid feeding.

Paphiopedilum Temperature range: Cool, also intermediate and warm for some. Check before buying.

Habit of growth: Mainly terrestrial, some epiphytic. No pseudobulbs produced. Popularly known as slipper orchids. A large and popular group with a wide range of colours. Flowers have a pouch-like lip. Flowering period winter, spring, summer or autumn, depending on cultivar.

Cultural hints: Compost of equal parts bark and peat, plus some charcoal. Keep in as small a pot as possible, as plants have a small root system. Plants do not have a resting period so water regularly all year round. Shade-loving plants, but good light needed in winter.

Phalaenopsis Temperature range: Warm.

Habit of growth: Epiphytic. No pseudobulbs. Thick fleshy leaves, often mottled. Produces an abundance of aerial roots. Excellent for growing on a plant tree or in hanging baskets. Popularly known as moth orchids. Plants flower at various times of year; blooms mainly white, pink or yellow.

Cultural hints: Needs plenty of humidity; be sparing with ventilation. Heavy shading from spring to autumn, and almost full light in winter. Keep compost steadily moist all year round – no resting period. Can liquid feed throughout the year. Re-pot annually, using equal parts bark and peat with some charcoal.

Pleione Temperature range: Very cool – only just frost free. Generally grown in an alpine house.

Habit of growth: Terrestrial. Pseudobulbs which last only one season. Deciduous, rest in winter. Flowers in spring. Low-growing plants. Popular species is *P. formosana* (pink and white), together with *P. f.* 'Alba' (white).

Cultural hints: Re-pot annually in spring, and remove old shrivelled pseudobulbs. Do not cover pseudobulbs with compost. Use a proprietary peat-based compost and half pots or pans. Keep compost steadily moist in growing season but do not wet the foliage. Grow as cool as possible.

Vanda Temperature range: Cool or intermediate; some species need warm conditions. Check before buying.

Habit of growth: Mainly epiphytic. Monopodial. Many aerial roots produced. Species flower at various times of the year, some blooming twice in one year. Many colours, including blue. There is the blue *V. coerulea* and also hybrids.

Cultural hints: Keep steadily moist all year round and reduce but do not stop watering in winter. Good light is needed for flowering, provide plenty of fresh air and feed in summer. Best in hanging basket to allow aerial roots to dangle. Use a bark/peat/charcoal compost.

27   Water plants

A pool can be very rewarding in a heated greenhouse, conservatory or sun room. One can grow water plants or aquatics, like the tropical water lilies, and add further colour by stocking it with fish.

Constructing a pool

A pool can be any shape desired; in a very formal setting it is best to go for a regular shape – square, rectangular or circular. In a more natural setting – for instance, in a bed planted with flowering shrubs and other exotic plants – an irregular shape is more suitable. If you intend growing water lilies and stocking it with fish, you will need a pool at least 45 cm (18 in) in depth.

A pool looks more natural if it is sunk into the ground so that the water level is at, or just below, ground level. However, some people may prefer to have a raised pool, especially in a formal setting (as in the centre of a paved area); in this instance one will not have to dig out a hole, but build it up from ground level using bricks or ornamental walling blocks. With a ground-level pool, however, it is possible to plant moisture-loving plants, such as ferns, in the moist soil around the edges.

To create a ground-level pool first dig a hole to the shape desired. If you wish to grow marginal plants around the edge of the pool, remember that they will need shallow water. Therefore, when excavating, make sure you form a 20 cm (8 in) wide ledge around the pool on which containers of marginal plants can be placed. Most need only a few inches of water over their roots.

When you have made the excavation you will have to line it. The easiest way these days is to use a butyl-rubber pool liner, or one of the cheaper heavy-gauge plastic or PVC liners. Unlike rubber, the last two need to be renewed after several years.

Liners mould to the shape of the excavation as water is added. They can be bought in any size, but make sure you buy one of sufficient size for your pool, taking the length, width and depth into account. They are supplied by aquatic specialists, whose catalogues generally give full instructions for making a pool in this way.

The edge of the liner extends over the edges of the pool and is hidden with paving slabs, irregular paving stones, rocks or soil. It is advisable to line the hole with 5 cm (2 in) of soft builders' sand before introducing the liner, to prevent stones from damaging it.

Raised pools, constructed of bricks, for example, can also be lined with these flexible liners, hiding the edges with the final course of bricks.

An alternative to making a pool with a flexible liner is to use one of the rigid pre-fabricated pools, obtainable in fibreglass or plastic. Such a pool is simply placed in a hole of suitable shape and size, making sure it is perfectly level, and packed firmly around the edges with soil. The edges can be hidden by the methods suggested for flexible liners. These rigid pools can be readily purchased from local garden centres.

The traditional method of making a pool is to line it with concrete; but in my opinion this is not worth all the hard work involved.

A *choice of plants*

For moist soil at the edge There are several suitable subjects for furnishing the immediate area around a pool:

Cyperus involucratus The umbrella grass, the leaves of which are arranged like the spokes of an umbrella. Can be grown in a cool greenhouse.

Ferns Various kinds (see Chapter 25 for a selection of genera). Most can be grown in a cool greenhouse.

Zantedeschia aethiopica (see marginal plants).

Marginal plants These are grown in the shallow water near the edge of the pool:
Cyperus Several of the sedges can be grown in shallow water and they have attractive grassy leaves. *C. involucratus* 'Variegatus' has green and white striped leaves and stems and can be grown in a cool greenhouse. The papyrus, *C. papyrus*, is a gigantic plant and suitable only for large structures which are kept very warm. The stems can reach a height of 3 m (10 ft). If you cannot manage this one, admire it in botanic gardens. *Zantedeschia aethiopica* the arum lily, which can be grown either in shallow water or in moist soil at the edge of the pool. A popular plant suited to the cool greenhouse, and bearing large white flowers.

Plants for deeper water Here we have all kinds of plants, from the tropical water lilies, to kinds which float on the surface and live completely submerged:
Eichhornia crassipes The water hyacinth. It floats in the water, has shiny leaves in rosettes and pale blue flowers. Of vigorous habit it is, nevertheless, easily controlled. Does not need conventional planting – drop it in to the water. Temperature as for tropical water lilies (see below).
Nelumbo nucifera Sacred lotus. Large leaves and pink flowers. Needs a large pool and temperature as for tropical water lilies, see below.
Nymphaea. This genus contains the tropical water lilies, which are not as difficult to grow as many people imagine. I am particularly fond of the blue-flowered ones, like *N. caerulea* (fragrant) and *N. stellata*. Both are ideal for a small pool or even a large tub.

Many of the *Nymphaea* hybrids are suitable only for larger pools, in the region of 1.8 by 1.2 m (6 by 4 ft) and above. Some well-known ones include 'General Pershing', pink, fragrant; 'Henry Shaw', blue; 'Missouri', white, nocturnal; and 'St Louis', yellow.

Tropical water lilies need a minimum water temperature of 18° C (65° F) and this means growing them in a warm greenhouse, although they are rested in a lower temperature for the winter (see planting aquatics).
Pistia stratiotes Water lettuce. A floating aquatic needing the same water temperature as tropical water lilies. Produces rosettes of pale green leaves. Just drop it in to the water – do not plant in the normal way.

Submerged aquatics These live under water and can be planted in containers. It is essential to have some of these to create a balanced well-aerated pool with clear water. There are many kinds, like *Cryp-*

tocoryne (needs warm water), *Myriophyllum* (species for cool and warm water) and *Vallisneria* (species for cool and warm water).

Planting aquatics There are special openwork containers (plastic baskets) for aquatics, obtainable from water-plant specialists or garden centres. Ordinary plastic pots could be used, although they do somewhat restrict root development. Use good-quality loam for planting – nothing else is needed.

The usual planting period is mid- to late spring. Aquatics, except the floaters, are planted in the containers just like any other plant but after planting place a layer of gravel over the loam to prevent it being washed out by the water and disturbed by the fish. Then lower the containers into the water. It is an advantage to repot most aquatics every two or three years, and at this time divided if they are becoming too large.

The tropical water lilies are treated in a somewhat different way. They are repotted each year in late winter or early spring. They make small tubers which are potted singly into 10 cm (4 in) pots of loam. Slightly submerge them in a tank of water, the temperature of which should be kept at 18–21° C (65–70° F), so one could start them off in a heated propagating case. When some leaves have been produced transfer to their usual containers in the pool. Simply knock them carefully out of their pots to avoid root disturbance. Put one water lily in one large basket. It is best not to put water lilies into too deep water when they first come into growth but gradually lower them as the leaf stalks elongate. This can be done by means of bricks under the basket; remove the bricks as growth develops until the baskets stand on the bottom of the pool. Start off with 15 cm (6 in) of water above the baskets.

Lift the baskets of water lilies in the autumn and allow them to dry out in the greenhouse. When the leave have died down lift the tubers carefully and store them for the winter in moist sand in the greenhouse, providing a temperature of 13° C (55° F).

Stocking the pool with fish

A pool is completed with the introduction of fish; they provide the necessary movement and give additional colour. Generally goldfish are to be seen in greenhouse pools, including the fancy kinds like fantails and veiltails. Koi carp are becoming popular and some of them are extremely colourful. All of these kinds are suitable for cool water but relish water in the region of 18° C (65° F).

Introduce fish to the pool only when it has settled down and the plants are growing well, especially the submerged oxygenators. The water in a new pool will quickly become like pea soup as green algae increase, but if a pool is well planted and has sufficient oxygenating plants, the water will clear of its own accord. On no account be tempted to change the water when it becomes green – be assured that it will clear naturally. This is the time to stock it with fish.

Fish can be fed daily in the spring and summer and far less in the winter. Feed only occasionally throughout the winter. Use a good proprietary fish food, either pellets which float on the surface and encourage fish to the top, or a finer granular type, especially for small fish. Live food is relished as a change of diet occasionally, like *Daphnia* or water fleas which can be bought from pet shops.

UTILITY CROPS

28 Fruits

Several hardy and tender fruits are suitable for growing in the green-house or conservatory and for most a great deal of heat is not required. A large greenhouse is not necessary to grow fruits because the larger kinds can be confined to pots. Those which I consider well worth trying are figs, grapes, melons, peaches, nectarines and strawberries.

Figs

There is no doubt in my mind that the best way to grow figs is in 25–30 cm (10–12 in) pots. If desired the pots can be placed out of doors in the summer to make more room in the greenhouse for other plants and returned in early autumn. Pot culture restricts the root system of figs and this results in more manageable plants and better fruiting.

Potting Pot-grown figs are generally available from garden centres and should be potted in late autumn, using well-crocked clay pots. I use a good-quality alkaline medium loam for potting to which is added some well-crushed brick rubble. If the loam is acid or neutral add some hydrated lime. Use pots only just large enough to take the root system as overpotting leads to vigorous growth at the expense of fruits. The compost should be firmed really well. Figs in pots are grown as bush trees which take up minimum space.

Cultivation Three crops a year are possible in a well-heated green-house but most gardeners aim for two crops – the first in early or mid-summer. To secure this, provide heat from late winter onwards. In an unheated house the second or main crop will ripen in late summer. So from late winter onwards maintain 10–15.5°C (50–60°F) for the early crop. Figs like a summer temperature of around 26°C (80°F) but at that time of year one relies on natural warmth.

In warm conditions provide plenty of humidity but keep the air drier when fruits are ripening. Shading is not necessary.

After the late-summer crop cease damping down and keep the compost only slightly moist. Give the trees a rest in winter – keep the greenhouse only just frost free. When growth commences in early spring increase watering and start damping down again. Also step up the temperature.

Repot the trees in mid-winter when necessary but only when the present pots are really full of roots and the compost is exhausted. In intervening years topdress with loam (to which some John Innes base fertiliser has been added) in the growing season.

Pruning Fruits are produced only on new growth and they start forming in the autumn, with more appearing in spring. These give you the two crops. Prune in summer by shortening back any vigorous new shoots to five or six leaves from the base. Thin out older branches if they are becoming congested. Aim to encourage a succession of new shoots which will bear fruits. Remove any weak or spindly growth.

Cultivars A number are available including 'Brown Turkey', generally considered the best; 'Bourjassotte Grise' which needs plenty of warmth; 'Brunswick', as good as 'Brown Turkey'; 'Negro Largo', which needs plenty of warmth; and 'White Marseilles' ('Marseillaise'), the fruits of which ripen yellow-green.

Grapes

A grape vine is ideal for training on the back wall of a lean-to or conservatory; if you do not have this kind of space, try pot culture. The latter is discussed later in this section.

Planting and training Plant in mid-winter in a well-drained soil border. Ideally the soil should be a good-quality loam and some well-rotted farmyard manure should be dug in prior to planting. If more than one vine is to be planted allow 1.2 m (4 ft) between each. After planting cut back the stems (known as rods) to 60 cm (2 ft). Train one strong new shoot vertically to horizontal wires spaced 30 cm (12 in) apart. The training wires can be taken right up the wall and under the roof to the ridge. Remove all other shoots.

Stop the side shoots when they are 60 cm (2 ft) in length. In the following winter cut these back almost to their base, leaving one growth bud, and reduce the length of the main rod by cutting it back to well-ripened wood.

In the second year the new side shoots are trained to the wires – tie them in a horizontal position. They may bear some fruits in the second year.

Winter pruning in the second and following years consists of cutting back all side shoots to one or two buds from the base. In late winter lower the main rod to a horizontal position (support it with a string attached to the roof) to encourage even breaking of the buds along its length. Re-tie when growth commences.

General cultivation Allow one bunch of fruits per side shoot in the second year, removing all others at an early stage of development. In subsequent years, two or three bunches of fruits can be carried on each side shoot.

Vine flowers need to be hand pollinated; gently draw your half-closed hand down the truss of flowers to spread the pollen. The resulting berries will need thinning to prevent overcrowding and to ensure a good size and well-shaped bunches. Thin out the centre of each bunch as soon as the berries reach pea size. Use fine-tipped vine scissors and do not touch the berries or you will remove the 'bloom'. Use a small forked stick to manipulate the bunch while thinning. Follow with a further thinning if necessary as the berries swell.

The side shoots will need stopping at two leaves beyond a bunch

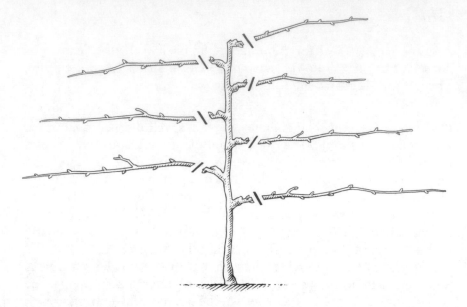

58 Winter pruning of established grape vine

of fruits, and sub-lateral shoots (which grow from the side shoots) should be pinched back to one leaf.

Provide grapes with good ventilation to prevent vine mildew. No artificial heat is needed in winter but if possible provide heat in spring when the vines are in flower. A minimum temperature in summer and autumn should be 13°C (55°F); natural warmth can be relied upon at this period.

When temperatures are reasonably high provide a humid atmosphere, but do not damp down while the vines are in flower – resume after petal fall. Also stop damping down when the fruits are ripening and increase ventilation. Provide plenty of water when the vines are in full growth and feed fortnightly until the fruits start to ripen.

Pot culture 'Black Hamburgh' is a good cultivar for pot culture. Pot in mid-winter, using a 30 cm (12 in) clay pot and John Innes potting compost No. 3. Stand the pots outdoors and take into the greenhouse in late winter, providing a temperature of 10°C (50°F) if possible, or even slightly higher.

The rod can be trained in a spiral fashion to a framework of bamboo canes. Side shoots will need thinning out to about 30 cm (12 in) apart and they should subsequently be stopped at two leaves

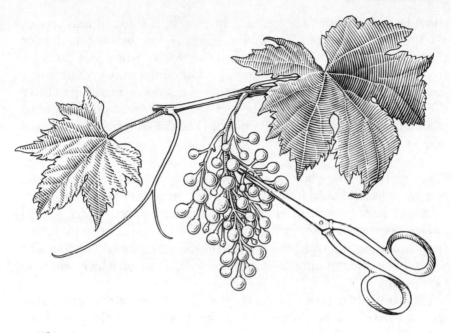

59 Thinning grapes

beyond a bunch of fruits. In winter reduce the rod by about half its length and cut back side shoots to one or two buds. The vine can be placed outdoors after fruiting until late winter.

Cultivars 'Black Hamburgh', black fruits, for unheated or slightly heated greenhouse; 'Buckland Sweetwater', white fruits, for unheated or slightly heated house; and 'Muscat of Alexandria', white, for a heated greenhouse – steady minimum temperature of 15.5° C (60° F) in spring and when ripening in autumn.

Melons

Melons, although tender, can be grown in a heated or unheated greenhouse – in the first instance plants can be started off earlier in the year. Choose suitable cultivars for the conditions you are able to provide (see list at the end of this section).

Raising plants If you have a heated greenhouse seeds can be sown in early spring and the resultant plants set out as soon as they reach a suitable size. For an unheated greenhouse sow seeds in mid-spring. Use 7.5 cm (3 in) pots for seed sowing, either bio-degradable or plastic, and John Innes potting compost No. 1. Sow seeds on edge, two per pot, and cover with 6 mm ($\frac{1}{4}$ in) of compost. Germinate in a temperature of 15.5° C (60° F). Remove the weakest seedling to leave the strongest. Or seeds may be pre-chitted (germinated on moist blotting paper) in a warm place indoors and the strongest ones potted off.

Planting The young plants need maximum light and frost protection. When well established in their pots, plant out. Melons can be grown in a soil border, well drained and manured, spaced 45 cm (18 in) apart. They can also be grown in 25–30 cm (10–12 in) pots (using John Innes potting compost No. 2) on the greenhouse floor, spaced 45 cm apart; or growing-bags may be used, most of which will take two plants.

Plant out when about 15 cm (6 in) tall. In a soil border plant on a mount of soil and in pots and growing-bags ensure the top of the rootball is slightly above compost level after planting. This is to ensure water does not lie around the base of the stems, which leads to collar rot.

General cultivation Provide horizontal wires for support, spacing them 30 cm (12 in) apart on the side of the greenhouse, up to the eaves or even higher. Tie in the main stem as it grows using raffia or soft string. When the top of the stem reaches the top wire pinch out the tip. Tie in the side or lateral shoots in a horizontal position. Their tips are removed beyond the second leaf, leaving them about 30 cm (12 in) long.

Keep the compost or soil steadily moist and avoid wetting the base of the stems. A good growing temperature is a night minimum of 13° C (55° F) and a day temperature of 15.5–21° C (60–70° F). But in summer an ideal range is 21° C by day and 15.5° C at night. Good light is needed but shade from very strong sunshine, and provide moderate humidity.

Melon flowers need to be hand pollinated. Male and female flowers form on the same plant and the females must be adequately pollinated. It is easy to tell the difference between the two – each female flower has a tiny embryo fruit behind it, while the male has only a thin flower stalk. Pollinate the flowers when the atmosphere is dry and they are fully open. Take off a male flower, remove the petals, and brush the centre of a female flower with it to transfer pollen. Pollinate four to six females all at the same time (using a different male for each) to ensure fruits develop uniformly. Allow only one fruit per side shoot.

60 *Melon fruits supported in nets*

When the fruits start to swell remove all subsequent flowers. Start feeding when the fruits have set, applying a weekly liquid feed, and stop when the fruits are virtually mature.

White roots will appear on the surface of the soil or compost, at which stage apply a topdressing of John Innes potting compost No. 2, 2.5 cm (1 in) deep, over the root area but keep it away from the base of the stems.

When fruits are the size of a tennis ball support them in net bags slung from the roof. As fruits start to ripen in late summer or early autumn reduce watering and keep the soil or compost on the dry side. Give more ventilation during ripening and keep the atmosphere dry. The fruits give off a strong sweet aroma when ready for picking and feel soft at the end furthest from the stalk.

Cultivars For a greenhouse without artificial heat: 'Charantais', 'Early Sweet' (F1), 'Ogen', 'Romeo' (F1), and 'Sweetheart' (F1). For a greenhouse with artificial heating, providing warmth in the spring and also during the ripening stage: 'Blenheim Orange Superlative', 'Emerald Gem', and 'Hero of Lockinge'.

Peaches and nectarines

These are grown in exactly the same way, hence the reason for grouping them together here. When fan trained they are ideal fruits for the back wall of a south-facing lean-to or conservatory. Alternatively they can be grown as bushes in pots. A wall space of at least 1.8 by 1.8 m (6 by 6 ft) is needed for each fan-trained tree. Peaches and nectarines can be grown in an unheated house and, indeed, it is best to have no artificial heat in the winter when they are resting. One can provide a little artificial heat in spring to prevent frost damage to the flowers; for example, a temperature of 7° C (45° F), and also in autumn to help ripening if necessary.

Planting and training Grow fan-trained trees (I will deal with these first) in a well-drained soil border consisting ideally of medium to heavy loam. Provide horizontal wires spaced 20 cm (8 in) apart for training.

Buy two-year-old fan-trained trees from a specialist grower and plant in late autumn or winter. The first pruning after planting is drastic; cut out the middle (vertical) branch down to the top side branches. Lightly cut back the two lowest branches and tie them horizontally to the supporting wires. Always make your cuts just above wood buds. These are the long thin ones, the flower buds being fatter and rounded. The remaining branches should be cut back to within a few inches of the main stem.

Many new shoots will be produced after this initial pruning and they must be thinned out (simply rub them out) to leave only sufficient to form a fan shape of main branches. Tie them into the wires as they develop, spacing them out evenly. Retain only those shoots which are growing upwards, downwards or sideways – not any sticking outwards – in order to form a perfectly flat fan of branches.

In the second winter the main branches will have extension growths and several shoots along their length. Some of these shoots may have flower buds and some can be allowed to fruit. Tie them in flat to the training wires.

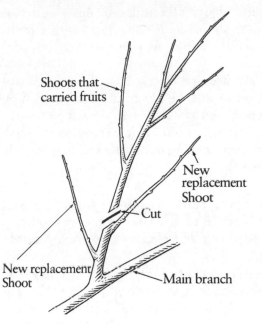

Shoots that carried fruits

New replacement Shoot

Cut

New replacement Shoot

Main branch

61 *Winter pruning of peach*

Routine annual pruning in winter consists of pruning shoots (produced on the main framework of branches) that have carried fruits. Cut them back to where new shoots have formed; these will replace the ones removed and bear fruits the following summer. So we have a constant succession of fruiting shoots: they form one year, fruit the next and are then cut back.

Routine care In the winter rest the trees (between late autumn and late winter) when they will need little or no artificial heat. Good ventilation on all suitable occasions should be provided in winter.

In the spring, when the buds are swelling, ventilation is reduced and a little artificial heat can be given. The trees benefit from being sprayed twice a day with water in mild spells. Pollinate the flowers by hand, using a soft artist's brush. Damp down in warm spells. Many new shoots are produced in spring and will need thinning – retain sufficient at the base of existing ones for next year's fruiting and remove the rest.

Thin the fruitlets over a period of time, leaving them evenly spaced on the shoots – for example, two or three per shoot.

In the summer spray the trees twice a day with plain water and damp down the floor. Provide plenty of ventilation night and day. Continue removing the surplus shoots and fruits. Feed with a high-potash fertiliser in the summer – apply as a dry topdressing and lightly prick into the soil.

Stop spraying when the fruits are ripening; and at this stage do not water the soil. Full ventilation should be given during the ripening stage. When fruits have been picked water heavily, continue to give full ventilation and spray the plants daily. When leaf fall occurs stop spraying and water only sufficiently to maintain the soil in a slightly moist condition during dormancy.

Pot-grown trees Grow in clay pots, starting off in 25 cm (10 in), and moving on eventually into 35 cm (14 in). Use John Innes potting compost No. 3. Crock the pots well and plant one- or two-year-old trees in the dormant season.

Grow as dwarf open-centred bushes. To form the main framework, or head of branches, select three to four strong branches and shorten them by half. All others, plus the main stem above them, are completely removed. Do this in late winter or early spring after planting. This pruning induces branching.

Routine pruning consists of keeping the centre of the tree open (free of branches), the removal of crowded or crossing shoots and the removal of dead or diseased wood. When the desired size has been reached remove shoots that grow beyond it – that is, cut them out completely. Old shoots that have fruited can be cut back to new ones. All pruning is done in the winter.

Cultivation is as outlined for fan-trained trees, except that potted trees could, if desired, be placed out of doors in summer when the fruits have set, to make room in the greenhouse for other crops. Chose a very warm, sunny sheltered site.

Cultivars Peaches: 'Bellegarde', 'Hale's Early', 'Peregrine' and 'Royal George'. Nectarines: 'Early Rivers', 'Lord Napier' and 'Pineapple'.

Strawberries

Forced pot-grown strawberries ripen several weeks ahead of outdoor crops. They are in the greenhouse from mid-winter to late spring. A minimum of 12 plants will be needed for a worthwhile crop of fruits.

Potting Buy rooted runners from a specialist grower in mid- or late summer and pot into 12.5 cm (5 in) pots, using John Innes potting compost No. 2. Stand them out of doors until mid-winter.

General cultivation Before housing the plants clean them up; remove dead leaves and spray with an insecticide to kill any aphids which may be braving the winter weather. Pot into 15 cm (6 in) pots, using JIP3. Set the pots on the staging or shelving, ensuring the plants receive maximum light. When growth starts a little heat can be provided – 4.5°C (40°F). Gradually increase so that by the time the plants are in flower, in mid-spring, a minimum of 15.5°C (60°F) is being maintained.

Hand pollinate the flowers with a soft artist's brush by dabbing the centre of each in turn. When half the flowers have set fruits, increase watering and give a liquid feed every 10 days from the time the first flowers open until the fruits start to ripen. Try if possible to maintain a temperature of 18°C (65°F) from the time the fruits start to colour.

After fruiting the plants can be planted in the garden – do not force them again. But root strong runners (plantlets) in 9 cm (3½ in) pots to give you plants for the following year. When the plantlets are well rooted pot on into 12.5 cm (5 in) pots and proceed as described above.

Cultivars The following are recommended for forcing: 'Cambridge Rival', 'Cambridge Vigour', 'Gorella', 'Pantagruella', 'Red Gauntlet', and 'Tamella'.

29   Vegetables

Amateur gardeners do not seem very adventurous when it comes to growing vegetables under glass. I find this somewhat puzzling, for in our temperamental climate one achieves much better results with protection. Apart from tomatoes (which are the most popular) and perhaps capsicums, aubergines, cucumbers and lettuces, very few vegetables are to be seen growing in amateur greenhouses.

I am recommending, therefore, a far bigger selection of vegetables suited to protected cultivation than is to be found in most other greenhouse books, and I hope this will stimulate gardeners into trying a wider range. Many of those I have recommended can be grown without artificial heat and occupy the house during the winter when, sadly, many amateur greenhouses stand empty and are completely unproductive. Other vegetables can be grown successfully with only a little artificial heat and are therefore an economical proposition.

Protected cultivation is suitable for two groups of vegetables: 1. Those which can be grown only for a short spell out of doors, because of our climate; for example, tomatoes, aubergines, capsicums, and Chinese cabbage. 2. Those whose season you want to extend (in other words, early or late crops) such as sweet corn, courgettes and French beans.

The type of greenhouse suitable for vegetable cultivation is one that permits maximum light to enter. A glass-to-ground house is ideal. A structure which, in my opinion, is excellent for vegetable cultivation without artificial heat is the walk-in polythene tunnel. Ideally, of course, this should be erected on the vegetable plot. Most vegetables are best grown in a well-drained, fertile soil border in the house; failing this, various containers can be used, like growing-bags, pots and ring-culture containers for some, such as tomatoes.

The heated greenhouse can be put to good use in late winter and spring for raising vegetables which are later to be planted in the open ground; the following table lists some of the vegetables which are treated in this way.

Vegetables which can be raised in the heated greenhouse

Minimum temperature 10° C (50° F)

Vegetable	Sow	Plant out of doors
Beans, French and runner	Mid/late spring	Late spring/early summer
Brussels sprouts	Late winter	Mid-spring
Cabbage, summer	Mid-winter/early spring	Early/mid-spring
Calabrese	Late winter	Mid-spring
Cauliflower, summer	Mid-winter/early spring	Early/mid-spring
Celery	Early spring	Late spring
Cucumbers, outdoor	Mid/late spring	Late spring/early summer
Leeks	Mid/late winter	Mid-spring
Lettuce	From mid-winter	Late winter onwards (cloches)
Marrows	Mid/late spring	Late spring/early summer
Onions	Mid/late winter	Mid-spring
Sweet corn	Mid/late spring	Late spring/early summer
Tomatoes	Early/mid-spring	Late spring/early summer

Vegetables for growing to maturity in a greenhouse
Aubergines

Popularly known as eggplants, and cropping in summer. They need similar cultivation to tomatoes and make a good companion crop as they also like plenty of warmth, sunshine and dryish air. A temperature of 15.5–21° C (60–70° F) is ideal with a minimum night temperature of 13° C (55° F). Some artificial heat will be needed early in the year.

Raising plants Sow seeds in early spring, spacing them 2.5 cm (1 in) apart on the compost surface. Use John Innes seed compost and a pot or tray for sowing. Germinate at 15.5–18° C (60–65° F).

Prick out seedlings into 7.5 cm (3 in) pots, using John Innes potting compost No. 1. Move on to 12.5 cm (5 in) pots when necessary, using JIP 2. When 15 cm (6 in) high, pinch out the tips to encourage branching.

Planting Plant in a soil border, growing-bags or large pots as for tomatoes (see Tomatoes). Plant when about 15 cm (6 in) tall and provide bamboo canes for support, or growing-bag crop supports.

General cultivation Spray open flowers with water to encourage fruits to set (when conditions are warm) or gently tap or shake each plant to ensure pollination. Carry out normal watering and feed weekly with a liquid tomato fertiliser when the fruits have set. Ventilate well in warm weather but shade from very strong sunshine. Cut fruits as they mature to allow further fruits to develop. For really large fruits allow only about six per plant and remove the rest.

Cultivars 'Black Beauty', 'Black Prince' (F1), 'Bonica' (F1), 'Dusky' (F1), 'Easter Egg' (F1), 'Long Purple', 'Moneymaker' (F1), and 'Slice Rite'.

Beans, climbing French

Early crops of climbing French beans can be grown in an unheated greenhouse or tunnel. Although dwarf French beans are also suitable for protected cultivation, higher yields can be expected with the climbing cultivars.

Raising plants Sow seeds mid- to late spring. Alternatively, sow in early spring in heat. If you can maintain a temperature of 10° C (50° F) a sowing can be made in mid-winter for a really early crop. Sow seeds individually in 9 cm (3½ in) pots, or use unit containers. John Innes potting compost No. 1 is recommended.

Planting Set out the young plants in a row, spacing them 30 cm (12 in) apart. Those sown in mid- to late spring are planted in late spring and harvested from mid-summer onwards; those sown in early spring in heat are planted in mid-spring when large enough and may need frost protection in an unheated house, but will crop in early summer.

General cultivation The plants can be trained up strings attached to a horizontal wire in the roof. Climbing French beans are self-pollinating so there is no need to carry out hand-pollination. Ensure good light and air circulation and a steady moist fertile soil.

Cultivars 'Blue Lake', 'Hunter', 'Largo' and 'Purple Podded'.

Capsicums

Capsicums or sweet peppers are becoming popular with amateur gardeners and are grown to crop during the summer. They need the same conditions as tomatoes and are a good companion crop – they also like warmth, sunshine and dryish air. A temperature of 15.5–21° C (60–70° F) is ideal with a minimum night temperature of 13° C (55° F). In the early part of the year some artificial heat may be required to maintain this temperature range.

Raising plants Sow seeds in early spring, spacing them out 2.5 cm (1 in) apart each way on the compost surface. Use John Innes seed compost and a tray or pot of suitable size. Germinate at 18° C (65° F). Prick out seedlings into 7.5 cm (3 in) pots, using John Innes potting compost No. 1. Pot on to 12.5 cm (5 in) pots when necessary, using JIP2. When the plants are 15 cm (6 in) high pinch out the tips to encourage branching.

Planting Capsicums can be grown in a soil border, growing-bags or in large pots as for tomatoes (see Tomatoes). Plant out when 15 cm (6 in) high and provide canes for support, or growing-bag crop supports.

General cultivation Spray open flowers with water to encourage fruits to set (when conditions are warm) or gently tap or shake each plant to ensure pollination. Water as normal and feed weekly with a liquid tomato fertiliser when fruits have set. Ventilate well in warm weather but shade from very strong sunshine.

Fruits can be picked when green (unripe) or red (fully ripe). Remember, however, that some of the modern cultivars have yellow fruits. I pick the first fruits when green, but of a suitable size for use, to ensure more fruits follow.

Cultivars 'Ace' (F1), 'Ariane', 'Big Bertha' (F1), 'Californian Wonder', 'Canape' (F1), 'Clio' (F1), 'Early Prolific' (F1), 'Gypsy' (F1), 'New Ace' (F1), 'Redskin' (F1), 'Worldbeater' and 'Yellow Lantern'.

Carrots

Early carrots can be obtained even earlier if grown in a moderately heated greenhouse, minimum temperature of 10°C (50°F).

Raising plants Sow stump-rooted forcing cultivars in the autumn for out-of-season use. Best results are obtained in a soil border but make sure it has not been freshly manured. Carrots like a deep well-cultivated soil. Sow in rows 10 cm (4 in) apart and thin out the seedlings as necessary. Carrots can also be grown in growing-bags.

General cultivation Ensure that carrots receive maximum light and ventilate on all suitable occasions. Keep the soil steadily moist. Pull the roots as soon as large enough to use – one generally uses them when quite small.

Cultivars 'Amsterdam Forcing 3', 'Nantes 5-Champion Scarlet Horn', 'Early French Frame', 'Early Nantes 2' and 'Parmex'.

Celery

Self-blanching celery can be grown in an unheated tunnel or greenhouse for autumn and early winter use. It may need some form of frost protection, however, in late autumn and early winter.

Raising plants Sow seeds in late spring for cropping in late autumn, and in early summer for cropping in early winter, including the Christmas period. Seeds should be sown thinly on the surface of the compost and do not need covering. Prick out seedlings into individual soil blocks at an early stage of their development.

Planting Celery likes a deep soil containing plenty of organic matter. Plant out at 30 cm (12 in) apart each way.

General cultivation Keep the soil or compost moist at all stages of growth. Plenty of water and feeding is needed in the growing period. In autumn and winter ensure a cool dry atmosphere and good ventilation.

Cultivars 'Golden Self-Blanching' and 'Lathom Self-Blanching'.

Chicory, sugar loaf

Sugar loaf chicory forms conical heads of pale green leaves and is self-blanching. Grown for autumn and winter salads in an unheated tunnel or greenhouse.

Raising plants Sow in summer for autumn and winter cropping, or in autumn for early spring use. Either sow seeds direct in a soil bed or raise seedlings in soil blocks or small pots and plant out when large enough – rather like lettuces.

Planting Sugar loaf chicory likes a fertile soil which retains moisture. Grow either in a soil bed or in growing-bags. Planting is the same as for lettuces (see Lettuces).

General cultivation (See lettuces).

Cultivars 'Crystal Head', 'Pain de Sucre' and 'Snowflake'.

Chinese cabbage

For summer, autumn and early winter harvesting in an unheated tunnel or greenhouse.

Raising plants Sow seeds from mid-spring to early autumn for harvesting between early summer and early winter. This crop takes from four to ten weeks to mature, depending on the time of year. Sow in soil blocks.

Planting Provide a fertile soil containing plenty of humus. Ideally, plant in a soil border. Space young plants 30 cm (12 in) apart each way.

General cultivation Chinese cabbage is a fast grower so water well. Keep conditions cool by providing good ventilation in summer and autumn – temperatures must be kept down.

Cultivars 'Chiko' (F1) and 'Nagaoka 50 Days' (F1).

Courgettes

Although courgettes are more often grown out of doors, they grow better, in my opinion, in an unheated greenhouse or tunnel, especially in a cold summer. I recommend growing the bush cultivars.

Raising plants Sow seeds in mid-spring and plant out in late spring. Harvest from early summer onwards. Alternatively, sow early in mid-spring in heat and plant out in an unheated structure when large enough. In this instance plants may need frost protection. Sow one seed per 9 cm ($3\frac{1}{2}$ in) pot.

Planting Plant out in a soil border at 60 cm (24 in) square. A moisture-retentive soil is recommended so incorporate plenty of organic matter prior to planting.

General cultivation The leading shoot can be trained up a string, even though we are growing bush cultivars; this results in better air circulation between the plants. Keep the soil steadily moist and ensure good ventilation. Pick fruits regularly when 7.5–10 cm (3–4 in) long to ensure a succession.

Cultivars You will find them listed under marrows or vegetable marrows in catalogues, for courgettes are true marrows. Try the following: 'Burpee Golden Zucchini', 'Gold Rush' (F1), 'Green Bush' (F1) and 'Zucchini'.

Cucumbers

Probably next in popularity to tomatoes but not quite so easy to grow. One cannot grow cucumbers successfully with tomatoes (although I have done so and achieved reasonable results) because cucumbers need a humid atmosphere. However, you can create a microclimate in a greenhouse by hanging some sheets of clear polythene around the cucumber plants in which the desired humidity can be created. A suitable temperature to maintain is 18–21° C (65–70° F) by day and a minimum of 15.5° C (60° F) at night. Artificial heat will be needed in the early part of the year. Open-pollinated cultivars are generally easier for the amateur than the F1 hybrids, although more and more of the latter are now listed in catalogues.

Raising plants A convenient time to sow seeds is early or mid-spring. Sow one seed per 7.5 cm (3 in) pot, ideally in soilless compost. Simply push each seed into the compost on edge. Open-pollinated cultivars germinate at 18° C (65° F) but F1 hybrids need 24° C (75° F).

Planting Plant seedlings when they have produced two true leaves. Cucumbers can be planted in growing-bags (two to three per bag), and in 22.5 cm (9 in) pots, using John Innes potting compost No. 3, or an equivalent soilless type. A soil border is also suitable, provided it has been well dug and enriched with well-rotted farmyard manure or garden compost. Set each plant on a mound of JIP3.

When planting ensure the top of the rootball is 12 mm ($\frac{1}{2}$ in) above the surface of the soil or compost to ensure water does not collect around the base of the stems, which can result in stem-rot. Space plants 60 cm (24 in) apart.

General cultivation Plants are trained to horizontal wires on the side of the greenhouse, spaced 30 cm (12 in) apart. Provide a warm humid atmosphere. Damp down the greenhouse twice a day and in warm weather spray the plants with tepid water twice a day. Lightly shade from strong sunshine. Feed weekly with a liquid fertiliser from about six weeks after planting; cease in early autumn. Keep the soil steadily moist but do not wet the base of the stems.

Train the main stem vertically to the wires and pinch out the tip when it reaches the top wire. Remove tendrils. Stop side shoots at two leaves beyond a female flower and tie them in horizontally to the wires. Some cultivars produce male and female flowers while others produce only females. Females are easily recognised – each has a miniature cucumber behind it. The males have only a thin flower stalk. If a plant has both male and female flowers do not allow cross-pollination to take place; it results in bitter, seedy and misshapen fruits. Remove the male flowers before they open.

When white roots appear on the soil or compost surface, topdress with similar compost, by spreading a 2.5 cm (1 in) layer over the root area but avoiding contact with the stems. Cut fruits when large enough for use to ensure more follow.

Cultivars There is a boom in F1 hybrids but open-pollinated cultivars are still grown by amateurs. Most F1 hybrids produce only female flowers. The following are recommended: 'Birgit' (F1) with all-female flowers; 'Conqueror', can be grown with tomatoes because it will tolerate less humidity; 'Fembaby' (F1), easier than most F1s; 'Femspot' (F1), produces mainly female flowers; 'Pepinex 69' (F1), mainly female flowers; 'Petita' (F1), easier than most F1s; and 'Sigmadew', easy to grow.

Endive

A lettuce-like plant grown for winter salads, cold or cool greenhouse.

Raising plants Sow in late summer either direct in a soil border or transplant as for lettuce (see Lettuces).

Planting Provide a fertile soil for best results and plant or thin out to 30 cm (12 in) apart each way.

General cultivation Provide the same conditions as for lettuces (see Lettuces). Endive can be blanched to remove bitterness; cover each plant, a few weeks before required for use, with a suitably large pot with the hole plugged.

Cultivars Grow the broad-leaved or Batavian endive.

Florence fennel

This is grown for its swollen stem base (or 'bulb' as it is sometimes called), and growth is better in an unheated greenhouse or tunnel than outdoors, especially in a poor, cool summer.

Raising plants Sow seeds in early or mid-summer for autumn use. Sow in a seed tray and prick out seedlings into soil blocks or bio-degradable pots.

Planting Plant out before the young plants become pot bound, in rows 38 cm (15 in) apart with 15 cm (6 in) between plants.

General cultivation Provide a fertile soil which retains moisture. Keep well watered while in full growth and ensure plenty of ventilation. Harvest when the 'bulbs' are about the size of a tennis ball.

Cultivars 'Contino', 'Sirio' and 'Zefa Fino'.

Forcing

Chicory and rhubarb can be forced in heat for autumn and winter use, grown specially for the purpose in the open ground.

Chicory This has parsnip-like roots and is raised from seeds sown out of doors in mid- or late spring. Lifting of the roots can start in mid-autumn, cutting off the leaves close to their base. Store the roots not required straight away for forcing in sand, in a cool frost-free place.

For forcing, place the roots vertically in a deep box of sandy soil, a few at any one time. The tops of the roots should be level with the compost surface. The bottoms of very long roots can be trimmed if required. Water the roots and cover with a 10 cm (8 in) layer of moist peat or substitute. Cover with an upturned box to exclude light, or place the box under the greenhouse staging, suitably blacked out. Provide a temperature of 7–10° C (45–50° F). Chicons (these are the blanched shoots which are produced for use) will be available in approximately four to six weeks. Cut them when 15 cm (6 in) long, before the leaves open. Discard roots after harvesting the chicons. Recommended cultivars: 'Apollo' and 'Witloof'.

62 *Chicory – the production of chicons*

Rhubarb Dig up crowns in autumn when the leaves have died down and lay them on the ground to subject them to frosts for a couple of weeks. Use only vigorous three- to four-year-old crowns.

Place the crowns in a deep box of sandy soil, ensuring the dormant buds are level with the compost surface. Water and keep moist and dark as for chicory. Provide a temperature of 7–15.5° C (45–60° F). The higher the temperature the quicker the stems will be produced. Stems will be ready for harvesting in five to eight weeks. Discard roots after picking. Good cultivars are 'Hawkes Champagne' and 'Timperley Early'.

Herbs

A selection of herbs for autumn and winter use is well worth growing in the greenhouse or tunnel. I can recommend the following:

Basil Can be grown out of doors (raised from seeds) in the summer.

Trim back and pot in early autumn and place in a cool greenhouse. Pick in autumn or early winter.

Borage Sow seeds in mid- or late summer out of doors. Pot in autumn and place in cool greenhouse.

Chervil Sow seeds in late summer in a cool or cold greenhouse and grow in pots.

Chives Pot garden-grown plants in autumn and place in a cool greenhouse.

Marjoram Sow sweet marjoram outdoors in late spring. Pot in late summer and place in cool greenhouse.

Mint Roots of garden mint or spearmint can be lifted in mid-autumn, boxed in potting compost and placed in a cool greenhouse.

Parsley Sow seeds outdoors in mid-summer, pot in late summer/early autumn and place in cold or cool greenhouse. Alternatively, sow direct in a greenhouse border.

Sage Take potted plants into a cool greenhouse in early autumn.

Savory Sow seeds of summer and winter savory outdoors in spring. Pot in early autumn and place in a cold or cool greenhouse.

Tarragon Pot young garden plants in early autumn, trim back the stems and place in cool greenhouse.

Thyme Pot garden plants of common thyme in early autumn and place in cool or cold greenhouse. Plants can be raised from seeds or cuttings in spring.

Lettuces

Lettuces are grown under glass for winter and spring use. There are cultivars for unheated and heated greenhouses. Make sure you choose the right ones. Above all, lettuces need maximum light, a dry atmosphere and fresh air for successful results.

Raising plants Sow seeds between late summer and mid-winter to produce lettuces between late autumn and late spring. The sowing time depends on the cultivar (see cultivars below). Sow small amounts of seeds (preferably in stages to provide a succession of plants) in a 9 cm (3$\frac{1}{2}$ in) pot of John Innes seed compost, or an equivalent soilless type. Germinate at 10–15.5° C (50–60° F). Prick out seedlings into soil blocks or small bio-degradable pots. Ensure maximum light at all times.

Planting Best grown in a soil border, ideally manured for a previous crop. Prick in a general-purpose fertiliser before planting and firm the soil well. Plant in rows 20 cm (8 in) apart, staggering the plants and spacing them 20 cm apart in the rows. After planting, the lower leaves should be just above the soil surface. Water. Good crops can also be produced in growing-bags – I use those which contained a summer crop of tomatoes or similar plants.

General cultivation Provide good ventilation on all suitable occasions and keep the atmosphere dry; damp conditions can result in botrytis and mildew. Keep the soil moderately moist at all times but do not wet the foliage. Harvest when you consider they are a suitable size. Unlike summer cultivars, these lettuces produce a loose, rather open heart.

Cultivars 'Cynthia' – sow mid-autumn to mid-winter; ready early to mid-spring; slightly heated greenhouse. 'Kelly's' – sow late autumn to mid winter; ready from mid-spring; unheated greenhouse. 'Kwiek' – sow late summer to early autumn; ready late autumn and early winter; unheated greenhouse. 'May Queen' – sow mid-autumn to late winter; ready early to late spring, unheated greenhouse. 'Novita' – sow early autumn to late winter; ready early winter to late spring; unheated greenhouse.

Mushrooms

Mushrooms can be grown under the greenhouse staging, suitably blacked out with black polythene sheeting. A temperature range of 10–15.5° C (50–60° F) is needed. There are two ways of growing mushrooms. The easiest way is to purchase proprietary mushroom kits or packs from a garden centre. They are ready to start into growth – just follow the maker's instructions and provide the right conditions. Such packs are generally available in a plastic bucket or special polythene bag. There is also the traditional way of growing which (let's not be secretive about it) involves quite a lot of work; it is dealt with in the following sections.

Growing medium This can be composted strawy stable manure, or plain composted straw. These materials are composted with an activator (there is a special one available for making a mushroom-growing medium).

Moisten the fresh manure or straw and add the activator according to instructions on the pack. Place material in a heap at least 91 cm (3 ft) deep and wide. The heap will ferment and become hot. Turn it completely after one week, at the same time moistening any dry parts. The inside should be turned outwards and the outside inwards. Repeat after five days, then twice more at least, again at five-day intervals. Composting takes three to four weeks. The material is ready for use when the straw is rotted and easily broken down, and the really fierce heat has subsided.

Place the growing medium in a large wooden box 30 cm (12 in) deep and make moderately firm. Place a soil thermometer in the medium and when the temperature settles down to a steady 21°C (70°F) go on to the next stage.

63 *Harvesting mushrooms*

Spawning You will have to purchase some mushroom spawn – it is generally supplied in blocks known as block spawn. Break the spawn into small pieces, the size of a walnut, and push them about 19 mm ($\frac{3}{4}$ in) deep into the compost, about 20 cm (8 in) apart each way over the entire area. Alternatively, grain spawn can be used (a granular type). This is worked into the top 2.5 cm (1 in) of the growing medium – scatter it evenly all over the surface first.

White 'threads' will be seen growing over the surface within about 10 days, which is an indication to carry out casing. Casing material is equal parts moist peat and chalk, well broken up to about pea-size particles. Spread a layer of this over the entire compost surface, about 3 cm ($1\frac{1}{4}$ in) deep.

General cultivation After about six weeks from casing you should be able to start picking mushrooms. Mushroom cultivation requires a moist atmosphere (so damp down regularly) and the growing medium should be kept steadily moist.

Harvest mushrooms by gently twisting and pulling. Their removal will leave holes in the casing material which should be filled with more of the same material. When the mushrooms have obviously finished (there will be a number of 'flushes' over about eight weeks) remove the compost and use it on the garden.

Onions, salad

Salad or spring onions are always welcome out of season and if you can maintain a temperature of 10° C (50° F) you will ensure supplies in the winter.

Raising plants Sow in early autumn in a soil bed, pots or growing-bags. Space rows (in a soil bed) 15 cm (6 in) apart.

General cultivation Keep the soil steadily moist but not too wet and ensure well-ventilated conditions. Pull the onions when large enough for use.

Cultivars 'White Lisbon' is the one usually grown.

Potatoes

If you have a greenhouse heated to about 10° C (50° F) for other plants you may like to try growing some early potatoes – to harvest as early as mid-spring.

Planting Tubers, or seed potatoes, are planted in mid-winter but first they need to be chitted. Lay them in a seed tray with the 'rose' end uppermost – the rose end is where the dormant growth buds are clustered. Place in a light airy frost-free place and within about two weeks shoots will appear. When they are about 12 mm ($\frac{1}{2}$ in) long the tubers are planted. Potatoes can be grown in large pots – a 20 cm (8 in) pot will hold three tubers and a 30 cm (12 in) pot will take five.

Half fill each pot with John Innes potting compost No. 3, space out the tubers evenly and cover with 5 cm (2 in) of compost. Water and stand them on the greenhouse floor or staging.

General cultivation Ensure maximum light at all times. As the shoots grow, topdress with more compost, a little at a time. Eventually the compost level should be within 2.5 cm (1 in) from the top of the pot.

Cultivars Choose early cultivars such as 'Arran Pilot', 'Epicure', 'Foremost' and 'Maris Bard'.

Radishes

For out-of-season crops in autumn and winter try to provide a temperature of 10° C (50° F).

Raising plants Start sowing in autumn and in succession throughout winter. Radishes can be grown in a soil border or in growing-bags. Sow thinly in rows 10 cm (4 in) apart and thin out resultant seedlings if necessary.

General cultivation Requirements are simple – ensure the plants receive maximum light, provide good ventilation and keep the soil moist at all times.

Cultivars 'French Breakfast', 'Helro' and 'Short Top Forcing'.

Sprouting seeds

Seed sprouting is becoming very popular and can be done at any time of year, although many people like to maintain a succession of sprouts throughout autumn and winter when fresh produce is not so plentiful. Basically, seeds are sprouted (germinated) in moisture and warmth and are used when the shoots are of a suitable length (a matter of a few centimetres). Seed sprouts are very nutritious and can be used in salads, sandwiches, etc. It is a very quick form of cultivation – a matter of a few days, the exact time depending on temperature. A good temperature range is 13–21°C (55–70°F). Buy only seeds intended for sprouting – they can be purchased from seedsmen and from health-food shops.

Methods of sprouting For a suitable method see types of sprouting seeds listed below.

Traditional – you will need a shallow tray with some absorbent material in the base such as flannel or layers of tissue paper. Sow the seeds thickly on the material, keep steadily moist and grow in normal light.

Jar method. You will need a jar such as a 2 lb jam jar. First, soak the seeds in water for a few hours to make them plump. Rinse and place a 12 mm ($\frac{1}{2}$ in) layer in the jar. Stretch some muslin over the top of the jar and secure with an elastic band. Rinse the seeds with water, morning and night; add the water and strain through the muslin. Drain off all water. Keep the seeds dark to ensure white sprouts; if in light the sprouts will be green.

Types of sprouting seeds The following are some of the most popular but there are many others available, plus mixtures of several kinds.

Adzuki beans – sprout in jar. Use when sprouts 1.8 cm ($\frac{3}{4}$ in) long; approximately four to six days.

Alfalfa – sprout in jar. Use when sprouts 2.5 cm (1 in) long; approximately five to seven days.

Alphatoco beans – sprout in jar. Use when sprouts 1.8 cm ($\frac{3}{4}$ in) long; approximately four to six days.

Cress – tray/absorbent material method. Use when 5 cm (2 in) high and seed leaves have been produced; approximately 15 to 20 days.

Fenugreek – sprout in jar. Use when sprouts 12 mm ($\frac{1}{2}$ in) long; approximately three to five days.

Lentils (whole) – sprout in jar. Use when sprouts 1.8 cm ($\frac{3}{4}$ in) long; approximately four to six days.

Mung beans – sprout in jar. Use when sprouts 1.8 cm ($\frac{3}{4}$ in) long; approximately four to six days.

Mustard –tray/absorbent material method. Use when 5 cm (2 in) high and seed leaves have been produced; approximately 12 to 15 days.

Rape – tray/absorbent material method. Use when 5 cm (2 in) high and seed leaves have been produced; approximately 12 to 18 days.

Sweet corn

Sweet corn crops earlier, and more reliably, in an unheated tunnel or greenhouse but needs headroom of 2.4 m (8 ft) at least.

Raising plants Sow seeds in mid-spring in soil blocks, one seed per block; or sow in 7.5 cm (3 in) bio-degradable pots.

Planting Plant in late spring before the blocks or pots become permeated with roots. Obviously needs to be grown in a soil border. Rows should be 45 cm (18 in) apart with plants 30 cm (12 in) apart in the rows.

General cultivation When the plants are in flower gently shake them to assist pollination. Do not spray with water for this purpose. The male flowers are at the top of the plants and the females lower down. Keep the soil steadily moist but not wet, ensure good ventilation and plenty of sunshine. Cobs should be ready for harvesting from mid-summer.

Cultivars 'Aztec' (F1), 'Earlibelle' (F1), 'First of All' (F1), 'Sundance' (F1) and 'Sunrise' (F1).

Tomatoes

Undoubtedly the most popular summer greenhouse utility crop. Tomatoes like warmth, sunshine and dryish air. An ideal temperature is 15.5–21°C (60–70°F), with a minimum of 13°C (55°F) at night. This is the lowest it should go, otherwise growth will slow down or stop. In the early part of the year some artificial heat may therefore need to be provided.

Raising plants Sow seeds in early spring. Space them 2.5 cm (1 in) apart each way on the compost surface. Use John Innes seed compost and a tray or pot of suitable size. Germinate at 18° C (65° F). Prick out seedlings into 7.5 cm (3 in) pots, using John Innes potting compost No. 1. Pot on to 12.5 cm (5 in) pots when necessary, using JIP2.

Planting Plant when about 15 cm (6 in) high. If the greenhouse is unheated it would be better to buy plants and plant them in late spring when the weather and soil have warmed up a bit. The various ways of growing tomatoes are listed below.

Fertile soil border – dig the border well and incorporate well-rotted farmyard manure, garden compost or composted bark. Apply fertiliser before planting, according to results of a soil test. (Soil-testing kits are available cheaply enough from garden centres). Try not to plant tomatoes in exactly the same part of the border each year as this can result in a build-up of soil-borne pests and diseases. Try to plan a three-year rotation. Plant the tomatoes 45 cm (18 in) apart each way.

Growing-bags – a popular method of growing tomatoes. They can be placed on the floor of the house, or on the staging if there is sufficient headroom. Most bags will take three plants, or four if 1.2 m (4 ft) long.

Large pots – tomatoes will be comfortable in 25–30 cm (10–12 in) pots. Use John Innes potting compost No. 2 or 3. Stand them on the floor, 45 cm (18 in) apart each way, or on a soil border on a sheet of polythene.

Ring culture – this is an excellent method of growing tomatoes (for full details see Chapter 9). Space rings 45 cm (18 in) apart each way. Plant tomatoes in JIP 2 or 3 and water well in. Thereafter, water only the aggregate base. Feeding of the plants is via the compost in the rings, using a liquid tomato fertiliser.

General cultivation Supports will be needed right from the start. Use 1.8 m (6 ft) bamboo canes, or grow-bag crop supports. Another method is to use strong garden twine – the lower end of a length of twine is buried under each plant when planting, and the other end secured to a taught horizontal wire about 1.8 m (6 ft) above ground level. The twine must not be too tight or too loose, because it is twisted around the plant as growth proceeds.

Rub out side shoots regularly (not for dwarf bush tomatoes). Keep the soil or compost steadily moist; do not allow it to dry out, and check ring-culture aggregate daily. Use water at greenhouse temperature. Try not to allow the temperature in summer to rise above 27° C (80° F); ventilate when this is reached. Shade only from very strong sunshine – light shading only as good light is needed. To pollinate the flowers gently tap or shake the trusses of open flowers, or spray with water (only in warm conditions). Use a proprietary liquid tomato fertiliser and start feeding as soon as the first fruits start to form. Apply fertiliser once a week. For the ring-culture method apply the fertiliser only to the compost in the rings. For plants in rings, pots and growing-bags feeding can be gradually increased with advantage to once every five days.

With standard (tall) tomatoes pinch out the growing point when five to six trusses of flowers have been produced. Stop feeding in early or mid-autumn.

As the lower fruits start to ripen a few of the lower leaves can be removed, especially if they are becoming yellow. This ensures good air circulation around the fruits. However, do not remove too many leaves – this can inhibit fruit development. Pick fruits as soon as ripe – red or yellow.

Cultivars 'Ailsa Craig', 'Alicante', 'Big Boy' (F1), 'Estrella' (F1), 'Eurocross BB' (F1), 'Golden Sunrise', 'Moneymaker', 'Piranto' (F1), 'Seville Cross' (F1), 'Shirley' (F1) and 'Sioux' (F1).

Bush tomatoes Although most people grow these out of doors, it is well worth growing them in an unheated greenhouse or tunnel for summer cropping, because they are less labour-intensive than standard (tall) tomatoes. Sow mid-spring and plant out late spring. Harvest from mid-summer onwards. Plants can be grown in a double row: 45 cm (18 in) between rows, with plants 38 cm (15 in) apart in the rows. Plants do not need stopping or supporting. I generally place straw around the plants to prevent the fruits coming in contact with the soil. Suitable cultivars are 'Red Alert', 'Sleaford Abundance' (F1) and 'The Amateur'.

Pinch out side
shoots

64 *Pinching out side shoot of tomato*

PART FOUR

Garden Frames and Cloches

30   Types of frames

A garden frame is a low structure providing protection for plants. It has many uses (as we shall see later) but basically it can provide suitable conditions for raising, growing and storing a wide range of plants. A frame can either be used on its own or in conjunction with a greenhouse.

Single span This type of frame is rather like a lean-to greenhouse, designed to be placed against a wall; but of course it is a low structure, typically about 45–60 cm (18–24 in) high at the back, sloping to something like 22–30 cm (9–12 in) at the front. It can also be used as a free-standing structure.

65 Single-span frame with Dutch lights

Double span A double-span frame can be compared to a traditional span-roof greenhouse, but again, of course, it is a low structure. The 'roof' slopes down on two sides, from a ridge to the side walls (in other words, it has a pitched roof). Typically it is about 45–60 cm (18–24 in) high at the ridge, sloping to about 22–30 cm (9–12 in) at the sides.

Lights A light is simply the lid or cover of the frame (the 'roof' if you like), consisting of a square or rectangular framework (generally made of the same material as the rest of the frame) which holds the cladding material – this may be glass or clear plastic. Lights either lift up or slide to one side (both in some models) for ventilation and access. I suggest you opt for a model with easily removable lights which will allow you to get into the frame for soil cultivation, planting and plant care.

Dutch lights are often used for home-made frames (see below) and consist of a simple timber framework holding a large pane of glass. The standard overall dimensions of a Dutch light are 1.5 m by 75 cm (5 ft by 2½ ft). The glass is held in grooves and is therefore easily

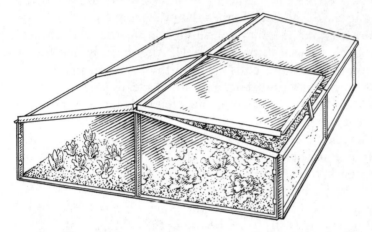

66 *Double-span frame*

replaced if broken. Dutch lights are not too easy to obtain these days.

Proprietary and home-made frames Most gardeners these days prefer to buy ready made frames, which often come in kit form – especially those with an aluminium framework. If you prefer timber framework there are frames available in western red cedar and other kinds of wood. If the frame is to be placed alongside the greenhouse it is obviously sensible, if only for aesthetic reasons, to buy one which has a framework made of the same material as that of the greenhouse. You will find that many greenhouse manufacturers also supply garden frames.

Proprietary garden frames may be clad with horticultural glass or with one of the rigid clear plastics, or even flexible plastics in some of the economy types. However, there is nothing to beat horticultural glass (as I said in Chapter 2): it retains heat better than plastics. Nevertheless, the latter are much safer if there are children around.

Frames may have solid sides and ends or glass/plastic. The latter let in more light, of course, which is especially important for winter cropping. However, these kinds of frames lose their heat more quickly than those with solid sides and ends – a disadvantage for winter cropping and storing. One final point concerning proprietary frames; most are portable so that they can easily be moved around the garden.

You may prefer to make your own frame. A glass-to-ground type can be quite difficult, unless you are skilled in carpentry; most people, therefore, prefer to build a permanent single-span structure. The sides and ends are easily constructed of bricks or building blocks, remembering to make the back higher than the front by at least 15–22 cm (6–9 in). First, lay a concrete foundation for the walls, about 7.5 cm (3 in) thick on well-rammed rubble. Alternatively, the frame could have timber sides and ends – I find that scaffold planks are ideal for this purpose. A timber frame should ideally still be placed on a concrete foundation – a strip of roofing felt laid on the foundation first will prevent rising damp.

The frame can be covered with Dutch lights, so make sure you take their size into account when building. The lights are simply laid on the front and back walls. To prevent gales from blowing them off, the lights should be held down with two lengths of strong wire running from one end of the frame to the other. One wire should be positioned about 15 cm (6 in) from the top of the lights, and the other the same distance from the bottom. Those wires must be really tight and can be secured to each end of the frame by hooks.

(For further details of materials used in frame construction refer to greenhouse construction materials in Chapter 2.)

31   Siting and equipping frames

Siting A frame can be placed against a wall of the greenhouse with the consequent advantage of securing added warmth; it will lose heat less quickly and will also absorb some heat which is lost from the greenhouse through the wall. A single-span structure is suitable for this purpose. Alternatively, a garden frame can be free-standing; for example, it could be placed in the vegetable garden, on a patio or terrace, or alongside a garden path. Wherever it is sited the frame must be in a sunny, open position but well sheltered from wind. If placed against a wall it should ideally face south or west so that it warms up quickly during sunny spells.

Base materials If you do not wish to grow plants in the soil you may like to consider some kind of material in the base of the frame on which to stand containers such as pots, seed trays, and growing-bags. There are several suitable materials: pea shingle, horticultural aggregate, gravel, weathered ashes or sand. A layer about 2.5 cm (1 in) deep will be sufficient, separated from the soil by a sheet of heavy-gauge polythene. This prevents the growth of weeds through the base material and isolates plants from possible soil-borne pests and diseases. Do not turn up the edges of the polythene otherwise excess water will not be able to escape.

Soil and its improvement If you have good garden soil you may wish to use this for growing plants in. Vegetable crops, for instance, are often sown direct into soil (see table). The soil must be well drained and of a good depth, especially for root crops like carrots. If you intend growing carrots, and other root crops, do not use manure prior to sowing; it results in deformed roots. Ideally, sow in soil that was manured for a previous crop.

Generally soil preparation consists each autumn of digging to at least the depth of a spade, and incorporating in each trench some well-rotted farmyard manure, garden compost or composted bark. Before sowing or planting, apply and prick into the surface a general-purpose fertiliser at a rate of 85 g per m^2 (3 oz per sq yd). If the soil is very poor you are advised to replace it with at least 30 cm (12 in) of good topsoil, or even John Innes potting compost.

The plunge bed This is a 30 cm (12 in) depth of material such as weathered ashes, pulverised bark or sand in the garden frame. It is used for plunging potted plants up to the pot rims to prevent rapid compost drying out and to protect pots and plant roots from frost. For example, alpines in pans are best plunged (see Chapter 19), and any pot plants. The plunge bed can also be used for bulb forcing (see Chapter 14). The plunge material should be kept steadily moist, but not very wet, and it needs to be placed on well-drained soil. Some gardeners prefer to have a special frame for plunging; there is no reason, however, why part of a frame should not be made into a plunge bed.

Heating A garden frame can be unheated but, as with a greenhouse, the provision of artificial heat during the autumn, winter and spring greatly increases the range of plants that can be grown. A heated frame can, in fact, be used for many greenhouse plants, provided there is sufficient headroom. There are various ways of heating a garden frame.

Electric warming cables – soil-warming cables can be laid beneath the soil or other base material; air-warming cables may be placed around the walls of the frame. Or one could use both. (See Chapter 6 for full details.)

Electric tubular heaters – these provide a convenient means of heating the garden frame. (See Chapter 6.)

Hot-water pipes – if the frame is positioned against a greenhouse wall, hot-water pipes (if used for greenhouse heating) could be run into it. These should run around the walls of the frame, in much the same way as in the greenhouse. (See Chapter 6.) Hot-water pipes can also be used for soil warming in a frame if they are buried under the soil or other base material.

Paraffin heaters – it is possible to buy small paraffin heaters for air heating, but leave a little air on at all times when in use to allow any fumes to escape. (See Chapter 6.)

32   General management

Ventilation As in a greenhouse, provide good ventilation consistent with maintaining the desired temperature. This is necessary to prevent a damp, stale atmosphere which can lead to diseases such as botrytis. It is especially important to ensure a dry atmosphere in an unheated frame during the winter. For most crops in the summer, during warm weather, one can remove the lights completely during the daytime to prevent excessive temperatures; possibly with the exception of the more tender vegetables and fruits like melons, cucumbers, tomatoes and capsicums. But even these need good ventilation in hot weather by opening wide the lights.

Most proprietary frames have facilities for providing varied openings. If no such facilities exist, as with Dutch lights, for example, use a block of wood for propping open the lights. Keep the lights closed during gales and fog and at night throughout autumn, winter and spring, but open during the day, as necessary, to maintain a fresh atmosphere, except during frosty weather.

Shading Plants in a frame are subjected to scorching during periods of strong sunshine in the spring, summer and early autumn, as with greenhouse plants, unless they are protected. There are several ways of shading plants in a frame. Liquid shading material can be applied to the glass; or shading netting, muslin or white polythene can be placed over the lights. Netting and other materials can be secured to the light along one edge and rolled back when not required. (See Chapter 7 for further details of shading.)

I would say that temporary materials, like netting, are best because they can be removed or rolled back during dull spells, but they are not so convenient as liquid shading which remains in place all summer. As with a greenhouse, the glass should be kept scrupulously clean for maximum light intensity within the frame – this is particularly important during the winter.

Insulation Some form of insulation is necessary during cold and frosty weather at night, to retain heat. The lights can be covered with a suitable insulating material such as old carpet or hessian. Even thick wads of newspaper will provide effective insulation. Hold in place with half bricks or similar weights.

There is no reason why bubble polythene cannot be used inside a garden frame, while heating is necessary, to conserve heat and reduce fuel bills. (For full details see Chapter 7.)

Watering By hand – really this is the same as outlined for greenhouse plants (see Chapter 11). Use a watering can (fitted with a rose for plants growing in the soil) or a gently running hosepipe. Do not wet plants in the autumn and winter – it can result in diseases such as botrytis. Lettuces, for example, are very prone to this trouble if the leaves become wet in the winter. The same applies to alpines – especially the woolly and hairy-leaved kinds.

Automatic – there are several automatic or semi-automatic systems which are suitable for frames (see Chapter 8); such as seep hoses which are good for watering crops in soil, and trickle and drip lines which can be used for watering soil beds or pots. You could also use an overhead sprinkler or mist system. This is recommended only for summer watering, during warm conditions; especially for plants which like to be sprayed with water and enjoy humid conditions. Capillary irrigation is suitable for pot plants, using capillary matting or sand moistened by means of a trickle line or seep hose. Such systems prevent the need to keep raising the lights as for hand watering, and they save the gardener a lot of time; but of course they are not selective and everything gets watered whether it needs it or not.

Soil care Really the same comments apply as for the greenhouse soil border (see Chapters 5 and 11). Dig and manure, ideally in autumn, and try to sterilise the soil with a horticultural sterilant. Apply fertilisers before sowing or planting. If artificial heating is to be used, by means of soil warming, then turn on several days prior to sowing or planting to ensure the soil warms up. A soil temperature of at least 10° C (50° F) is necessary. If you are unable to sterilise the frame soil, it is best to replace it every few years with fresh topsoil or potting compost or alternatively move the frame to a fresh position.

General maintenance Above all keep the glass clean all the year round. At least once a year thoroughly scrub the inside and outside, using disinfectant and plenty of water. Repair any cracked or broken panes of glass before the winter sets in. Treat timber frames regularly with a suitable horticultural wood preservative. If algae present a problem (green film or slime) wash the structure with a horticultural algicide. Moss and liverwort forming on the base material should be scraped off, topping up with fresh material if necessary. Regularly raking the base material will prevent moss or liverwort becoming established.

33 Making the best use of a frame

A garden frame can be used in conjunction with a greenhouse or as a means of protection in its own right. A heated and unheated frame can be used for many of the greenhouse plants included in the preceding chapters, the only limitation being headroom. A heated frame is especially useful for securing early vegetables like beetroots, carrots, lettuces, salad onions and radishes. Even an unheated frame will ensure vegetables earlier than those grown in the open ground. Vegetables such as bush tomatoes, frame cucumbers and melons are ideal for unheated frames. but the plants should be raised in heat. The accompanying table gives plenty of ideas for cropping in heated and unheated frames the year round. There is certainly no need to let this valuable structure stand empty for any part of the year. Apart from cropping, there are other uses to which a garden frame can be put.

Growing pot plants Provided there is sufficient headroom and suitable temperatures, all kinds of pot plants can be raised and grown in a frame. (See Chapters 14, 15, 16 and 17 especially, for ideas and cultural details.) Bulbs are an ideal choice, together with calceolarias, primulas, cinerarias, begonias, pelargoniums, streptocarpus, coleus, fuchsias, as well as alpines (Chapter 19) and cacti and succulents (Chapter 21).

Raising summer bedding and other plants Provided suitable temperatures can be maintained a frame is ideal for raising many plants from seeds, such as summer bedding plants (see Chapter 13). You can also raise a wide range of vegetables for later planting out in the garden (see Chapter 29).

Vegetative propagation Stem cuttings of both hardy and tender plants (softwoods in spring and early summer, semi-ripe in summer and early autumn, and hardwoods in autumn and winter) can be successfully rooted in heated or unheated frames. (Full details are given in Chapter 10). Of course, soil-warming cables in the frame provide ideal conditions for rooting and there is no reason why a mist-propagation system should not be installed if you plan to use the frame for a lot of vegetative propagation. Mist and bottom heat create the ideal conditions for rooting cuttings. You could root cuttings direct in a bed of cutting compost in the base of the frame, or in containers like trays and pots.

Hardening plants An unheated frame is necessary for hardening plants raised in a heated greenhouse prior to being planted in the garden, such as summer bedding plants and vegetables. It does not matter if the plants are tender or hardy – if raised in heat they will need to be gradually acclimatised to outdoor conditions before being planted out. This avoids giving the plants a nasty shock which would happen if they were to be transferred suddenly from a high temperature to much cooler conditions.

Move plants from the greenhouse to the cold frame three to four weeks before they need to be planted out in the garden. For the first few days, the frame lights should be kept closed; then they can be opened slightly during the day but closed again at night. Over a period of several weeks the lights are gradually opened wider during the day until eventually they are left off altogether, but are still closed again at night. Several days before the plants are to be planted, the lights are left off at night also.

Remember that any tender plants – summer bedding, and vegetables such as tomatoes, capsicums, aubergines and marrows – should not be planted out until all danger of frost is over (late spring or early summer in cool temperate climates). If a frost is forecast when these plants are hardening off in a cold frame it is wise to cover the lights at night with some kind of insulation material (see Chapter 32) to ensure the plants are not frosted. Do not leave the lights open at night until you are sure there is no longer danger of frost.

Overwintering plants A garden frame makes an ideal storage place for resting and dormant plants over the winter; it also gives you more room in the greenhouse for plants which are used for display.

If the frame is heated you can store tender plants like pelargoniums, fuchsias, and tender bulbs, corms and tubers. Most need only frost-free conditions and should be put into the frame in early autumn. Hardy plants like chrysanthemum stools can be overwintered in a cold frame, together with hardy bulbs (in containers) which have finished flowering. All stored plant material needs good air circulation and a dry atmosphere, so ventilate accordingly.

A selection of crops to grow to maturity in a garden frame

Crop	Cultivar(s)	Unheated frame	Heated frame	Harvest
Anemone coronaria	De Caen Group St Brigid Group	Plant tubers early to late autumn		Mid-winter onwards (flowers)
Aubergine	'Duskey'	Plant young plants late spring	Plant mid-spring	Summer
Bean (dwarf French)	'The Prince' 'Masterpiece'	Sow mid/late spring	Sow late winter/early spring	Late spring/mid-summer
Beetroot	'Boltardy'	Sow early spring	Sow late winter	Late spring/early summer
Capsicum	'Early Prolific'	Plant late spring	Plant mid-spring	Summer
Carrot	'Amsterdam Forcing 3' 'Early Nantes 5'	Sow late winter/early spring	Sow mid/late winter	Early spring onwards
Cauliflower	'All the Year Round' 'Snowball'		Plant early/mid-spring	Early summer
Chicory (sugar loaf)	'Pain de Sucre' 'Crystal Head'	Sow summer		Autumn/winter
Convallaria (lily of the valley)	–	Plant mid-autumn, cover mid-winter		Spring (flowers)
Corn salad	–	Sow early autumn		Autumn
Cucumber	'Telegraph'	Plant late spring (raise in heat)		Summer

Crop	Cultivar(s)	Unheated frame	Heated frame	Harvest
Endive	Batavian	Sow late summer		Autumn/early winter
Iris (Dutch, Spanish, English)	–	Plant bulbs early autumn		Early summer (flowers)
Lettuce	'May Queen'	Sow mid-autumn/late winter		Early/late spring
	'Diamont'	Sow mid-autumn/mid-winter		Late winter/mid-spring
	'Kwiek'	Sow late summer/early autumn		Late autumn/early winter
	'Windermere'	Sow mid-autumn		Late spring
Melon	'Ogen' 'Sweetheart'	Plant late spring (raise in heat)		Late summer
Onion (spring)	'White Lisbon'	Sow late spring	Sow late winter	Winter/spring
Parsley	'Bravour' 'Curlina'	Sow late summer or early spring		Autumn and spring
Radish	'Cherry Belle' 'French Breakfast' 'Prinz Rotin' 'Scarlet Globe'	Sow late winter/early spring	Sow mid/late winter	Late winter/early spring onwards
Spinach (winter)	Broad-leaved prickly 'Norvak' 'Sigmaleaf'	Sow late summer/early autumn		Winter

Crop	Cultivar(s)	Unheated frame	Heated frame	Harvest
Tomato (bush)	'The Amateur' 'Alfresco' 'French Cross' 'Sleaford Abundance'	Plant late spring (raise in heat)	Plant mid-spring	Summer
Turnip	'Purple Top Milan' 'Snowball 'Tokeyo Cross'	Sow late winter/early spring	Sow late winter	Late spring
Violet	–	Plant early autumn		Winter (flowers)

CLOCHES

34   Types of cloches

Cloches are low structures used to cover plants, not only for weather protection but to extend vegetable and flower crops seasons – early crops or late. Cloches are used extensively in the vegetable garden. Let us first, though, consider the various types available.

Tent These cloches often consist of two glass sheets held together with special wire clips or fittings. The main ones available are the Chase cloche fittings. Tent cloches may also be made of rigid clear plastic sheets. However, glass is the best material for cloches of all kinds, for it retains heat better than plastics. Tent cloches are placed end to end to form a continuous 'run', the ends being closed with sheets of glass or rigid plastic.

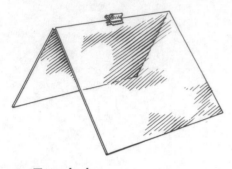

67 *Tent cloche*

Barn These, like tent cloches, are a traditional shape. They generally consist of four glass sheets held together with special wire clips or fittings – again Chase cloche fittings are advised. Incidentally, if you want to make up tent or barn cloches using Chase fittings you have to supply the glass or rigid-plastic sheets. This type of cloche has two side walls and is therefore higher than a tent cloche, and also wider. These cloches are also placed end to end to form a continuous 'run', the ends closed with sheets of glass or rigid plastic.

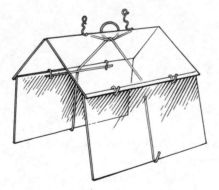

68 *Barn cloche*

Low polythene tunnels These consist of a long sheet of clear or white polythene stretched over galvanised-wire hoops. The polythene is held in place with thinner wire hoops or twine. The edges of the polythene can be buried in the soil, but they will have to be lifted up for access and to provide ventilation. The ends are either buried in the soil or tied to a wooden peg inserted securely in the ground.

69 *Low polythene tunnel cloches*

Variations There are many proprietary variations on the above types. For example, it is possible to buy tent-shaped cloches consisting of a wire framework covered with flexible polythene; or tunnel-shaped cloches formed of corrugated plastic sheeting or polythene-covered wire netting (the wire being sandwiched between two sheets of polythene). Some proprietary cloches are moulded rigid plastic and come in various shapes. It is possible to buy tall cloches for protecting tomatoes and similar tender plants.

Cloche clips Chase cloche fittings or clips can be bought to make up glass/rigid clear plastic tent and barn cloches (see above). You supply the glass. There are, however, other kinds of metal cloche clips available – but again you have to supply the glass or plastic. It is possible to make up many shapes and sizes using these clips.

Floating cloches This is a fairly recent idea – at least for the amateur gardener – for in fact it has been used by commercial growers for some years now. The floating cloche is polythene film which has thousands of tiny slits per m². It is laid over a seed bed after sowing vegetables, flowers, etc, and can also be laid over young plants after planting out. Lay it loosely and bury the edges in the soil to hold the film in place. The floating cloche does not restrict growth, for as the plants grow they lift it and cause the slits to open slowly and evenly – the film 'grows' with the plants. It is generally kept over the plants right up to harvesting or flowering time – at least in the case of low-growing plants. As the slits open so air is able to circulate and rain penetrate.

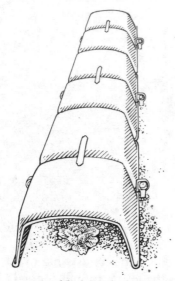

70 *Moulded rigid-plastic cloches*

35   General management

Siting Choose a warm sunny site for your cloches and avoid an area overhung with trees. It must also be sheltered from winds otherwise the cloches may be damaged during gales. If there are wind problems it may be advisable to erect a wind-break on the windward side of the site, using, for example, wind-break netting supported on a timber

framework. For long-term protection, a screen of conifers is recommended.

If possible avoid siting cloches in a frost pocket – this is a low-lying
area where cold air drains down and collects. Ideally, choose a well-
drained fertile piece of ground. If the drainage is good the soil will
quickly warm up in the spring and therefore early sowings and
plantings will have a good start.

Erecting cloches Always follow any erection instructions supplied
with cloche kits. It is best to set cloches in place at least three to four
weeks before you wish to start spring sowing so that the soil becomes
suitably warm and dry. Always leave a comfortable working space
between rows of cloches.

Soil preparation and care The soil needs to be thoroughly prepared
before setting up cloches. You should aim to maintain a highly fertile,
well-drained soil, as for frame cultivation (for further details see
Chapter 31).

Watering There is no need to remove cloches to water plants. Water
can be applied overhead and it will enter the soil, and therefore the
root area, at the sides of the cloches. A garden sprinkler can be used
for applying water.

Alternatively you could lay a seep hose between rows of cloches,
connected to an ordinary hose-pipe. Mulching the soil helps to conserve moisture. A strip of black mulching polythene could be laid
down the length of each row, and the young plants planted through
it. The cloches can then be put in place. Make sure the soil is moist
before laying the polythene. Very little additional water is needed
with this system – but keep an eye on the soil for water needs. It is
also a good idea to mulch the soil between rows of cloches, in this
instance using straw if available.

Ventilation As in a greenhouse, adequate ventilation of cloches is
necessary to prevent damp stale conditions. Many cloches have an
integral ventilation system; for example, adjustable top panels. If not,
then leave a slight gap between cloches during warm weather. If using
low polythene tunnels the way to provide ventilation is to lift up the
sides. Avoid ventilating during very windy weather otherwise damage
may occur to both plants and cloches.

Weeding and feeding Weeds grow very well under cloches! Therefore carry out a regular weeding programme otherwise young plants and seedlings may quickly be choked by weed growth. Either hand weed or, preferably, hoe regularly between the plants to kill weeds as they are germinating. Hoeing also produces a loose surface tilth which helps to conserve soil moisture. Use an onion hoe for cloche work. A polythene mulch will, of course, suppress weeds (see the entry on watering). When in full growth plants will benefit from regular feeding. I prefer to use a liquid fertiliser, applying it to the soil during the growing season. Feeding every seven to ten days will not be too much for the majority of vegetables and flowers.

Raising cloches to give headroom Sometimes it is desirable to keep cloches over crops right up to harvest time; for example with tomatoes, capsicums, aubergines and other tender plants. Eventually these tall crops will touch the glass but it is often possible to raise cloches on bricks to give more room. I have also seen tomatoes grown in a trench about 30 cm (12 in) deep with a row of cloches over the top; a good way, it seems, to provide more headroom for plants. Remember, however, that there are tall cloches available for crops like tomatoes and capsicums.

De-cloching crops If you are starting off plants under cloches with the intention of removing them later, bear in mind that plants should not be suddenly exposed to outside conditions – this will give them a shock and may slow down their growth. Instead, gradually acclimatise plants to normal open-air conditions by increasing ventilation bit by bit over a period of at least a week.

Storing cloches Cloches should ideally be in use all the year round but, if there is a period when they are not in use, make sure they are stored safely to prevent them being damaged. First, though, thoroughly clean the glass or plastic. Traditional tent and barn cloches, made of glass, are stacked on end, inside one another, on a firm level surface and should be stored in a sheltered part of the garden to prevent wind damage.

36   Uses

Aim to keep cloches in use all the year round; for example, cover, throughout autumn and winter, seeds sown in the autumn, and cover seeds and young plants sown or planted in the spring. In the summer, use cloches for covering tender crops like melons and tomatoes. Cloches provide protection from cold weather and excessive wetness and this induces good growth. A range of vegetables and flowers which can be grown under cloches is given in the table at the end of this chapter.

Protecting tender and young plants Cloches can be used for covering newly sown seeds or newly planted young plants. They can be left on until the plants are well established and then transferred to other crops which would benefit from protection (see accompanying table). Single tent or barn cloches can be used to protect tender plants which have been planted out in beds and borders, until they become established; for example, fuchsias and pelargoniums. Single cloches can also be used to protect certain alpines from excessive wetness over the winter, especially those kinds with woolly or hairy leaves.

Propagation I have already mentioned that cloches can be used to cover all kinds of seeds sown in the open ground, to provide optimum conditions for germination and establishment. However, cloches are also valuable for various forms of vegetative propagation, particularly for rooting semi-ripe cuttings. Cuttings of hardy plants can be successfully rooted, such as shrubs and particularly evergreen kinds – cuttings of these, taken in mid-autumn, root very well under low polythene tunnels. Semi-ripe cuttings of tender plants such as pelargoniums, calceolarias, heliotrope and gazanias, taken in late summer, will root within a few weeks under cloches. Cloches can also be used to cover beds of hardwood cuttings of shrubs over the winter to protect them from excessive wetness.

Flowers for cutting Cloches can be used to cover *Anemone coronaria* planted in the autumn, to ensure clean, good-quality flowers for cutting in the winter and spring. Use cloches also to cover clumps of *Helleborus niger*, the Christmas rose, lily of the valley, violets and polyanthus during the autumn, winter and spring to protect the flowers from inclement weather and to prevent mud splashes. Also cover autumn-sown hardy annuals which are grown for cutting (see accompanying table).

Strip cropping This technique is used mainly in the vegetable garden to minimise movement of cloches. For example, you could have three parallel strips of land per row of cloches, with adequate pathways between. The cloches are then moved from one strip to another as required for covering crops. In other words, you could sow seeds in

Year-round cropping under cloches

Crop	Cultivar(s)	Sow/plant
Anemone coronaria	De Caen Group St Brigid Group	Plant tubers late summer/early autumn
Beans, French and runner	'Masterpiece' 'Enorma'	Sow late spring
Beans, broad	'The Sutton'	Sow late autumn
Beetroots	'Boltardy'	Sow mid-spring
Brussels sprouts	'Peer Gynt' (F1)	Sow early spring
Cabbage, summer	'Greyhound' 'Golden Acre – May Express' 'Hispi' (F1)	Sow early spring
Calendula	'Art Shades' 'Fiesta Gitana'	Sow late summer
Carrots	'Early French Frame' 'Early Nantes 5'	Sow early spring
Cauliflower, summer	'All the Year Round' 'Snowball'	Sow early autumn

the first strip and cover with cloches; when the young plants are established sow seeds in the next strip and move the cloches over these; then when the plants are established sow the third strip and move the cloches across.

Ripening and drying Cloches can be used for ripening the fruits of outdoor tomatoes in the autumn. Cut the ties, remove the canes, gently lower the plants on to a layer of straw on the ground and cover with cloches. Also use cloches for drying off bulbs and tubers such as onions, shallots, dahlias and gladioli. Lay them out in a single layer under cloches – preferably not on the soil but in, for instance, shallow trays.

Cloches on	Cloches off	Harvest
Late summer/early autumn	Mid-spring	Winter/spring (flowers)
Late spring	Early summer	Mid/late summer
Late autumn	Mid-spring	Late spring
Mid-spring	Late spring/early summer	Summer
Early spring	Mid-spring	Autumn onwards
Early spring	Mid-spring	Summer
Late summer	Mid-spring	Spring (flowers)
Early spring	Mid-spring	Early summer
Early autumn	Mid-spring	Early summer

Crop	Cultivar(s)	Sow/Plant
Centaurea cyanus	'Blue Diadem' 'Polka Dot Mixed'	Sow late summer
Cucumber	'Telegraph Improved'	Plant late spring
Godetia (*Clarkia*)	'Azalea Flowered' 'Sybil Sherwood'	Sow late summer
Larkspur (*Consolida*)	Hyacinth flowered Stock flowered	Sow late summer
Leeks	'Autumn Mammoth-Argenta'	Sow early spring
Lettuce, summer	'Fortune' 'Salad Bowl' 'Susan' 'Windermere'	Sow early/mid-spring
Marrows	'Green Bush'	Plant late spring
Melons	'Sweetheart' (F1)	Plant late spring
Nigella	'Miss Jekyll'	Sow late summer
Onion, salad	'White Lisbon'	Sow early autumn
Peas	'Feltham First'	Sow mid-autumn
Radishes	'French Breakfast'	Sow early spring
Spinach, summer	'Sigmaleaf'	Sow early spring
Sweet corn	'Sundance' (F1)	Plant late spring
Sweet peas	Many available	Sow early spring
Strawberries	Many, e.g., 'Redgauntlet'	Plant late summer
Tomatoes	'Harbinger' 'The Amateur' (dwarf bush)	Plant late spring

Cloches on	Cloches off	Harvest
Late summer	Mid-spring	Spring (flowers)
Late spring	Leave cloches on all summer	Summer
Late summer	Mid-spring	Spring/summer (flowers)
Late summer	Mid-spring	Spring/summer (flowers)
Early spring	Mid-spring	Autumn/winter
Early/mid spring	Late spring/early summer	Early summer onwards
Late spring	Early summer	Summer/autumn
Late spring	Leave cloches on all summer	Late summer
Late summer	Mid spring	Spring (flowers)
Early autumn	Mid-spring	Spring
Mid-autumn	Mid-spring	Spring/early summer
Early spring	Mid-spring	Mid-spring
Early spring	Mid/late spring	Late spring/summer
Late spring	Early summer	Summer
Early spring	Mid/late spring	Summer (flowers)
Mid-winter	Early summer	Late spring/early summer
Late spring	When plants touch glass; otherwise leave on all summer	Late summer/mid-autumn

General Index

(Numbers in italics indicate a line drawing.)

Index of Plant Names